Victorian Society Papers
Seven Victorian Architects

The Euston Propylaeum by Philip Charles Hardwick (Photo RIBA) and the Thiepval Arch by Lutyens (Photo Commonwealth War Graves Commission)

WILLIAM BURN
PHILIP AND PHILIP CHARLES HARDWICK
SYDNEY SMIRKE · J. L. PEARSON
G. F. BODLEY
ALFRED WATERHOUSE
EDWIN LUTYENS

Seven Victorian Architects

Edited by
JANE FAWCETT

Introduction by
NIKOLAUS PEVSNER

with 119 illustrations

THE PENNSYLVANIA STATE UNIVERSITY PRESS
University Park, Pennsylvania

Copyright © 1977 TRUSTEES OF THE VICTORIAN SOCIETY

Published in the United States of America by
The Pennsylvania State University Press

Library of Congress Catalog Card Number 76–42090

International Standard Book Number 0–271–00500–9

Printed in England

Contents

Introduction   6
NIKOLAUS PEVSNER

I   William Burn: 8
the country house in transition
DAVID WALKER

II   Philip and Philip Charles Hardwick: 32
an architectural dynasty
HERMIONE HOBHOUSE

III   Sydney Smirke: 50
the architecture of compromise
J. MORDAUNT CROOK

IV   John Loughborough Pearson: 66
noble seriousness
DAVID LLOYD

V   George Frederick Bodley: 84
climax of the Gothic Revival
DAVID VEREY

VI   Alfred Waterhouse: 102
civic grandeur
STUART ALLEN SMITH

VII   Edwin Lutyens: 122
the last High Victorian
RODERICK GRADIDGE

ACKNOWLEDGMENTS AND NOTES ON THE TEXT   137

CHECK-LISTS OF CHIEF WORKS   148

SOURCES OF ILLUSTRATIONS   157

INDEX   157

Introduction
NIKOLAUS PEVSNER

My Inaugural Lecture as Slade Professor in Cambridge in 1949 dealt with Matthew Digby Wyatt, not a good architect but an interesting man. I analysed his buildings exactly as I would have done if the object of the lecture had been an architect of the fourteenth century. The students who were present thought this was a huge joke, and they laughed and laughed – so much so that I had to step down from my platform and say: 'This is not funny.'

How much has that changed in less than thirty years! Now a large number of students choose Victorian architects as their subjects for theses, the Department of the Environment lists and grades Victorian buildings as appreciatively as those of a more remote past, and the Historic Buildings Council gives its grants to the owners of nineteenth-century houses without any anti-Victorian bias.

I think I am fair in saying that this change of heart and of eyes is due to quite some degree to the Victorian Society. The present volume is a joint enterprise of the Society and Thames and Hudson. It is dedicated to seven Victorian architects, all of them, except for one, not yet treated by full-scale books. They are in chronological order: William Burn, the Hardwicks, Sydney Smirke, Pearson, Bodley and Waterhouse. Generationally, there are three born between 1780 and 1800, three born between 1815 and 1830: Burn born 1789, Philip Hardwick 1792 and Smirke 1798, and then Pearson 1817, Bodley 1827 and Waterhouse 1830. Odd man out is Lutyens, born in 1869.

All seven have certain qualities in common but differ radically in other qualities. The one universal Victorian quality is of course historicism, that is the conviction that serious architecture must be inspired by styles of the past. Individually however there is a world of difference between Pearson's adherence to the English and French High Gothic of the thirteenth century or Bodley's adherence to the English Decorated and Hardwick's use of an English Baroque for the Goldsmiths' Hall, Tudor for the Hall and Library of Lincoln's Inn, Gothic for the Stockport Grammar School and Doric for the railway and dock architecture. The confrontation between two styles sometimes even took place in one and the same building. Waterhouse is the most telling case (though Webb had preceded him). Waterhouse combined Gothic with Georgian-shaped windows, and he, unlike others, formulated this attitude. He said: 'Whenever I thought that the particular object in view could not be best obtained by a strict obedience to precedent I took the liberty of departing from it.' The point is illustrated less by Waterhouse's most conspicuous buildings—the Manchester Town Hall, wholly Gothic, and the Natural History Museum, wholly Transitional between Late Norman and Early English—than by his university buildings and hospitals.

Waterhouse built hardly any churches, Pearson and Bodley on the other hand hardly any mansions, let alone public buildings. The mentality of the Victorian church designer was indeed very different from that of the Victorian secularist. The church architects were more earnest and disciplined, the secularists more enterprising. But the layman would be wrong, if he thought that the great church builders were copyists of the past. Far from it. A man like Pearson was so steeped in the thirteenth century's elements that he could use them for buildings which taken as a whole had no period authority. St Augustine, Kilburn, is the finest example and indeed one of the finest parish churches of any age. Other churches of his are less daring in plan and elevation, but equally noble. Among the most outstanding elements was rib vaulting (as against open timber roofs) and thrilling vistas into subsidiary rooms, also vaulted.

In another way Bodley was just as Gothic and yet just as original. It is surely a surprise for anybody that Pendlebury and Hoar Cross were designed by the same architect and built during the same seventies, the former severe, lofty and unadorned, the latter gorgeously decorated. Albi Cathedral must have been the inspiration for both Pendlebury and Pearson's St Augustine.

Of Pearson's oeuvre a considerable part was church restoration, and it remains baffling that he should not have shown more respect for the medieval buildings he was commissioned to restore. The case of Peterborough is telling.

But enough of styles and enough of churches. The social, the technological and the functional aspects of Victorian architecture are as interesting. Take building types: Hardwick and the Docks, Hardwick and the railway terminal (Euston), Smirke and the British Museum library, Smirke and a bazaar, Smirke and working-class housing. Waterhouse and hospitals, Waterhouse and the Natural History Museum, and so on. The Natural History Museum had an iron skeleton, and iron was also structurally used by Hardwick in the St Katharine's Dock for the Tuscan columns supporting the upper storeys, and by Smirke for his bazaar in Oxford Street.

Other Victorian aspects are the coming of the architectural journals – the *Builder* was started in 1843 – and the belief and disbelief in competitions. The story of the Carlton Club is significant. The selection committee invited fifteen architects but came to nothing like a unanimous choice. Thereupon a new competition was announced, this time for all members of the Club to agree on an architect, not a design. Sydney Smirke got the highest vote and designed the new premises. An unsuccessful architect called it a farce and a 'flimsy blind to screen some intended favouritism'. The most notorious competition was that for the Royal Exchange.

Finally a reminder of the frequency of dynasties of architects. The Scotts and the Waterhouses are the best known and the most lasting. But Barry's two sons followed their father, and Philip Hardwick's father as well as his son were architects.

I have made a point in this preface to collect my facts – nearly all of them – from the chapters of the book. By doing so I hoped to convince readers of the wide range of matters of interest represented by Victorian architects. And the ones presented here are only a sample. One could without much effort produce a volume with another seven, say Brooks, Lamb, Lethaby, Paley and Austin, Prior, Salvin and Teulon. These seven are just as much in need of monographs as the seven of this volume. The Victorian Society is ready for them.

I

William Burn
the country house in transition

DAVID WALKER

William Burn was born in Edinburgh on 20 December 1789, the son of Robert Burn (1752–1815), an architect of modest distinction and a prosperous builder. A conversation piece, painted probably about 1805, shows a stout father with palette at an easel, and a slightly built, very earnest-looking son with a portfolio. In 1808 his father sent him to Robert Smirke's for three years, where, with C. R. Cockerell and Henry Roberts, he learned what they described in 1844 as 'important lessons' – including, perhaps, the art of pleasing 'men whom it was proverbially impossible to please', and Toryism.[1] It was a busy office, large but closely related – Robert Smirke's younger brother Sydney arrived a few years later. At Smirke's Burn worked on Covent Garden and Lowther, and formed what appears from the Edinburgh National Monument correspondence to have been a close friendship with Cockerell. On his return he set up an office at the family building and marble-cutting premises in Leith Walk. The first work with which his name has been connected was the remodelling of the Binns for the Dalyells, but the date (*c.* 1810) suggests he merely completed work initiated by his father or, more probably, designed the additions made in the 1830s. Between May and August 1812 he designed the Exchange Assembly Rooms at Greenock (destroyed) and by the following January was sufficiently esteemed in his native city to be included among those invited to report on the layout of Calton.

In 1814 he took a large house at 78 George Street (from which he moved along to No. 131 in 1822) and designed his first church, the tall-spired Greek Ionic parish church at North Leith; and in the same year designed his first known country house, Gallanach, Argyll (for Dugald Macdougall). With its symmetrical castellated elevation and bow-ended room shapes in the late eighteenth-century tradition, reminiscent of John Paterson rather than Robert Smirke, Gallanach gives virtually no hint of the highly developed house plans which were to begin appearing in a few years time. In 1816 he designed the Neo-Perpendicular St John's Episcopal Church and Grecian Merchant Maiden Hospital (destroyed) in Edinburgh and the very grand Custom House at Greenock. But in that same year he was narrowly defeated by W. H. Playfair in the Edinburgh University competition which inaugurated a long and in time bitter rivalry between the two architects and brought about his well-known abhorrence of competitions, leading eventually to an almost total avoidance of public and commercial commissions after 1844. Churches, terraces, banks and public buildings continued to flow freely from his pen for the next thirty years, but this brief essay must be confined to his country houses to the design of which he was in time to devote himself exclusively. They were the mainstay of his practice from 1817 when, probably thanks to his father who had made proposals for it in 1803, he received his first major country house commission, Saltoun.

5, 6, 7

After that he never looked back. By 1820–21 he had three large houses on hand; in 1823 three more; in 1824 another four; and in 1825 no fewer than six, enabling him to take a lease of Hermiston House on the Riccarton estate, where, as business permitted, he lived the life of a country gentleman. Thereafter he averaged three to four large houses a year.[2] What was the secret of his success? Robert Kerr said of

8

1 WILLIAM BURN. *Bust by Thomas Campbell*

2, 3   BURN. *Dupplin. North and south fronts*

him that 'he had so thoroughly acquired the mastery of that particular problem of plan . . . that I may safely say no one else could hope to compete with him'. Burn knew his clients, the minutiae of their regularly ordered lives, their desire for privacy from both their servants and their constant round of guests. His houses never sacrifice convenience or privacy to showy geometrical planning or symmetry for symmetry's sake. They consist almost exclusively of rectangular apartments assembled with the most compelling logic and economy in the sequence in which they were to be used, a sequence which, together with complex considerations of service and privacy dictated the entire plan form of the house and offices. Burn seldom built higher than two storeys and attics, and basements were avoided wherever possible, partly to preserve the privacy of the gardens where they adjoined the principal apartments, partly because he nearly always made a point of providing the servants with decent accommodation. Almost invariably he planned outwards from the family bedroom from which master and mistress progressed to their separate dressing rooms. In the smaller houses these were private sitting rooms as well, but in the larger ones they usually open into a private room for the master and a boudoir for the mistress where they could be comfortable until the principal rooms warmed up, or simply alone. In many this private suite forms a wing of its own, and is often skilfully linked en suite to the principal rooms so that the mistress seldom needed to appear in hall or corridor unless going out. Of several large Burn and Bryce houses has it been recalled that in winter the principal rooms were used only when there were guests, and so well had the servicing been thought out that they scarcely saw any servant but the butler unless the number of guests was exceptional. The privacy of these apartments was external as well as internal. Almost from the first Burn positioned the entrance so that the possibility of callers looking in was minimized; and frequently the house and approach was disposed so that the area of garden adjoining the principal and private apartments was hidden from their sight. But part of his success was more personal. T. L. Donaldson described Burn as

frank and plain-spoken, occasionally even to roughness . . . no flatterer . . . somewhat impulsive, and gifted with great shrewdness and common sense . . . he was a man of the highest integrity and independence, and so far from leading his clients into needless or extravagant outlay, he would demur to any unnecessary expense or an expenditure beyond his employers' means. . . . And it is well known that, being required to prepare designs for an useless and costly object . . . he purposely delayed beginning and appealed to the son to advise the father to give up the intention.

Nor, as the ultimate extension of protecting the privacy of his clients, did he ever publish or exhibit: he refused election to the Royal Scottish Academy in 1829. Everything in the period covered by this essay was handled personally; he rose early, and 'rain, snow or frost never kept him in'. He first drew small-scale plans washed in red accompanied by a perspective, usually in pencil, sketched as Donaldson says 'with great accuracy and neatness' as a basis for discussion. Many of these went to working drawing stage without modification, but with others, again in Donaldson's words,

he was untiring in his endeavour to meet the wishes and tastes of his employers, and he has shown me numerous sketches of subjects varying in plan and even in style to realise their wishes, nay caprices.

'I will do anything you do desire' wrote Burn to a difficult client, Dundas of Ochtertyre, who eventually cancelled his house.[3] Many of these sketch plans got no further; but if proceeded with, Burn (Donaldson again)

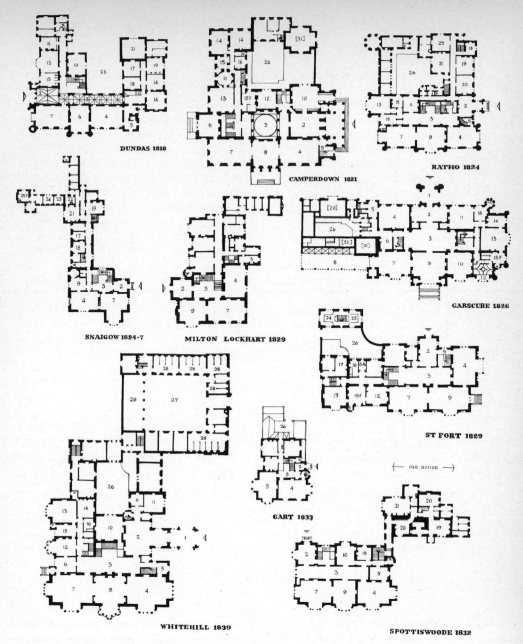

DUNDAS 1818

CAMPERDOWN 1821

RATHO 1824

SNAIGOW 1824-7

MILTON LOCKHART 1829

GARSCUBE 1826

ST FORT 1829

GART 1833

WHITEHILL 1839

SPOTTISWOODE 1832

OLD HOUSE

4   BURN. *Plans of ten houses to show comparative planning. South is at the bottom
except for Dundas (east) and Whitehall (east-south-east). Re-drawn from his original
working drawings. 1 Carriage-porch; 2 Entrance hall; 3 Saloon or hall; 4 Dining
room; 5 Dinner service; 6 Ante-room; 7 Drawing room; 8 Conservatory; 9 Library;
10 Billiard room; 11 Private sitting, writing or business room; 12 Boudoir; 13 Family
bedroom; 14 Bedroom; 15 Dressing room; 16 Bathroom; 17 Ladies' maid; 18 Butler;
19 Housekeeper; 20 Servants' Hall; 21 Kitchen; 22 Scullery; 23 Game larder;
24 Dairy; 25 Laundry; 26 Servants' Court; 27 Stable Court; 28 Stables; 29 Coach
houses. Square brackets indicate upper parts of rooms at a lower level. In the Snaigow
plan 19–25 are conjectural as this end of the house was extended and re-arranged c.1902
and earlier: Burn's working drawings seldom have the destination of the rooms marked.
As built Snaigow had two windows of three lights instead of a single four-light at the
dining room.*

following the example of his master, Sir Robert Smirke, drew out the plans with the minutest accuracy, dimensioning with his own hand every part and detail with peculiar clearness so as to afford no excuse to the builder for any mistakes or blunders.

5, 6, 7   His expertise in planning was not acquired instantly however. At Saltoun sketch plans were prepared in October 1817[4] for a client (Fletcher of Saltoun) who was just coming of age and went to working drawings the following year. His work there, Perpendicular Gothic with a hint of the elder Smirke's cubic style about it, was on the model of the Elliots' Taymouth Castle (1806–10) with angle towers, a cloistral entrance arcade and a central lantern tower, all skilfully grafted into the angle of the old L-shaped house enlarged by his father. The interior is of impressive competence with richly vaulted apartments and ingeniously planned services, but perhaps too spacious to be of real comfort, the central saloon being, as James Dunbar-Nasmith has observed, 'quite literally a gothic version of the dome of St Paul's' with a circular gallery and a vaulted ceiling high up; heat loss was considered, however, for the square lantern is double-glazed by an inner octagon. For the future much the most interesting feature was the last minute provision of the private apartments. As first drawn the principal floor consisted almost entirely of very grand public rooms. Pencilled in, however, is the division of the smaller second drawing room in the old house as family bedroom and dressing room, a small adjoining chamber off the dining room being now requisitioned as a bathroom. This, together with the oval ante-room linking the small drawing room with the principal one, provided the characteristic Burn private suite of family bedroom, bathroom, dressing room and private sitting room or boudoir opening directly into a single large drawing room.

4   Later in the same year he designed Dundas Castle (for James Dundas), externally a weakly detailed essay in the elder Smirke's early Lowther idiom. Yet, however inferior artistically to Saltoun, Dundas is perhaps more significant for the future in that its lower, more intimate two-storey scale, the near-symmetrical block of three principal rooms (here facing east), the large family bedroom flanked by dressing rooms (here an integral part of his plan from the start), and the asymmetrically-

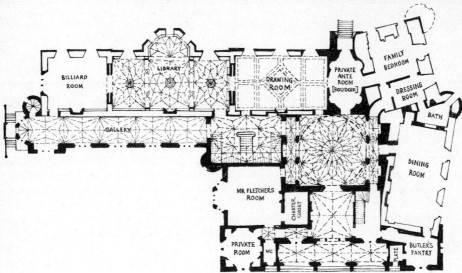

5, 6, 7   BURN. *Saltoun. North front, library and ground plan*

placed square tower were to be recurring features of his larger houses.

The general style of Dundas was repeated in his unexecuted design for Arisaig of December 1819. Its plan is not known, but in the same year he designed Adderstone in Northumberland, a simple Greek house with a rectangular central hall squared off by columnar screens and domed, and a top-lit staircase which neatly pushes out the adjoining room as a projected centre. In 1821 Burn enlarged and elaborated this design in his plans for Camperdown, Dundee (for Viscount Duncan), the exterior of which is Wilkins' Grange Park translated from Doric to Ionic, but with a more complex relationship of house and portico; and as finally

4

revised (December 1823) with the pilastrade omitted except at the central features. Here he perfected his classic plan type. The private apartments grouped around the family bedroom are now expressed as a separate wing, but are linked en suite with the public apartments in the main block, each opening into the other in logical sequence from family bedroom to dining room.

The origins of this type of plan have not yet received the study they warrant. Neither the private bedroom suite at main floor level nor the private wing was a new idea. Many well-arranged eighteenth-century examples are to be found wherever the house was large enough on plan. Robert Adam's Mellerstain (1770) is a particularly good example of the former arrangement with the rooms en suite much as they would be in a Burn plan except that the bedroom opens directly into the drawing room and the breakfast room is at the other end of the house. Many later Adam plans, such as the triangular Walkinshaw of 1791, are excellent and indeed improved variants of the same sequence, except that the importance of having the principal and private apartments out of sight of the main entrance as at Mellerstain was more often than not sacrificed to brilliant geometric planning. Adam's ex-assistants Paterson and Crichton tended to follow Adam in this respect, though Crichton was markedly less skilful in his planning and neither achieved quite the same clarity of arrangement. In Archibald Elliot's earlier houses the private apartments tend to become more extensive occupying the greater part of one side of the house, but he usually placed them adjacent to the dining room rather than the drawing room and allowed the entrance hall to break the sequence of the principal apartments in a way Burn almost always avoided: but at the reconstruction of Minto (1814) he produced a very well arranged V-plan with the private apartments in one wing and the principal apartments in the other, all en suite very much as Burn would have ordered them, and completely hidden from the main entrance in the angle. An earlier and perhaps more significant version of the same idea is William Atkinson's very skilful double courtyard plan for Scone (1803) where the private apartments form a single clearly recognizable architectural unit adjacent to the main block of principal apartments and not, as usually the case in earlier houses with private wings, one of two externally identical wings allocated to the purpose. Privacy was well considered, most of the principal and all of the private apartments being out of sight of the main entrance. Closer to Burn's Camperdown plan than any of these are those of Wilkins' Neo-Tudor houses at Dalmeny (1814) and Dunmore (1820) where the public and private apartments are strung out in a long unbroken right-angled enfilade, the ground floor being only one room deep, all looking out on to the park, and well away from the main entrance so that callers could not look into them. All of these plans are considerably more sophisticated than say Wyatt's Ashridge or Smirke's Lowther where the private apartments are in the vicinity of the main entrance. At Camperdown Burn followed Wilkins' general arrangement, reversing it to suit the different approach and shortened Wilkins' inconveniently long and somewhat institutional lines of communication by deepening the plan and grouping secondary apartments to which a view was of less consequence on the courtyard side. In Burn's plans the suite associated with family bedroom was always given privacy from the younger members of the family as well as from guests. Unlike Atkinson and Elliot he never provided more than one large bedroom at principal floor level, other members of the family being accommodated in the upper floor of the private wing with a stair for the exclusive use of the family, or, as at Camperdown, completely out of earshot elsewhere in the house.

The slightly earlier Blairquhan (1820, for Sir David Hunter Blair), Burn's next Gothic house,[5] is not quite so sophisticated in its planning. In its arrangement of

8 BURN. *Carstairs. Watercolour*

central hall and imperial staircase and clearly defined wing of private apartments it
recalls Camperdown, though hall and staircase are not enclosed by a complete
periphery of rooms, there being only two principal rooms en suite (here facing
west) instead of three; the staircase is thus lit by an oriel bay on the north instead of
a lantern light. In designing the elevations of Blairquhan, Burn looked to Wilkins
yet again for inspiration – this time to Dalmeny Park, in his East Barsham mode,
even to the extent of having higher gables than the roofs warrant. Blairquhan is not
so well informed in detail as Dalmeny, but the logic of the plan is reflected in the
neatly composed entrance elevation which, in its basic concept of a main block
with an asymmetrically placed centrepiece balanced by a lower family wing
terminating in a tower, appears to derive from Atkinson's Scone. From the
centrepiece projects a big carriage porch, while above and behind it the central
saloon rises as a lantern tower as at Saltoun. Carstairs (1821, for Sir Henry   8
Monteith) is an elaborated and reversed version of Blairquhan, with the central
tower brought forward immediately behind the carriage porch and flanked by bay
windows with gables above. It is clumsier than Blairquhan however; the gables
would have been better omitted, and the octagonal angle turrets at the northern
angles of the main block are too emphatic for the rest of the design. Internally
Carstairs is lavish, with four very large principal rooms to the south; the central
hall is given up, a vaulted corridor runs longitudinally through the centre of the
house with an immense imperial staircase at its eastern end.

Stylistically, the most singular feature of Carstairs was the Jacobean treatment of
the gables of the south front. They are amongst the earliest examples of the revival
of that form in the country. Sir Richard Morrison's Miltown (1818) and
Kilruddery in Ireland (published by Neale 1821) and St Julian's Underriver in Kent
by J. B. Papworth (1818–20) are the only executed houses built anew in Jacobean
style which have yet come to light, though Repton had proposed an Elizabethan
house for Great Tew as early as 1803.[6] This theme was further pursued at Riccarton
(for Sir William Gibson Craig) for which Donaldson gives 1823 and Small (*Castles
and Mansions of the Lothians*) 1827. The drawings are lost and the house was razed in
1956. It incorporated an early sixteenth–century tower house recased to match the
new house which was otherwise decidedly English Jacobean with shaped gables
and dormer gablets over the first-floor windows; porch and angle pinnacles were
still Tudor. Jacobean details, particularly strapwork crestings, are again in evidence
at Lauriston (1825, for Thomas Allen). It also incorporates an old tower house, the
rubble walls of which were now accepted unrefaced as a picturesque antiquity.   15

9   BURN. *Garscube. North front*

4   Ratho (1824, for John Bonar) has Jacobean gables but is still battlemented Tudor. The plan is interesting in that it was the prototype for many others. Like Camperdown, Ratho enters on the east with three principal rooms *en axe* on the south, and an office court on the north, with luggage porch at the north-east angle; but the circulation space consists of a hall corridor with staircase on the north in T-plan arrangement. John Dobson used a similar plan-type from the same year, but he treated the flanks symmetrically also, even at Tudor-Jacobean Lilburn Tower of 1828.[7] At Ratho only the south front is symmetrical with centre bay-window and gable: the money would not run to an entrance tower, carriage porch or private wing, but the entrance front was quite resourcefully treated. Both the entrance and the north-east bay of the court are advanced; the former has tall octagon angles and the latter a slight increase in height, thus giving a suggestion of Burn's favourite two-tower arrangement. In the following year he produced an elaborated version of this design with a tower and carriage porch of Carstairs type for Moncreiffe, but only a lodge was built. Drumfinn (later Aros, 1825, for Hugh MacLean, demolished) resembled Ratho in plan with the addition of a north-western private wing as at Camperdown. The entrance bay was more ambitiously treated as a tower, but the detail was otherwise weaker.

4, 9   Garscube (reconstructed for Sir Archibald Campbell, demolished by the University of Glasgow, 1955) was the last and much the finest of this early series of Neo-Tudor houses.[8] His first design was Neo-Greek, fifteen windows long with hexastyle Ionic portico. Although the working drawings were complete by May 1826, a Tudor design was got out in October. There was no wing, a lavish suite of private apartments with a very secluded boudoir forming the eastern part of a big main block. The familiar secondary tower had an ogee roof and the entrance tower, advanced as at Drumfinn, had a carriage porch ground floor. Thus all the elements of his previous designs were gathered into one sweepingly successful composition. The detail, too, showed great advances, reflecting the material published by Britton and Pugin in the intervening years. The entrance front was still battlemented, but the southern garden front, two bays with Jacobean gables on the right of the central turret-flanked gable balanced by a single bay, another turret and a conservatory on the left, hints at the later façades of Dupplin. The

2, 3   interior had a complete periphery of rooms to the top-lit central hall and staircase; reticent by the standards of Saltoun and Carstairs, it nevertheless contained features of special interest, particularly the Jacobean pendants of the saloon lantern.

16

10   BURN. *Kimmerghame. Watercolour showing unexecuted design*
11   BURN. *St Fort. South front*

The Jacobean influences are even more marked in the contemporary reconstruction of Fettercairn (for Sir William Forbes) where the entrance tower also has a shaped gable; the sketch design for Kimmerghame (June 1828, not proceeded with) developed this theme further with a similar but taller tower (possibly inspired by Britton's engraving of Audley End) and a conservatory terminating in another tower. The design otherwise resembles the more mature Dupplin, drawn one month earlier. But here we should look again at the influence of Sir Robert Smirke. Dr Crook has pointed out to me that *c.* 1821, the year of Burn's Jacobean gables at Carstairs, Smirke probably built a Jacobean house on

Castle Green at Hereford. In 1824, the year of Ratho, Smirke built Edmond Castle in Cumberland, very similar in style to the Fettercairn and Kimmerghame designs. Moreover Edmond Castle's plan-type as extended in 1844–46 is closely related to that of Ratho but has a set-back wing, a common feature of Burn houses from the 1830s onwards. Dr Crook tells me that this plan-type was evolved by Smirke, parallel with, and perhaps even in consultation with, Burn and Dobson. Smirke must have visited the north several times during this period, and Burn was certainly occasionally in London, where he doubtless saw plans of work in progress; probably Smirke should therefore be credited with a share not only in the creation of the Jacobean style but also in Burn's renowned expertise in house-planning,[9] although it may be observed that his large Kinfauns design of 1820 still did not include a private wing en suite with the principal apartments. Sir Robert, however, never equalled Burn's confident handling of the Jacobean idiom at Dupplin (1828–32, for the Earl of Kinnoul, main block burned out 1934, demolished 1967). The centre of the main block was only two rooms thick, the central hall of Burn's early houses being given up in favour of a hall corridor on the north front with separate stair hall at the south-west; and for the first time the luggage entrance is clearly featured in a slim turret of its own. The wing at the south-west (a survival from the old house recased) was a mansion in itself and the office court had a further range of bedrooms on the north side. The composition of the north front with the characteristic primary and secondary towers was a little strung out, mainly because the position of the offices, originally designed to be at right angles to the north front, was altered after work began, probably in order to sink the office court to a lower level.

At Dupplin Burn's Neo-Jacobean is mature, less directly derivative but suaver in proportion than George Webster's Eshton and Underley of 1825–27 and much more consistent than Rickman's exactly contemporary Matfen. It is much closer to John Dobson's Lilburn of the following year in its level of accomplishment. In the same year, 1828, Gillespie Graham began an equally mature but quite different house at Murthly (demolished)[10] and Robert Reid the inferior but equally Jacobean United College building at St Andrews. Why, as late as 1828, in Scotland – where there were no original Jacobean gables to copy? That question is not easily answered, for the Elizabethan and Jacobean material included by John Britton in the second volume of *Architectural Antiquities* had been published as long ago as 1809, while T. H. Clarke's rather slight *Domestic Architecture of the Reigns of Queen Elizabeth and James I* was not published till 1833. In 1828 Robert Lugar had published his reconstruction of Markyate Cell, Herts (1825–27), in *Villa Architecture,* but its brick Jacobean has little in common with the Scottish designs. Burn visited London in 1827, but there is every indication the Britton and Neale were all he had; if the assurance of Dupplin surprises, it seems to be but a reflection of the cautious way he had, step by step, progressed towards Jacobean just as the Tudors had done. It comes as a shock to find that its façades are a direct expression of its plan without any large-scale borrowings. The entrance tower roof comes from Aston Hall, and the main door-piece appears to have been built up from several sources. Of the interior we know all too little. The ribbed ceilings pencilled on the plans show a good knowledge of Elizabethan and Jacobean patterns, but these could easily have been derived from several old Scots houses on which he had been consulted, particularly Niddrie Marischal (1823 onwards) where he had reproduced original ceilings already in the house. The Dupplin main staircase was most revealing; as in that at Niddrie Marischal, the fret patterns of the balustrades were adapted from Britton's plate of the staircase at Crewe, while the ceiling was improvised from both Jacobean and Neo-classic details.

12 BLORE *and* BURN. *Freeland. South front in original condition*

The Dupplin formula was repeated in condensed form at St Fort (1829, for A. C.   4, 11
Stewart, demolished) with a single large tower combining the features of the
Dupplin ones and strapwork crestings to the bay windows. The interior had a
central corridor lit from the staircase at the western end which echoed the Dupplin
one with a more personal fretwork design; the principal rooms were indecisive in
style, mainly Neo-Greek but with simple Jacobean ceilings in the principal
apartments. One chimney-piece, however, was Louis Quinze, a feature repeated in
many later houses. In the same year Burn designed a convincing symmetrical
Jacobean front for Ribston, Yorkshire, and in 1830 a small towerless edition of St
Fort for Dunskey, neither of which was executed. Thereafter, despite the excellent
Madras College at St Andrews (1832), the wells of Jacobean inspiration ran nearly
dry. Spottiswoode (1832, for John Spottiswoode, demolished) had Jacobean gables
and a central cupola but the windows were Georgian sashes to match the old house
(retained as offices) – an unhappy compromise. The house was, unusually, of three
storeys with the private apartments on the first floor; on the main floor it had a
stairhall and a narrow range of ancillary accommodation on the north side of the
hall corridor which was lit from the west. The entrance was at the north-west and
the three-room south front was symmetrical, with centre gable on the Ratho
model.

Concurrently Burn had been developing what contemporaries called his
'cottage houses'. In 1823–27 he was called upon to design a number of smaller
houses, the most interesting of which was Snaigow (1824–27 for Mrs Keay,   4, 13
reconstructed 1962). As built it was unattractive in its dark red stone, but the
simple, almost Cotswold Tudor idiom, arrived at after much experiment, was
interesting for that date. The plan, entrance on the east, L-shaped suite of three
principal rooms, two on the south, one on the west, with service wing on the
north, formed the prototype for many others. Freeland (1825, reconstructed for   12
Lord Ruthven, enlarged later by R. R. Anderson and again for Strathallan School),
designed in conjunction with Edward Blore and the prototype of that architect's
Goodrich Court, is a large house in similar 'vernacular' Tudor vein, and more
convincingly Neo-medieval than Burn's more ambitious Tudor houses prior to
that date. It suggests that Blore might have had a hand in the creation of his cottage

19

style. Duntrune (1826, for Graham) has a small version of the Ratho plan, asymmetrically treated. Pitcairns (1827, for J. Pitcairns) is a larger, more compact Snaigow, a little thin but of interest in that in general arrangement it is the immediate prototype of his first Scots-Tudor house, Milton Lockhart.

There was no historical precedent for Scots-Tudor. Scotland, except at Pinkie and the Kirkwall Earl's Palace, had rarely used mullioned bay windows. But, thanks to Sir Walter Scott, the demand for Scots houses was growing. Such houses did not lend themselves to expected standards of daylighting and Blore and Atkinson in their work at Scott's own Abbotsford had indicated a Scots-Tudor compromise in 1816 and 1822–23.[11] Burn followed their lead in additions at Riccarton and Niddrie (1823), Brodie (1824; originally with Jacobean gables, removed 1846) Pinkie, Lauriston and Dalhousie (1825); but it was not until May–June 1829 that he designed completely new houses in the Scots-Tudor (or by 1829 more properly Scots-Jacobean) vein: Milton Lockhart (with Pitcairns-type

13　BURN. *Snaigow. Drawing showing scheme of 1824 as revised c.1827*
14　BURN. *Riccarton. (Note how the courses are lined up with the glazing bars.)*

15　BURN. *Tyninghame, an*
old photograph showing the
cantilevered terrace round the
principal apartments, since
removed
16　BURN. *Milton Lockhart*

plan, for W. Lockhart, demolished) and Faskally (for Archibald Butter) which has, most unusually, the porch inserted in the suite of three principal rooms on the south. By the end of the year he was emboldened to design the immense Tyninghame (reconstructed for the Earl of Haddington), almost French in its tourelles, but in detail decidedly Jacobean. It was arranged round a courtyard open to the south, with the entrance front to the north and the principal rooms in the old house facing west. The interior, except for the magnificent Jacobean staircase, is simple with some very clever ceilings. Sprott (reconstructed for J. Sprott) followed in 1830 in a dourer, more Scottish idiom with unmullioned windows, the more graceful Auchmacoy in Aberdeenshire with mixed Scots and English features in 1831. Auchmacoy (for J. Buchan, interior classical) is of particular interest in that its style was immediately taken up by the Aberdeen architect John Smith at Easter Skene (1832), Balmoral I (1834), Slains (1836) and so on, finally culminating in his son's Balmoral II in 1853: Smith's initial acquaintance with the style derives from

15

17 BURN. *Lude. North front*

his having been consulted on Burn's Jacobean schemes for Robert Gordon's College at Aberdeen and for Fintray House (jobs he eventually secured for himself) in 1828–30. In the same year as Auchmacoy (1831) Burn experimented further with the corbelled angle turret theme, only tentatively introduced at Tyninghame, in a design for the entrance front at Kilconquhar (for Sir Henry Bethune, revised before execution in 1839), but the turrets were rather slim. Those in his additions to Stenhouse (1836, for Sir Michael Bruce, demolished) and Castle Menzies (1836, revised 1839, for Sir Niel Menzies) square (copied from the original house) and round respectively, are more convincing. By 1837 at Invergowrie House (reconstructed for A. Clayhills) he is using them freely and expertly, and it is now chiefly by the layout, proportions, finishes and the precision that came of a Neo-Greek training, rather than by non-Scottish detail, that we recognize the exteriors as patently Early Victorian.

Burn built no large new houses in the middle 1830s: most were houses in the four- to ten-thousand-pounds price range.[12] In 1832 he built two good ones, Auchterarder (for James Hunter, internally remodelled with the addition of a *porte-cochère* and winter garden by Burnet Son and Campbell (1886–89), Jacobean in detail but crow-stepped with a Scots tower, and Dawyck (originally Posso, for Sir J. Nasmyth, extended 1898 by J. A. Campbell) which, while retaining the double gable and dormer motif of the entrance front at Tyninghame, shows a developing Scots vocabulary with corbelling from the round to the square. Not all had turrets or towers, however. Lude (1837, for J. J. McInroy) is in many ways the classic Burn house of the mid-1830s, Scots-Jacobean with crow-stepped gables, Baroque door-piece, Spottiswoode-type plan with symmetrical south front and a neatly segregated service court with the housekeeper's and butler's corridors at right angles. Yet though Lude is, in a quiet way, a distinguished house, the lack of large commissions to stir Burn's imagination resulted in some rather dull houses all with plans deriving from Snaigow, Ratho or Spottiswoode. The Ratho-Spottiswoode types were capable of a good deal of variety, with the position of the entrance and family wing and/or offices shuttled about from north to east to west; the Snaigow type was capable of very little. In all the main elements were becoming disturbingly familiar. Moreover, Burn seems to have been the victim of his own anxiety to please. The Dundas of Ochertyre correspondence shows that after the contracts were settled he allowed the client to change the Jacobean gables ('I much prefer the old crow-toes') and cut out the servants' hall ('I find they eat exceeding well in the kitchen') doubtless to the detriment of the design.

In 1839 that discerning critic Lord Cockburn, who had earlier been a client, noted these developments with disapproval in his *Circuit Journeys*:

22

I am sorry to see so many of Burn the architect's repetitions of himself throughout this picturesque district. There is one of his gimcrack cottage houses at Fascally, two if not three about Urrard [Urrard, 1831, Killiecrankie Cottage, 1825, and presumably Strathgarry] and one at Lude, all the same and none in keeping with a rough climate and situations of romantic wilderness.

Cockburn's own house, Bonaly (for which Burn made a cottage design in 1826), was a convincing tower-house designed by William Henry Playfair in 1836. Playfair was closely following Burn's stylistic career, but his approach was different and his commissions fewer but larger. Burn designed modern houses with straightforward functional plans in Jacobean style, Playfair, like Devey later, houses which he hoped would in time be mistaken for originals. In his additions at Grange and Prestongrange (1830–31) he came far closer to the qualities of original Scottish work than Burn (both were outdone by David Hamilton at Dunlop in 1833) but his attitude is best shown by the picturesque bi-axial plan of Brownlow Hall, Lurgan County Armagh (1833), of which he himself wrote 'my Elizabethan child . . . more like an Old Manor House than any modern attempt I have yet seen'. By 1834 he was turning his mind to an even bigger Elizabethan child, Donaldson's Hospital, Edinburgh (begun 1842), in 1836 the Scots-Jacobean Barmore (Stonefield) and in 1838 the remodelling of Floors.[13] Burn's astonishing success in 1838–41 after the cottage houses of the mid-1830s dismayed him. In April 1841, instructed to reduce the plans for Donaldson's, he wrote bitterly

Burn meantime carries everything before him, generally however creating horrid blots on the landscape wherever he is employed, and is again becoming more purseproud and ostentatious and overbearing than ever. His utter want of Genius is only to be equalled by his copious supply of impudence.[14]

Yet while the 'cottage houses' – The Gart and Inverawe (1833), Monkrigg (1834), Bourhouse and Tyneholme (1835), Anton's Hill (1836), Ninewells and Finnart (1839), Cardrona (1840) – were being churned out to clients comfortable as never before, Burn had a new theme for bigger houses in gestation. In 1833 he had turned to English-medieval-castellated at Inverness County Buildings, rather in the manner of Robert Smirke's Kinfauns and the assize courts at Carlisle, and in 1834 made sketch proposals for rebuilding Beaufort Castle in a similar vein. In 1835 he pursued this line further with proposals for an asymmetrical addition at Knowsley, rather in the manner of Robert Smirke's Eastnor, for the Earl of Derby. But more significant for the future were two sketch proposals of 1832 for Jacobeanizing Dalkeith Palace, one based on Wollaton, the other a much brighter design closer to his designs of 1839. Its features were largely taken from Winton House (1620) which he had sketched in March 1829. His work at Drumlanrig (1830, for the Duke of Buccleuch), a commission he took from Atkinson in 1828, must also have suggested the possibilities of seventeenth-century Scottish-Jacobean. The first executed hints of it are at Netherby (1833) in Cumberland for Sir James Graham, work which, as Sir Nikolaus Pevsner has remarked, one would without hesitation date *c.* 1850. His three largest commissions of the time were the immense but short-lived entrance wing at Arthurstone (1836)[15] somewhat in the Dupplin manner with an ogee-capped tower corbelled from the canted to the square, Duncrub (1837; for Lord Rollo, replaced by Habershon thirty years later) and Balcarres (1838, for James Lindsay, much enlarged by Bryce 1863–67), but these give little indication of further development.

The great turning point in Burn's career was his engagement to complete Harlaxton in 1838. Anthony Salvin had begun it in 1831 for Gregory Gregory, but in that year he and his builder Mr Weare departed, having got roughly half-way

4

18 BURN. *Harlaxton. The staircase*

with the building of this gigantic pile which rivalled in extent, and in assurance
surpassed, the great prodigy houses of the reigns of Elizabeth and James I. It
occupied Burn's attention until at least 1853. For a house where the architects are
known, Harlaxton is quite remarkably full of unanswered questions. Exact dates
for the interiors are lacking, we do not know how or why Burn got the job, nor to
what extent he executed designs already made or interior work already ordered.
Only the drawings for its carcase survive in the Salvin collection at the RIBA,
while the Burn collection contains not a scrap of drawing relating to it. Nor do we
know what hand Gregory had in the design himself, for Loudon in 1832 tells us
that Gregory 'studied the subject for several years previous to commencing it'; the
houses he visited included Burghley, Montacute, Rushton, Wollaton, Cobham
and Audley End, and if Harlaxton is carefully scrutinized, detail echoes from all of
these will be found there. The *Civil Engineer and Architects' Journal* of 1839 tells us
only a little more than is apparent from Salvin's drawings, that Burn was engaged
to 'erect what remained to be done in strict conformity with that half or portion
which had been built by Mr Salvin. Mr Blore was also called in but for consultation

only'. Recently Mrs Jill Allibone has found what may be an important clue as to the interior work : that Salvin was for some weeks in Munich and Southern Germany during his tenure of the commission. She has also found however, from the 1841 census return, that the work force contained no foreign names. That does not, however, by any means preclude the possibility of Burn having inherited drawings or arrangements already made in Bavaria or elsewhere on the Continent. It does suggest a possible explanation for the extraordinary Continental Baroque illusionism of the Cedar Staircase, which, as Christopher Hussey has remarked actually surpasses authentic productions of Zimmerman and the Asams. The Louis Quinze Rococo interiors fit more easily into the British historical pattern as Benjamin Dean Wyatt in his interiors at York (later Stafford) House, Apsley House and Crockford's Club and Belvoir had established the fashion in the later 1820s. Burn had himself been fitting Louis Quinze chimney-pieces from the very same years and was to achieve further French interiors of almost equal splendour at Montagu House, Whitehall (1859, for the Duke of Buccleuch; demolished), and the still extant 18 Carlton House Terrace (1863, for the Duke of Newcastle).

18

Externally, Burn's hand is chiefly evident in the outworks. The astounding Mannerist forecourt lodges and gateways on the main approach, challenging comparison with the most extravagant of Italian Baroque garden architecture, are from his office. Without parallel either before or after in Burn's œuvre, they are possibly the work of John Bryce (1805–51), younger brother of his partner-to-be David Bryce. Work by him of similar character and power, though not on so extravagant a scale, can be seen at Glasgow Necropolis; he might also have provided some hint for the Vanbrugh school architecture of the kitchen garden. The rest of the work, the Wollaton-inspired entrance to the service court (1843, echoing similar features in his designs for Dalkeith and Madras College, St Andrews) and the east terrace, have much more of the tightly disciplined Grecian-trained restraint which we associate with Burn composition and detailing.[16]

At Harlaxton Salvin and Gregory between them opened Burn's mind to possibilities hitherto undreamed of, and rekindled an imagination dulled by Scottish clients who wanted no more than his most comfortable plan-types reproduced as inexpensively as possible. In 1839 he designed four large houses, Muckross (Co. Kerry, for H. A. Herbert – working drawings February), Falkland (or Nuthill, for O. Tyndall Bruce – working drawings April–May), Beaufort (complete reconstruction for Lord Lovat – working drawings July) and Whitehill (for R. B. Wardlaw Ramsay – working drawings August). In the same year Christopher Turnor requested sketch plans for a new house at Stoke Rochford, Lincolnshire. All are Jacobean.

Beaufort was not carried out. The plans show a garden front with square and octagonal angle towers (à la Netherby), the entrance front being parallel with a carriage porch rather like that at Whitehill, though the other details are closer to Falkland. The other three houses are similar in layout, each with the entrance front at right angles to the garden front containing the three principal rooms, with one wing of the office court at right angles to form a two-sided entrance forecourt. Muckross, however, with principal rooms on the west and entrance on the north, is a reversal of the other two, which have their entrance on the north but their principal rooms on the east, with the family apartments to the south and west. In detail the plans are very different. Whitehill is Ratho enlarged with a very feminine private suite incorporated in the main block, Mr Ramsay's room being at the other end of the house.[17] At Falkland Mrs Bruce's suite is within the main block, while Mr Bruce's is in the link to the service court with his sitting room adjoining the passage to the women servants' wing, doubtless to discourage dalliance there.

19　BURN. *Falkland. View from south-east*
20　BURN. *Whitehill. East front*

Falkland and Whitehill are English-Jacobean in general character with their big mullioned bays, but many of the details are Scottish. The idea of the bays flanked by square pepper-pot turrets at Falkland presumably derives from the flanks at Audley End, but the elaborate crow-stepping, the magnificent chimneys, the cornice and arcaded balustrade of the entrance front tower (containing the service

19 stair to the dining room) are all Scottish, based on Winton House. Falkland composes extremely well all round, particularly on the west side, where the composition builds up from the women servants' wing, clinging to the slope of the den, to Mr Bruce's wing, and then up to the *corps de logis*, asymmetrically composed with the staircase and other features of the plan very neatly expressed in the elevation. The interior is also very distinctively detailed with very delicate plasterwork, reflecting the large volume of Elizabethan and Jacobean information Robinson, Richardson, Shaw and Nash had made available from 1833 onwards, and was further embellished by Robert Weir Schultz for Lord Bute from 1887.

4, 20 Whitehill is Falkland enriched and enlarged but is not so effectively sited. The entrance front is similar in arrangement but the single-storey entrance hall of Falkland is replaced by a projected entrance feature with an elaborate Dutch gable (apparently derived from those of the Wollaton pavilions) and a carriage porch, while the tower has a first-floor oriel. Its plan is deeper than Falkland, and it has attic dormers; the centre of the east front is not recessed, and it has a trefoil bay in the middle. The south front is equally lavish with another elaborate centre bay, here extending through two storeys. Whitehill is more varied in detail than

26 Falkland, doubtless reflecting the material which had been published in the few

21   BURN. *Muckross*
22   BURN. *Stoke Rochford*

months between them. The interior again had very pretty Jacobean ceilings. The exterior is, alas, now much cluttered and the ceilings either enclosed or destroyed.

The sketches at the RIBA suggest that the Muckross commission may have come to Burn through Harlaxton, for they show a Harlaxton-type tower behind the carriage porch. But as finally revised (June 1841) it is much the simplest of the three with a south front of three bay windows with three straight gables above and simple square chimney shafts; the entrance front repeats the Whitehill formula but the tower is replaced by a gable and the carriage porch (not executed until 1861 by William Atkins of Cork) is simplified and without columns. Muckross is an extremely satisfying design; its simple distinction has almost the quality of original work and anticipates Devey's houses later, though, of course, the layout is unmistakably Early Victorian. The interior is simpler than its two contemporaries, but again delicate and distinctive.

The Gregory connection brought Burn further Lincolnshire commissions. The working drawings for Stoke Rochford were finalized in 1841; Rauceby (1842, for Anthony Wilson) and Revesby Abbey (1844, for J. B. Stanhope) followed in quick succession. Stoke Rochford is externally a reshuffling of the elements of Whitehill and Falkland with the crow-steps, Winton detailing of the chimneys, carriage porch and tower omitted. The east front is similar to that of Falkland, but slightly stiffer, mainly due to the elongation of the pepper pots. The south front is plainer, but the entrance front, here on the west, rivals its prototypes with its enriched version of the Whitehill Dutch gable and near-symmetrical treatment, balanced on the north by a large wing containing services and private apartments, and on the

23 BURN. *Dartrey. Drawing by Burn showing the south front*

south by a low orangery. The forecourt is grander than at any of its predecessors, with tall piers and splendid iron work.[18] Revesby returns to the shaped gable theme, again with enriched chimneys; the arrangement of the entrance front is Muckross reversed with the carriage porch much elaborated in Dietterlinesque manner. Like Harlaxton, both these houses show extraordinary changes from their predecessors in interior décor, Louis Quinze interiors being intermingled with the Jacobean at Stoke Rochford, and Viennese and German Baroque at Revesby. Of Burn's ability to produce such exotic décor to gratify the individual stylistic wishes of his clients, his sources, and any assistance he might have obtained, we require to know a great deal more. Rauceby is more in the Muckross vein, but with a different plan and no carriage porch.

Concurrently with these, he had in hand additions to Raby Castle (1844, for the Duke of Cleveland) which were necessarily castellated, the reconstruction of Prestwold (1843, for C. W. Packe) and the very simple Redrice (1844, for Thomas Best), both in the subdued Italianate tinged with a Greek sharpness of detail he had evolved in his buildings for the Bank of Scotland; Prestwold is very elegant, a three-storey palazzo with recessed centres on the west and south into which Tuscan porch and conservatory features are inserted, and a Raphaelesque central hall.[19]

23   His first designs of 1843 for Dartrey (Co. Monaghan, for the Earl of Dartrey, demolished) were also classical, but the executed scheme was Jacobean with a recessed symmetrical front to the garden. Calwich (for A. Duncombe, demolished) and Bangor Castle (Co. Down, for R. E. Ward, now the Town Hall), both straight-gabled Jacobean, followed in 1846–47, and Calton Mohr (later Poltalloch, for N. Malcolm, gutted) in 1849.

Burn's splendid scheme for extending and recasing Eastwell (1848–50, for the Earl of Winchelsea, recast 1926) being only one-quarter executed, Poltalloch is the

24, 25   last major Jacobean house to fall within this review. The plan and composition follow well-tried patterns: main block entered on the east, with principal rooms on the south, balanced by a wing at the north-west and a court of offices at the north-east forming the familiar two-sided forecourt, the luggage entrance being contained in an octagonal clock turret echoed by a lower one at the angle of the offices. The south front was reminiscent of the corresponding (east) fronts at Falkland and Stoke Rochford with advanced bay-windowed ends. The pepper pots were replaced by small pinnacles, however, and the gables were trefoiled. The formula was repeated at the more ambitious brick-built Lynford (1856–61, for S. Lyne Stephens). Poltalloch, although a very pleasant design, was a little weak

28   compared with its predecessors. The interior was entirely Jacobean.

24, 25 BURN. *Poltalloch. Entrance and garden fronts*

Poltalloch was built five years after Burn had moved to London and has been taken out of sequence to keep Jacobean and Scots baronial developments consecutive. The later development of the Scottish side is intimately bound up with David Bryce (1803–76). Bryce was, like Burn, the son of an architect-builder and 'somewhat rough in manner'.[20] He trained with his father, but moved to Burn's, where by 1829 he enjoyed a very privileged position as his chief clerk, being allowed to carry on a modest practice from his house in Castle Street. In the spring of 1841 Burn had a serious breakdown in health with clients and builders clamouring for drawings,[21] and by May of that year Burn was describing Bryce as his partner. What influence Bryce had on Burn, if any, is hard to guess now; but the great Elizabethan palace he built at Langton (for the Marquis of Breadalbane, largely destroyed) in 1862 had the Whitehill version of the Wollaton gable, while his strongly Mannerist Unitarian Church in Castle Terrace and Neo-Baroque interior at 87 George Street (both in Edinburgh and of 1835) are interesting in relation to such things as the Harlaxton lodges. David's brother John, practising in Glasgow, had, as we have seen, also shown remarkable interest in Mannerism and Baroque in his McGavin monument of 1834 and Screen of 1836 in Glasgow Necropolis.

29

26   BURN. *Fonthill. Drawing by Burn showing unexecuted 1849 scheme*

By June 1844, with the bulk of his business now in England, Burn moved to Stratton Street, London, where he became not William Burn, architect, but William Burn Esq. He left Bryce in charge of the Edinburgh office. That he regarded the Scottish business as of equal importance is shown by the fact that he immediately sought out R. W. Billings and financed *The Baronial and Ecclesiastical Antiquities of Scotland*, published under their joint names by Blackwood in 1848–52; but in 1850 the Burn and Bryce partnership was broken. A sufficient reason is that by 1847 the Edinburgh office was busier than the London one, with Bryce now being commissioned directly. But that there were other differences between them, some of which certainly relate to their work for the Duke and Duchess of Buccleuch, is hinted by Burn's letter to Blackwood in July: 'I have closed my partnership with Bryce it being utterly impossible to go on with him.'[22] And in September, evidently feeling his interest in Scotland at an end, he extricated himself with difficulty from his partnership with Billings and Blackwood.

The first hints of Bryce taking an independent hand in country house work within Burn's practice appear in the entrance front of Kilconquhar, redesigned in 1839 when Burn had his hands full with his four Jacobean giants. This has the canted bay corbelled to the square which was to be characteristic of Bryce throughout his career. Finnart (1839) has a cottage version of the same feature with concave corbelling, and of this, too, Bryce built a large edition at Invermark Lodge (Glenesk) in 1847. The extensive alterations and additions at Thirlestane (1840, for the Earl of Lauderdale) appear to be Burn, at least in the initial stages, for his neat pencil studies for it are preserved at the RIBA.

Seacliff (1841, for George Sligo, extended later and now burnt out) was a large Scottish baronial house with many details characteristic of Bryce later. It may be that Bryce owed his characteristic motifs to Burn, but the fact that Burn did not use them at Fonthill suggests otherwise. Donaldson listed Carradale (1844, for R. Campbell), Inchdairnie (for Mrs Aytoun, burnt), Leny (for J. B. Hamilton) and Clatto (for J. Low, recently altered), all 1845,[23] as Burn's but John Bryce Jr. claimed them for his uncle at the latter's death. Clatto looks as if built much as Burn sketched it out; Leny also looks rather like him, but has some Bryce details, including his characteristic bay. Carradale is a low white harled house with square and circular angle turrets. Inchdairnie had a lavish Burn-type layout, but the elevations were characteristic Bryce.

While Bryce was enjoying unparalleled success, Burn suffered what must have been the greatest disappointment of his career. About 1847 he was commissioned to design an immense palace at Fonthill for the Marquess of Westminster, which

reached working drawing stage in 1849. Surprisingly for such a site, the style was   26
Franco-Scottish, the first of its kind—Bryce was to make the style his own later,
with the other leading members of the Edinburgh school quickly following. It was
to have had a two-storey symmetrical main frontage, basement and high attics with
advanced turreted ends and main floor balcony; the entrance front was to have a
giant carriage porch tower, a secondary tower and a picturesque array of French-
roofed offices forming his favourite two-sided forecourt. A chapel, whose apse
formed the centre of the east front, was included; one of the variant studies has
French flamboyant tracery. The detail was mixed, some of it, like the tower top,
going back to Winton House and other Scottish exemplars, and some to the early
French Renaissance. The much smaller executed house (1856, demolished 1955)[24]
reflected its author's disappointment, but at Buchanan (designed 1851–53, for the
Duke of Montrose) he had his second chance.

His neat preliminary perspective[25] shows a shortened Fonthill. It lacked the
basement which gave such a proud, dramatic uplift to the Fonthill design, but
would nevertheless have been a fine design with its mullioned bays and rich French
dormers. The plan was an enlargement of Poltalloch's with the offices less happily
pushed round the north side and playing no part in the main composition. It was
regarded by Kerr as the ultimate in perfection with a western private family wing
which formed a sizable mansion in itself.

Alas for Burn! He built the house, but his client wanted plate glass and fewer bay
windows. The design was quite ruined; an abortive attempt was made to restore
character by the use of hammer-dressed masonry, while the main front, redesigned
asymmetrically with a vestige of the original design at one end and a top-heavy
corbelled turret clawing the other, was a disaster. The dark stonework merely
accentuated the bleakness of its plate glass windows. It was gutted, unlamented, in
1955. The shell still remains.

Burn was the victim of his own anxiety to please. It was a situation his ex-
partner would have handled better ('Mr Bryce . . . allowed no obstacle to stand in
his way and was permitted to do what other men would not have dared to suggest')
and except in the case of a few exceptional clients it was a similar story elsewhere.
Sandon (1851, for the Earl of Harrowby) shows his struggle to cope with the
incongruity of plate glass in Jacobean design, and so does Idsworth (1852, for Sir
J. C. Jervoise). He excelled again at Lynford, Montagu House, Narford and in a few
other works, but thereafter the neat preliminary perspectives become fewer;
probably the later works, as Donaldson hinted, are mainly MacVicar Anderson
and William Colling under Burn's direction. After Burn had died (15 February
1870) Charles Barry Jr, who chaired Donaldson's memorial lecture, commented:

He was – I was going to say – more a man of business than an artist: but that would
certainly not be right or fair, because many of his works have very high artistic
merits.

He might have added that he had been in the forefront of the revival of
Jacobean, both English and Scottish, of Mannerism and Baroque and had excelled
in Louis Quinze décor. But it is as a planner that Burn's greatest importance
consists. He played a central role in the transition of the country house from the
rigid formality of the eighteenth century to the comfortable asymmetry of the
nineteenth. Above all, he was adept at reconciling the conflicting requirements of
his clients – for grandeur, privacy, outlook, guests' accommodation, logistic
convenience and segregation of servicing. Indeed, his thinking on how buildings
should function was on a more sophisticated level than that of any previous British
architect.

II

Philip and Philip Charles Hardwick

an architectural dynasty

HERMIONE HOBHOUSE

The nineteenth century is full of architectural dynasties—the Cundys, the Barrys, even the Burtons, are obvious examples. Few such dynasties, however, last as long as the Hardwicks, or furnish such clear illustration of the work available for architects, and the style in which it was fashionable to carry it out.

I propose to deal only with the last two generations of Hardwick architects, Philip (1790–1870) and his son Philip Charles (1820–90). Detailed consideration of all their works is clearly out of the question on the present occasion, though this is something that I would like to attempt in due course. I feel, however, that even a list of their works would help in the re-assessment of two architects who have suffered much, perhaps unfairly, through the swings of architectural fashion, and whose works have been so extensively destroyed for the same reason.

It is indeed difficult to give more than a list of major works when dealing in a single article with architects who together practised for more than fifty years. Both were prolific and ran a varied practice with vigour and success. In the middle period of the practice, from about 1843 till about 1850, it is difficult not to agree with H.-R. Hitchcock's dictum that the name 'Hardwick must stand for father and son'.[1] Nonetheless, I hope to disentangle the threads of the practice in the middle years, and try to assess the role played by each architect.

Like most architectural dynasties, the Hardwicks were descended from a successful builder, Thomas Hardwick I (1725–98). He came from Herefordshire, and settled in Brentford where he is known to have been responsible for the rebuilding of two local churches. He apprenticed his son, Thomas II (1752–1829), to the leading government architect Sir William Chambers. Young Thomas was also entered at the Royal Academy Schools, and sent on the extensive Italian tour which was an essential part of any young architect's education.

Thomas II had a distinguished and successful career, holding a number of surveyorships, many of which passed down in his family for three generations. He held government office as Clerk of the Works at Hampton Court and at Richmond, and designed a number of official buildings including a new shire hall for Dorset, and a new gaol for Galway. He restored or repaired a number of London churches, and we are perhaps most indebted to him for saving the great Norman masterpiece of St Bartholomew the Great, Smithfield, from total collapse. He seems to have instilled the art of 'judicious repair' into his son, Philip, and indeed this antiquarian interest in preservation and sympathetic restoration passed to both son and grandson, and make some of their restorations difficult to identify as such.[2]

He was a diligent and accurate draughtsman, filling several sketchbooks with drawings of Paris made on a visit when he was over seventy. Earlier sketches reveal an interest in Adam's work, and like many contemporaries he was interested in the picturesque. He had a number of distinguished pupils, including J. M. W. Turner, whom he persuaded to turn to painting rather than architecture, Samuel Angell (1800–66), and his son Philip.

Philip Hardwick's education also included enrolment at the Royal Academy Schools, and travel in both France and Italy. He began his independent practice in

27, 28 PHILIP *and* PHILIP CHARLES HARDWICK

29   PHILIP *and* PHILIP CHARLES HARDWICK. *Euston Station, London. The booking hall*

1816, at the age of twenty-four, as Surveyor to the Bethlehem and Bridewell Hospitals.

At this period the appointment of surveyor varied from institution to institution. Generally speaking, however, Hardwick seems to have acted as both architect and surveyor to the various bodies who employed him. Thus he carried through major building programmes such as the new Goldsmiths' Hall; he was responsible for the refronting and internal reorganization of many of the St Bartholomew's buildings, and yet he was also employed on such mundane and

33

30, 31   PHILIP HARDWICK. *Goldsmiths' Hall, London. Façade to Foster Lane, and elevation of staircase*

practical matters as the schedules of dilapidations for the large amount of small town property owned by such institutions, and on the surveys of country estates.[3] Indeed, his reputation as a practical businessman and his acknowledged skill in negotiation obtained for him the posts as a salaried surveyor which gave him his major opportunities as an architect. Both Philip and later his son Philip Charles looked to the City as the major source of work, and many of the latter's country houses were built for City bankers.

Philip Hardwick's first major commission was his appointment as architect and surveyor to the St Katharine's Dock Company, set up in 1825, to build a new set of docks immediately east of the Tower. Over 1,250 houses and tenements had to be removed, and Hardwick's first role was that of surveyor in the negotiations for purchase. The engineer was Telford, who had prepared the original scheme in 1824.[4] The plan was unusual in that the goods were intended to be hoisted straight into the warehouses, without any preliminary sorting on the quayside. Unlike those of earlier docks, therefore, the warehouses rise almost directly from the water's edge, with hoists and cranes on the side of the warehouse itself.

Hardwick produced a severely functional design, the only ornament being the setting back of the brickwork to provide space for the cranes. The walls are massive, 4 ft at the bottom narrowing to a mere $2\frac{1}{2}$ ft at the top. Despite his admiration for the French use of cast iron seen on his visit in 1815,[5] he used brick vaults for the basement, and above that substantial wooden beams for the floors of the upper storeys. He did, however, use cast-iron Doric columns to carry the open water fronts necessitated by the absence of any roadside track, and smaller cast iron columns to support the floors above.[6]

In February 1829 Hardwick was elected Surveyor to the Goldsmiths' Company, a post which he held for nearly forty years 'with ability, fidelity and zeal'.[7] The Company had been considering the question of rebuilding the Hall in whole or in part since the beginning of the century, and Hardwick, in one of his practical and well considered surveys, reinforced by a second opinion from his father-in-law, John Shaw, advised the Company on the existing site and foundations. Use could

be made, he pointed out, of such historic and expensive fittings as the ceiling and wainscoting of the Court Room, which could be re-erected. The accommodation and circulation was based on careful research into other City Halls, into Liverpool Town Hall, and detailed study of his clients' requirements.

The Goldsmiths' Hall is primarily a ceremonial building, and as such it is very successful. The visitor passes through a vestibule into the grand staircase hall, up the stairs—which branch into two halfway up—and into a fine first-floor balcony giving on to the main reception rooms. The staircase is lit by a lantern with four of Hardwick's favourite semi-circular windows, heroic in scale and divided by wrought-iron tracery. Unfortunately, the columns which carry the roof, originally designed by Hardwick in scagliola or to be painted to resemble Italian marble,[8] were clad in real marble of a less attractive colour during redecoration by one of his successors. The result has been to make the entrance unnecessarily ponderous.

For the Livery Hall itself Hardwick provided two designs, of which the Company picked the more elegant version with plain Corinthian columns between the windows, rather than a more elaborate Italianate décor with heavy panels between the windows and an enriched cornice.

'Chasteness and elegance', in one of his own favourite phrases, are also displayed by the main façade, though it would perhaps be better without the trophies and the heavy balconies between the Corinthian columns. The capitals are modelled on those of Mars Ultor at Rome.[9] The slightly top-heavy effect given by the ornamented capitals and simple basement was compared by one critic to 'a man in a full-bottomed wig, terminating below not exactly *in piscem*, but in a pair of nankeen trousers'.[10]

City opinion generally seems to have been favourable, and was reflected in Hardwick's employment in 1832 by the Committee of the City Club. This was a

30

31

35

32 PHILIP HARDWICK. *The City Club, London. Dining room*

group of bankers who wished to found a club with more conveniently sited
premises in rivalry to those in Pall Mall. The club-house in Old Broad Street is
another striking example of Hardwick's skill in handling public buildings. The
elegant masculinity of the staircase which rises to a landing and then divides into
two flights to reach the drawing rooms catches exactly the right note for the semi-
private nature of club premises, and is as fine as anything Barry created in Pall Mall.
In the coffee room, Hardwick opened up one wall with three giant semicircular-
headed windows, reminiscent of Adam's orangery at Kenwood. The fortunate
outcome of the long battle to save this important building means that at least one of
Hardwick's major works will survive.[11]

As successful, though humbler in concept, are two contemporary buildings
for St Bartholomew's Hospital, where Philip Hardwick had succeeded his father in
April 1826. His first employment was the rebuilding of the main gateway in 1834,
and the addition of rooms above, which he designed so harmoniously that the
whole entrance is usually attributed to 1702. However, there seems little doubt
from the Hospital records and from the Charity Commissioners' report of 1840
that this building is largely by Hardwick.[12] At the same time he designed new
accommodation for the medical school, now absorbed into other buildings or
demolished.

Shortly afterwards, he made a plan for the extension of the hospital northward
and westward on to Smithfield. He considered the question of a new grand front,
but true classicist that he was, rejected the idea because the frontage was irregular.
Instead he built a new lodge to the north of the gateway, and a much-needed new
ward block at right angles to the main frontage, designed in his most restrained
classical idiom to accord with Gibbs's existing buildings. The rather ragged
frontage to West Smithfield was pulled together by a rusticated screen wall,
broken by his favourite semi-circular arches; he stuccoed the wall of St
Bartholomew the Less to accord with the other buildings. This work, as well as a
minor addition by his son P. C. Hardwick, who succeeded him as Hospital
Surveyor (1856–71), is recorded on a plaque facing Smithfield.[13]

Hardwick's practice was primarily and most successfully institutional, but he
had a small domestic clientele. He designed Lord Sefton's house in Belgrave
Square, with a classical façade so restrained that the only emphasis is given by the
twin-columned *porte-cochère*. Behind he designed a stable yard in a more relaxed

33   PHILIP HARDWICK. *Lord Sefton's house, Belgrave Square, London*

and light-hearted style, with a hexagonal clock tower and hexagonal clock over the entrance from the mews. When the Duke of Wellington dismissed the difficult Benjamin Dean Wyatt, in August 1842, he appointed Hardwick as surveyor. By this time Wyatt had completed Apsley House, and Hardwick's only major commission was the building of upper storeys to the west wing of Stratfieldsaye House in 1845, for which he designed gables to match those elsewhere.[14]

These buildings had all been carried out in a classical idiom, but Philip Hardwick also handled a version of the English vernacular Gothic with skill and competence. His earliest essay in this style is the very successful grammar school at Stockport of   34
1830–31, for the Goldsmith's Company – demolished in 1923. This building, of which his characteristic careful sepia sketches perhaps give an unduly picturesque impression,[15] is a well-planned and straightforward school building in a sixteenth-century Gothick dress of stock brick with stone dressings, with no concessions to 'Gothic' planning. The schoolmaster's house has the porch of a sixteenth-century manor house, while the schoolroom has an open timber roof, and a double height four-light mullioned bay window. The windows have leaded panes and moulded dripstones over, the doors have four-centred arches with ornamented spandrels.[16] These were all details collected by the meticulous Hardwick in his sketchbook.[17] In the next twenty years they became a commonplace of village schools, alms-houses and other buildings whose purpose merited the style, but in 1830 they were sufficiently 'unique and novel' to cause the Stockport builder to lose £266 6s 3¾d. on the contract, because of the difficulty of 'calculating anything near the real cost . . . [of] working the stone in the various forms of antique architecture'.[18]

A year or so later Hardwick restored Babraham House in Cambridgeshire for J. Adeane Esq.,[19] and in 1840 carried out a major re-organization of Westwood Park, a fantastic Elizabethan hunting lodge, in Worcestershire.[20] This contract is important not so much for Hardwick's additions to this rather gloomy red brick and red sandstone pile, as for the interest taken by his son in the work, shown by his sketches of the twin gatehouses with their curious and elaborate superstructure,   35
and their ogival roofs. They were clearly the inspiration for Philip Hardwick's 1844 sketch of Hall,[21] and for the turrets of P. C. Hardwick's Great Western Hotel of 1851–53.

Philip Hardwick's conversion to the Gothic style was never more than skin-deep—literally, for his Gothic buildings have symmetrical plans under their   37

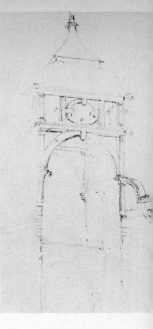

34   PHILIP HARDWICK. *Stockport School*
35   PHILIP CHARLES HARDWICK. *Drawing of detail from the gatehouse of Westwood Park*

trappings of gables and bay windows. This is particularly true of the new buildings he was engaged to design for Lincoln's Inn in 1839.

The Society had been considering the lack of accommodation for some time, and a plan was prepared by John White[22] for extending the existing hall, which was submitted to Hardwick for his opinion. He criticized the plan because it did not 'sufficiently divide the rooms and offices . . . the accommodation is inadequate for the business of the Society' and because, in modern terms, the circulation was ill planned. He ended with the diplomatic comment that 'if economy be a principal object I am not aware that a more economical plan could be produced'.[23]

Poor White and his 'patchwork' plan were dismissed, and the Benchers commissioned Hardwick to prepare a new scheme for a Hall and a Library, not only on a more generous scale but on a different site to the west of the Inn, next to Lincoln's Inn Fields.[24] Two lesser commissions were given to him in 1840, to design temporary courts, and to complete Stone Buildings to the south in the manner of Sir Robert Taylor. This was carried out in 1843–45. The work on Stone Buildings, however admirably performed, is a mere pastiche in 'strict adherence to Sir Robert Taylor's architecture',[25] while the Hall, despite its revival style, is an original and interesting building. It is particularly interesting since it was Hardwick, whom it is tempting to consider as a classical architect, who suggested the 'Collegiate style of Architecture . . . of the period towards the end of the sixteenth century before the admixture of Italian architecture',[26] though his exact responsibility for the details of the building is shrouded in some confusion.

Philip Hardwick's plan and report were considered by a Special Council in July 1842. As usual he had done careful research, and was able to assure his clients that the 'Principal entrance [to the Great Hall] is on one side, following the example of nearly all the Ancient Halls in this country', while before designing the Library he had investigated the British Museum, and the Inn's existing Library.[27] On 1 February 1843 the contractor George Baker was appointed, and on 20 April the foundation stone was laid. Shortly afterwards Hardwick's health deteriorated and control of the work is said to have passed to his son Philip Charles, then barely twenty-one.

36

Contemporary opinion gave Philip Charles the credit for completing his father's building,[28] and indeed he did rather more, since various alterations to the internal arrangements and to the ornaments were made in the course of building.[29] The interior of the Library was particularly altered: it was originally planned with a single gallery approached by means of circular staircases in the corner turrets; the ground floor bookshelves were originally to be no higher than shoulder-height, but an additional intermediate cast-iron gallery was added. Philip Charles also took the opportunity to make the ornament more vigorous and more correct.

The new buildings were basically T-shaped in plan, a symmetrical layout conceived by the elder Hardwick. The Library, later extended by G. G. Scott, lies across the top of the T, with the Hall occupying the stem, and private accommodation for the Benchers cleverly fitted in between. Both Hall and Library are high two-storey chambers with open timber roofs, and they stand on a podium containing stewards' and service accommodation. The original 'design' was expanded into working drawings by John Loughborough Pearson, engaged for the purpose in 1842, and he remained the assistant in charge of the job until the 'building was far advanced'. Pearson appears to have been in control during the interregnum, probably during the summer of 1843 when the elder Hardwick had already been taken ill and the younger was also away from the office sick.[30]

On his return, Philip Charles took over from Pearson, and 'the crowning features and all the fittings were carried out from his designs'. This probably explains the changes in the detailing, and the more 'Gothic' and medieval character of the completed building. This attention to detail was noticed by contemporaries. The *Builder* commented at the end of an ecstatic review:

36 PHILIP *and* PHILIP CHARLES HARDWICK. *Lincoln's Inn, London. Entrance and Hall* 39

The bolts, hinges, latch and escutcheon are admirably designed and executed, and this is the case . . . throughout the building. Every lock, every knob, is different, and is full of the right feeling. So too with the stone spandrels of the various door-heads, every one is varied, shewing there has been no lack of pains to produce a perfect whole.[31]

Philip Charles was responsible for a number of smaller commissions at Lincoln's Inn, including the railings for the new buildings, the Steward's block to the north-west, and the new gateway on to Lincoln's Inn Fields. These all show the interest in Jacobethan details which were to be developed in his later work. Thus the Hall is built in red brick decorated with unfinished lozenges in black bricks which he also used at Aldermaston Court; Madresfield repeats the interest in moulded octagonal chimneys of different patterns, his castellated rainwater heads can be found elsewhere.

Lincoln's Inn Hall also demonstrates very dramatically the Hardwicks' liking for 'signing' their buildings. 'P.H.' is worked into the black brick ornament as boldly as any Elizabethan gentleman ever worked his name or his motto into the parapet of his new country house.

From 1843, when he left Blore's office in which he had been a pupil, until at least 1854, Philip Charles Hardwick shared an office with his father. They do not ever seem to have gone into formal partnership, probably because the father's health degenerated so dramatically after 1843. It is clear, however, that the son carried out a lot of the father's work, doing both designs and supervision, and he seems to have gradually 'inherited' much of his father's practice, as the latter's health deteriorated. The *Builder* stated categorically in its obituary of the elder Hardwick in 1870 that in 1847 his spinal complaint became so serious 'that he was compelled to confine himself to such practice as could be followed in his own room', but in fact he does seem to have continued practising for several years longer, at least taking the responsibility for work, and even making visits to the country for important clients.[32] The confusion between the work of father and son is made worse by the similarity of name, which misled both contemporaries and modern authorities.[33]

There are in fact a number of works dating from the 1840s on which both father and son worked. Hall, near Barnstaple, a large stone Jacobethan house resurrecting a medieval house on the same site, was designed by Philip Hardwick in 1844,[34] but was only completed to the design of the son in 1847–49, by the addition of the Great Hall.[35] The original sketch shows the house with ogival towers copied from the Westwood gatehouses (later omitted), as well as high gables copied from Crewe Hall, and P. C. Hardwick's favourite type of moulded chimneys. The house itself is formal, but the plan is made asymmetrical and more interesting by the Great Hall with its open roof and niche, and windows in the decorated style.

The other major commission on which both father and son worked was, of course, Euston Station.

Philip Hardwick was an important figure in the early railway age – he was surveyor to the embryo Great Western, as well as to the Euston group. His role as surveyor was crucial, and he negotiated successfully with several obstructive landowners on behalf of the railway. For the termini at London and Birmingham he designed two triumphal arches, one in 'chaste and elegant' Greek Doric for Euston Square, and an Ionic arch incorporating the station master's office and a booking hall for Birmingham.[36] He saw immediately that public prejudice against the new form of travel could best be overcome by architectural *panache,* and having created the arch in a characteristic gesture he designed a medal for presentation to the directors at the opening of the railway in September 1838. The

37   PHILIP HARDWICK. *Euston Station, London. Propylaeum.*

Doric propylaeum flanked by two small lodges on either side stood alone on the   37
north side of Euston Square in the heroic isolation necessary to show it off to
advantage. A contemporary critic wrote:

We here behold the full majesty and severity of the order exhibited upon a scale
that renders it truly imposing. Till now, we had nothing that could convey an
adequate impression of the majesty of a Doric portico. . . . We have the effect not
only of magnitude, as well as of forms, but that also arising from breadth of light
and shade, heightened by that of great depth, and the contrast of perspective.[37]

The very success of the railway destroyed much of the effect of the arch. In
1838 Hardwick was commissioned to design two hotels flanking the entrance,
originally to be the Adelaide and the Victoria Hotels, later combined as the Euston
Hotel,[38] and in 1842 extensions to the passenger shed were approved,[39] and a
Euston Station Improvement Committee was instructed to provide a scheme for
extensions both at Euston Grove and at the Camden goods yard. In April 1846 the
Board approved his plans, which included a Great Hall and a 'Great Room for
Public Meetings' as well as a new booking office and a set of royal apartments.[40]   29
     In July, however, the London and Birmingham amalgamated with the Grand
Junction and the Manchester and Birmingham Companies to form the London
and North-Western Railway. Owing to Hardwick's failing health the consequent
enlargements to the projected station – for which a contract had already been
signed – were entrusted to his son. Though Philip Charles adhered to his father's
plans, he enlarged the buildings by adding a storey and rearranged the Great Hall
internally, and redesigned the elevations and interior decoration in a classical
Italianate style instead of his father's heroic Greek.
     Euston Station provides a unique and fascinating opportunity to compare the
solutions of two architects, but a detailed analysis is outside the scope of this
study.[41] Several different styles were involved in the design of the Board Room, at
the end of the Great Hall. In the Great Hall itself Philip Hardwick had designed the
roof to be carried on four groups of columns, and to be lit from either side with
three of his favourite semi-circular windows. His son's plan dispensed with the
pillars, had blind first-floor walls – intended to be covered with frescoes – and
square clerestory windows under a coffered Italian ceiling. The angles were filled
with panels by the fashionable sculptor John Thomas, portraying the spirits of
London and Lancashire, Liverpool and Birmingham.[42]
     Philip Charles inherited his father's connection at Paddington also, and was
engaged to design the Great Western Hotel, the second of the great terminal hotels   38, 39
to be built in London. The Great Western is extremely important in the
development of luxury hotels, but this is no place to discuss the significance of its   41

38, 39 PHILIP CHARLES HARDWICK. *Great Western Hotel, Paddington, London. Dining room and façade*

planning and conception – something that will be done in Christopher Monkhouse's forthcoming work on the history of the hotel. Less obvious in its present 'shorn' condition is the importance of the Hotel as a trend-setter in architectural fashion. H.-R. Hitchcock has pointed out that it is 'notably Second Empire *avant la lettre*,[43] and there is undoubted French influence, something that was to recur later at Rendcomb. It also owes a great deal, however, to the towers at Westwood, and at Crewe, showing that whatever the origin of the silhouette of the tower roofs, the inspiration came from native sources, collected by P. C. Hardwick in his own sketchbook.

The son's practice falls into two groups, each with a distinctive style. He built a considerable number of banking houses in the 1850s and 1860s at a time when the conception was growing of a bank as a purpose-built structure, and not a converted dwelling-house. In 1855 he was appointed surveyor to the Bank of England after C. R. Cockerell's resignation; he built the two branches at Hull and Leeds, and converted Uxbridge House in Burlington Gardens, to a West End
41 branch in 1855.[44] In 1864 he built a new banking house for Barclay and Bevan in Lombard Street, whose elaborate Italianate façade was 'arranged to show clearly the object for which it is built'. Despite the traditions of the Renaissance palazzi on which it was based, the *piano nobile* was the ground floor banking hall, not the first
40 floor offices.[45] The following year he designed a similar building for the Union Bank, crowned this time with a high French mansard roof instead of a classical cornice, which dominated the Poultry, glowering between Wren's doomed St Mildred, Poultry, and Soane's Bank of England, as yet its modest original height.[46]

Philip Charles inherited a number of his father's surveyorships, either formally or informally, but on the whole his work for St Bartholomew's Hospital, and the Duke of Wellington was of a minor nature, as was what he did for the Goldsmiths' Company in his father's name.[47] He had, however, a far larger country-house practice than his father achieved, often for City men, and he was also responsible for a large number of church restorations and rebuildings. This is partly a reflection of the work then available, though the younger Hardwick's interest in religion doubtless influenced his church work.
42 In 1848–51, he rebuilt Aldermaston Court, gutted by fire in 1843, for D. H. D. Burr. Only the renowned and magnificent staircase with its carved balusters and newels, and the stable court, survived from the earlier house, and he used them both

40 PHILIP CHARLES HARDWICK. *The Union Bank of London, Poultry*
41 PHILIP CHARLES HARDWICK. *Barclay and Bevan's Bank, Lombard Street, London*

to inspire the style and planning of the new one.[48] From the brick and stone of the
stables he derived the black-diapered red brick and stone-mullioned windows of
the garden front, though the elaborate and exaggerated tower with its blind stone
tracery and curious bastard North French spire is all his own. Behind the 'prettily
pink and cream and lacy front'[49] the house is conveniently and regularly planned
round a double height hall with a minstrels' gallery, whose balustrading and
carved figures derive from those of the famous staircase. In restoring the stairs, he
made no attempt to restore the elaborate plaster soffits with their pendants, using

43

42   PHILIP CHARLES HARDWICK. *Aldermaston Court*

throughout the interior restrained Jacobethan motifs, except in the French
fireplace in the Hall.

There were a number of other essays in the Jacobethan style, not all as successful
as Aldermaston, possibly because he was so often at his best as a restoration or
conservation architect, and those country houses where he started from a virgin
site did not give him the same inspiration. Gilston Park, in Hertfordshire, is similar
to Aldermaston in general handling, but here he used random rubble with ashlar
facing and stone carving instead of brick. The roofline is mellowed by the use of
stepped gables as well as straight.[50]

Enormously solid, as befitted the residence of the Governor of the Bank of
England, was Addington Park, Buckinghamshire (now demolished), built for
J. G. Hubbard, Lord Addington (1805–89). Only the stables and some lodges
remain and they are more Jacobethan in style than the mansion, for which the style
chosen was 'the later Gothic of France'.

As in all P. C. Hardwick's country houses, there was the inevitable tower, ever
more overbearing with its high mansard slate roof, which had to be blown up
when the house was demolished in the 1930s. There was the usual blue-faced clock,
the castellated rainwater heads ornamented with J.G.H., and the usual plethora of
lodges, cottages and outbuildings without which no Victorian country house was
complete.[51]

His country houses in this French style are the least successful: one of his obituary
notices suggested that he turned to Gothic from classical architecture – his first
love – because it was cheaper in execution, and therefore more popular with
clients. The Abbots, Sompting, near Worthing, is certainly an awful warning
against ostentation on the cheap. Superficially it is picturesquely attractive in his
Royal Academy drawing, and from outside even the restless main façade and the
absurdly elaborate skyline have interest, but internally the planning is impossibly
inconvenient to accommodate the height of roof, towers and gables, and the detail
is mean and dull.[52]

His most successful new country house is his only classical one – Rendcomb,

43

44

43 PHILIP CHARLES HARDWICK. *The Abbots, Sompting*
44, 45 PHILIP CHARLES HARDWICK. *Rendcomb, near Cirencester. Stables and house*

near Cirencester, which he designed for Sir Francis d'Avigdor Goldsmith, MP in
1864–67.[53] Again it is a complex of buildings, a fine classical country house of Bath 45
stone in the Barry style, on a superb site, classical lodges to all the drives, cunningly
fitted into the landscape, estate cottages in a modest vernacular adaptation of the
contemporary model dwelling for rural employees, and an unexpected and most
successful French Renaissance stable yard

The stable yard is an elaborate quadrangle with high dormers on the first floor 44
and round French lunettes above them. The entrance on to the village street is a
classical gateway, with over it the tower from a French château, whose parti-
coloured slate roof is crowned by an English classical lantern. On the opposite side
of the yard an identical classical arch, with all the austerity and dignity of his
father's railway arch, gives on to the private drive which leads across a bridge with
vigorous cast-iron balustrading to the house itself.

An earlier drawing reveals that the tower was something of an afterthought, and

45

it is indeed a far less integrated feature than either Cubitt's towers at Osborne or Barry's at Trentham. Rendcomb's plain balustraded skyline, even with its elaborate chimneys, does not absorb and point up the tower as Hardwick's Gothic houses do. The planning is very simple, the circulation is grandiose, with an open marble staircase reached through a series of marble halls.

Hardwick had other aristocratic patrons for whom some of his church rebuilding was carried out. One of these was the fourth Earl Spencer, for whose brother[54] his father had negotiated with Barry over the purchase of land for the building of Bridgewater House.[55] From this utilitarian beginning the elder Hardwick had gone on to advise on the refurbishing of Spencer House, taking enormous and characteristic trouble over the matching of silk for the ballroom and the correct repainting of Athenian Stuart's sofas and other furniture.[56] He attended the Stowe sale – 'a most melancholy picture' – in 1848, but found little there to buy for Lord Spencer or anyone else.

In 1851 Lord Spencer commissioned P. C. Hardwick to design a new billiard room for Althorp. Hardwick gave it a coved ceiling with double bands of floral mouldings, reminiscent of the Euston Shareholders' Room, and a library gallery similar to that at Lincoln's Inn. This modest classical box, with a Venetian window on one side and blind arcading on the other two, spoilt the north façade of Althorp and was demolished forty years later.[57]

Hardwick designed the village school for Little Brington, Northants, in 1850. It still stands, and is reminiscent of the Stockport school, but it has a very fine curvilinear window instead of the latter's domestic Tudor. He also built one of his characteristic brick lodges with elaborate barge-boardings,[58] and Little Brington Church too, of which only the tower now remains. This is ironical, for his brief was how best to 'contrive a place for the bells without either tower or bellcote'. His first solution was a *clocher* behind the porch, 'not a common place ... but occasionally its position'. Here he seems to have decided that he must have a tower, and not only a tower but one with a spire. Despite his client's opposition he persisted: 'The effect of so small a tower as that proposed for Little Brington, is never, I think, good without the spire. .... A large tower with bold parapet and pinnacles looks very well without a spire.' And then with some relief (for Lord Spencer was a client who knew his mind): 'I am glad it is popular now for I think it will be greatly improved when the spire is finished.'[59]

He seems to have employed the bellcote design for St James, Upper Stowe, attributed to his father but more likely to have been designed by him. With its timber porch, its Gothic door key with cruciform wards, east window of five lancets, and twin windows under a single internal opening, it has the modest charm of his other small churches.

He did a large number of ecclesiastical restorations, some in the metropolis, and others of tiny country churches. The sympathy commended by Hitchcock in the father's restoration of St Anne's, Limehouse, in 1852[60] is shown by the son's handling of All Saints', Aston Upthorpe, the unusual Cromwellian chapel at Littlecote[61] or St Martin's in the Bullring, Birmingham, with its outdoor pulpit and its carefully restored arched tomb recesses.[62]

He carried out a series of important commissions in Ireland at Adare, County Limerick, for the third Earl of Dunraven, from 1851 till 1866. There is no room here to go into the work in detail, and it has been very well covered by John Cornforth in *Country Life*.[63] A large series of drawings has survived, very typical of Hardwick – it includes full size details of furniture not only for the house but for the school, masonry and ironwork details, and door hinges, as well as elegant client's drawings for completed buildings. He was also responsible here for

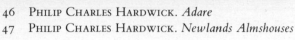

46   Philip Charles Hardwick. *Adare*
47   Philip Charles Hardwick. *Newlands Almshouses*

48   Philip Charles Hardwick. *Madresfield Court*

Elizabethan parterres for which he did a number of alternative schemes. One parterre has survived, on the south front; there may have been others which have disappeared with the changes in garden fashion. Hardwick's meticulous antiquarianism shows through in a note on a drawing – 'outline of old battlements of the Tower to be exactly reproduced.'

He first came in contact with the Earl of Dunraven, an interesting and unusual Irish landlord, through a common interest in religion. The Earl was much concerned with the religious problems of his tenantry and commissioned Hardwick to restore two ancient abbeys in the village used as churches for the two communities. The Augustinian Abbey provided the Protestant church and the family mausoleum, the Trinitarian abbey had been turned into the Roman Catholic parish church in 1811, and was restored by Hardwick again in the 1850s. Hardwick was also commissioned to design a Roman Catholic cathedral at Limerick.[64]

He was employed on the completion of Adare Manor, work begun under the   46 second Earl in the 1830s by James Pain and continued by Pugin. Hardwick started in 1850 on the west end of the south front and the important and characteristic Wyndham Tower,[65] with its castellated parapet and steep French roof rising to an ironwork crest. He was engaged at Adare until 1862, and in a comment that will serve for much of the rest of his work, a modern writer has called his work at Adare 'both more correct and more fashionable [than the earlier restorations] but . . . also . . . colder and drier'.[66]

Hardwick also worked on the repair of the Octagon roof at Wynyard, County Durham, the seat of the Marquis of Londonderry, and on the restoration of Long Newton Church and the building of a family mausoleum in 1859,[67] a commission possibly inspired by his successful and impressive town hall at Durham of 1851.[68]   47

His work for the Beauchamp family is an interesting mixture of new work and restoration, and a detailed examination of it throws much light on his methods. In 1862 he was commissioned to build the Newlands Almshouses, complete with church, trustees' meeting room and warden's house. He created an interesting and varied complex, with the almshouses grouped round an open courtyard facing south, entered through a towered gateway. One wing is occupied by the warden's house, immediately adjacent to the trustees' meeting room, with its hammerbeam timber roof, its founder's portrait framed in Gothic leaf tracery, and its fireplace complete with encaustic tiles decorated with the Beauchamp arms. From the board room a brick half-timbered passage leads to the mortuary chapel (built from the medieval timber and daub church of St Leonard's moved from its original site) and thence to the new stone church with its octagonal spire. An oriel window in the west wall connects the infirmary with the church in the manner of Philip II's bedroom at the Escorial. The almshouses themselves are grouped in fours, entered through a wide pointed archway containing the four doors to the flatted dwellings. The most unsuccessful element is the gateway tower, which is large and square with, rising from it, not a mere spire, but one of Hardwick's favourite North French roofs, complete with lanterns in the sides, and a line of ironwork on the crest.[69]

The Beauchamp family, who had built the almshouses, then asked Hardwick to undertake the repair of Madresfield Court, their famous medieval house largely rebuilt in the sixteenth century and later modernized by the addition of tall sash windows. It was still standing within its moat, and could be approached only by its drawbridge; basically it was an ancient structure. Under the patronage of the fifth and sixth earls, Hardwick totally reconstructed the house, 'the principal lines of the old building being followed', only two rooms remaining unaltered, and even one of those being given new windows. Today the house looks more 'ancient' than when Hardwick started, medieval and sixteenth-century features from the old house being re-used, and others imported from interesting local buildings. Work went on from 1863 to 1875, beginning with the roofing over of the courtyard,[70] going on to the enlargement and rebuilding of the dining hall, and the reconstruction of the Long Gallery and the rooms under it. On the site of the large dining room, to the extreme right of the garden front, he built two suites of bedrooms. He finished this phase of the work in 1865 with the reorganization of the offices, later completed by the erection of a roofed Gothic timber bridge.

On the accession of the sixth earl in 1865, the rebuilding continued with the making of a chapel out of part of the old library in 1867, and the pulling down of the two Georgian drawing rooms with the plastered walls and sash windows, and the building of a Jacobethan wing in red brick with stone mullions at right angles to the garden front, containing book room and drawing room, in 1866–67. This wing was crowned with its elegant *flèche* in 1875. At the same period the wattle and daub walls of the garden front were replaced by brick and stone.

The result of fifteen years' patient reconstruction is an agreeable asymmetrical building, containing remnants of medieval planning and medieval construction. It raises all the philosophic and aesthetic problems of restoration, but the skill and love with which it was done cannot be denied and are characteristic of P. C. Hardwick at his best.[71]

Hardwick built a number of schools, commissions which gave him the opportunity to design well-articulated groups of Gothic buildings whose functions were relatively closely allied to their style – in contemporary terms at least – and where his favourite towers could be used to their best advantage. His first large academic building was the Royal Freemasons' School at Wandsworth (1851),

47

48

49 PHILIP CHARLES HARDWICK. *Charterhouse School*

sometimes attributed to his father, and possibly influenced by the latter since the façade is symmetrical, though carried out in the son's exuberant red brick with black diaper work, and a central tower complete with harsh triangular oriel window, a conical roof with gabled dormers and chimneys, corbelled turrets at each corner.[72]

More interesting in plan and altogether less harsh was the College of St Columba, near Dublin,[73] where he had an opportunity to group the buildings round a quadrangle, using a variety of treatments to make his point. In 1854 he exhibited a design for the Clergy Orphan School at Canterbury, rather harsher and less romantic in treatment.[74]

His major school commission was, however, the new Charterhouse buildings at   49
Godalming in 1865–72. He exploited the opportunities of this commission to the full. There are long ranges of gabled medieval buildings, lit by rows of two- and three-light windows, in which the boys ate, slept and worked, with masters' houses and a chapel. His favourite towers, each one slightly different in style and emphasis, are used to punctuate the groups, with the highest tower, in the Early English idiom, proclaiming the entrance doorway.

The buildings were planned round an open quadrangle, happily untouched by recent school extensions, and this approach is still impressive. One wing of the quadrangle, balancing but not symmetrical, contains the chapel, complete with nave, aisles and transepts, while the other contained the headmaster's house, with accommodation for boarders behind. The *Builder* thought that the Great Hall was 'not made sufficiently distinctive', but went on to admire the 'free use of bow-windows, oriels, gabled dormers, octagon chimney shafts, and a generally ruddy, thoroughly old English tone about the buildings which are designed in the style of the domestic architecture of the late Decorated period'.[75] One may argue about the 'old Englishness' of the tone of Charterhouse, but it is difficult to disagree with a modern authority who has called it 'a brilliant study in symmetry . . . probably the most picturesque of the nineteenth-century public schools'.[76]

The Charterhouse buildings were not only one of his greatest works, they were also one of his last. In 1872, at the age of fifty, he married an heiress from Somerset and settled down near Bath, abandoning most of his professional practice, though completing work for important clients, and continuing with his benevolent and charitable work for the profession. Like his father, he spent his later years in increasing ill-health, but unlike his father he had no son to carry on the practice. None of his children trained as an architect, and he was the last of an able, conscientious and competent dynasty, inspired on occasion, which produced a number of great buildings, and many interesting ones, epitomizing the trends and varying ideals of their profession for over a century.   49

Sydney Smirke
the architecture of compromise

J. MORDAUNT CROOK

Dynasties, as we have seen, are common enough in British architectural history: the Adams, the Cockerells, the Hardwicks, the Scotts, the Waterhouses – to mention only a few. It was the peculiar structure of the architectural profession which produced them. As the nineteenth century progressed the architect became very much a member of the Victorian professional class, separated by institutional barriers from less acceptable groups, such as engineers, surveyors, contractors and builders. Specialization had fragmented the eighteenth-century tradition. At the same time two pillars of the eighteenth-century system survived right to the end of the Victorian period: patronage and pupillage.[1] The noble patron and the family practice remained key factors long after British architecture is popularly supposed to have gone over to the 'goddam bourgeoisie'. In its fashionable upper ranges at least, and particularly in the secular sphere, High Victorian architecture still had its roots in the Regency. The Picturesque was still a dominant aesthetic category. And at the top of the profession there were still architects called Wyatt, Barry, Pugin and Smirke. But in each case they were men of smaller stature. T. H. Wyatt and Matthew Digby Wyatt clearly lacked the genius which created Fonthill and Heveningham. The talents of Charles Barry Jr, E. M. Barry and E. W. Pugin were derivative and synthetic – hardly the qualities which produced the Houses of Parliament. And in Sydney Smirke the limitations of a second-generation mentality are only too apparent.

Sydney Smirke's credentials as an Establishment architect were impeccable. Besides boasting the customary letters RA, FRIBA and FSA, by the end of his career he was a Trustee of the British Museum, a Trustee of the Soane Museum, Treasurer of the Royal Academy, Gold Medallist of the RIBA and President of the Architects' Benevolent Society.[2] He came of a family which was numerous, talented, ambitious and almost embarrassingly well-connected. He was born in London in 1799, the fifth son of Robert Smirke RA (1751–1845), an able illustrator, satirist and intriguer, privately known as 'the Abbé Seyes of the Royal Academy'.[3] One of his elder brothers became Sir Edward Smirke (1795–1875), antiquary and Attorney-General to the Prince of Wales.[4] Another, the short-lived Richard Smirke (1778–1815), a friend of Samuel Lysons, was employed as a topographical artist by the Society of Antiquaries.[5] One of his sisters, Mary Smirke, translated *Don Quixote* and privately practised as an artist with some success.[6] Another, Sarah Smirke, married into a great family of building contractors, the Bakers of Rochester and London. Their descendants included the architect Sir Herbert Baker (1862–1946).[7] It was the Bakers who gave Sydney Smirke his first major commission – the reconstruction of the Oxford Street Pantheon (1833–34). But the most distinguished member of the clan was undoubtedly Sir Robert Smirke RA (1780–1867), the leading Greek-Revivalist of the Regency period and joint-monopolist, with Nash and Soane, of the immense patronage of the Office of Works.[8] From the start Sir Robert took a close interest in the career of his much younger brother – 'little Syd' as he used to call him. So did the Smirkes' close friend Joseph Farington, 'Dictator of the Royal Academy'. At the age of ten young Sydney, 'very tractable and sweet', was packed off to Eywood, the Herefordshire

51 SMIRKE. *British Museum, London. The Reading Room showing intended decoration to the dome*

seat of the Harleys, to study under a private tutor with Lord Oxford's eldest son.[9]
Eight years later he entered brother Robert's office as an articled pupil, at the same
time joining the Royal Academy Schools, where he won the Gold Medal in 1819
with a drawing of 'Pliny's Villa'. Then away he went for several years to Italy and
Sicily, sketching, measuring and absorbing the antique, returning in 1827 to step
into one of the choicest possible posts for a young architect, a Clerkship of the
King's Works.[10] In 1832, however, the Office of Works was reorganized and his
post summarily abolished. This was no more than a temporary set-back. He had
already begun his career as assistant and heir to Sir Robert Smirke, a career which
eventually brought him within an ace of knighthood, and even carried him
beyond his elder brother's achievements, to the Professorship of Architecture at
the Royal Academy.

So Sydney Smirke's inheritance was a rich one. But it was very slow in coming.
He waited twenty years to inherit his brother's appointments as Architect and
Surveyor to the Inner Temple, the Duchy of Lancaster, the British Museum and
the General Post Office. All these architectural plums were plucked during the
early 1840s. They coincided with three more lucrative commissions: the
restoration of York Minster, the redevelopment of Lord Exeter's property in the
Strand and the extension of Bedlam Hospital, Southwark. His career was now well
and truly launched. And as if to celebrate his belated independence, he married – at
the age of forty-two. It was a dynastic marriage – in keeping with the whole of his
career – to Isabella Dobson, daughter of that veteran classicist, John Dobson of
Newcastle.[11]

Tory patronage was the basis of the Smirkes' architectural careers. Sir Robert
Smirke's chief patrons had been the Earl of Lonsdale and Sir Robert Peel. Almost
inevitably it was Sydney Smirke who designed Peel's new portrait gallery at
Drayton Manor, Staffordshire (1844–48),[12] and the nearby Grammar School at
Tamworth (1851).[13] In the same way, he designed Wellington Pit and 20 Irish
Street – both on the Lonsdale Whitehaven estate – as well as Lonsdale's new
hunting box at Barleythorpe in Rutland (1847)[14] and the nearby School House at
Oakham (1850–55).[15] Peel's successor as leader of the Tory party was Lord Derby.
And it was Derby's father, the long-lived thirteenth Earl, who turned out to be

Sydney Smirke's most persistent benefactor. Although nominally a Whig, he lacked his son's dedication to politics – one obituarist called him 'inconspicuous . . . noiseless and unobtrusive'.[16] His real passion was zoology. But in his Lancashire kingdom he was also something of a keen builder. In this way Sydney Smirke came to design alterations at Knowsley Hall and a house nearby for R. Earle Esq. (1842), the assembly rooms, hotel and athenaeum at Bury (1846–47), rectories at Halsall (1844–45), Burscough (1848) and Treales (1858) and three small churches, Holy Trinity, Bickerstaffe (1842–43),[17] St James, Westhead near Lathom (1850–51) and Christ Church, Treales (1855). Other Tory patrons included the Duke of Newcastle (alterations at Clumber Park *c.* 1832), Sir Thomas Lethbridge (alterations at Basing Park, Hampshire),[18] and Sir Edward Kerrison (Oakley Park, Suffolk, *c.* 1830) and his son-in-law, Lord Henniker (Thornham, Suffolk, *c.* 1837).

Piece by piece Sydney Smirke built up a flourishing practice. It was not enormous – no more than eighty separate commissions have so far come to light, as against some two thousand apiece for Sir Arthur Blomfield and Ewan Christian. But his work covered a very wide range. Besides private houses and churches there were government contracts like the Custom Houses at Bristol, Newcastle, Shoreham and Gloucester, and the Parkhurst Juvenile Reformatory in the Isle of Wight (1837–46),[19] suburban developments such as The Park, Ealing (1846), and Lord Radnor's estate at Folkestone (1850s), institutional jobs like the alterations to Bridewell Hospital, Blackfriars, and the House of Occupation, Lambeth,[20] and public works like Brookwood Cemetery near Woking and the Horticultural Society's Galleries at Kensington. But one building type Sydney Smirke made very much his own: the metropolitan club house. Even more than Decimus Burton or Sir Charles Barry, the Smirkes deserve to be remembered as architects of London's clubland. In this new sphere of urban design their old Tory connections certainly paid off. Sir Robert Smirke designed the original United Services Club in Charles Street (1817), the first Carlton Club in Pall Mall (1833–36) and the old Union Club in Trafalgar Square (1822–25), besides acting as judge in the Athenaeum Club competition. Both brothers co-operated in designing the Oxford and Cambridge Club, Pall Mall (1836–37). Sydney Smirke designed the old Conservative Club in St James's Street in conjunction with Disraeli's kinsman George Basevi (1843–45), as well as the second Carlton Club in Pall Mall (1847–56) after Basevi's fatal accident. He also competed, unsuccessfully, in the Reform Club competition. In several of these commissions the influence of Sir Robert Peel is very much in evidence. All in all, from the reconstruction of the Pantheon to the remodelling of Burlington House, Sydney Smirke's was a prosperous and successful life. Not surprisingly, when he died at Tunbridge Wells in 1877 he was worth £80,000.[21]

Such is the skeleton of this man's career. What of his architectural achievements? It would be wrong to think of him merely in terms of family influence and Tory patronage. At least one of his sponsors, Lord Radnor, was a Radical Whig. His talents certainly merited patronage. His *Suggestions for the Architectural Improvement of the Western Part of London* (1834) anticipated several developments associated with the Metropolitan Improvements of the mid-Victorian period. In particular his ideas on the subject of rehousing the poor influenced Chadwick's celebrated report of 1842, and eventually bore fruit in the 'Model Houses for Families' designed later in the 1840s by a fellow pupil of Sir Robert Smirke, Henry Roberts.[22] As so often in his career, here again he was indebted to his brother's training: the planning of Henry Roberts's pioneering lodging house in Bloomsbury owes just a little to Sir Robert Smirke's galleried almshouses at Ledbury, Herefordshire (1822–25).[23]

Like his brother, moreover, Sydney Smirke was a master of constructional techniques in a variety of building materials. One of his most elaborate rescue operations took place at Lambton Castle, Durham, where he succeeded his aged father-in-law as architect in 1862. Much of the house had apparently been undermined by coal seams not far from the surface. 'So much,' we are told, 'were the walls and ceilings shaken, and into such chasms and fissures were they riven, that it is matter for astonishment that so much remained standing.'[24] Two of his ecclesiastical commissions resulted directly from his reputation as a constructor. At St Mary, Theydon Bois, Essex (1850), he was called in to replace a church designed only six years previously by Abbott and Habershon. 'Judging from Joseph Clarke's report in 1849,' remarked Goodhart-Rendel, the first building 'was disgustingly and abominably ill-constructed.'[25] At St Mary the Virgin, Andover, Hants (1840–46), two walls collapsed during the progress of the work before Sydney Smirke was summoned to the rescue of Goddard and Livesay's over-ambitious design.[26] And in the Round Reading Room of the British Museum he produced one of the greatest monuments of mid-Victorian cast-iron construction. As with so many of his contemporaries, however, the boldness of his structural solutions was counter-balanced by caution and conservatism in design. He was a typical product of the age of historicism. At the RIBA, he read papers ranging from a disquisition on Assyrian sculpture (1850) to 'Technical Observations on the Architecture of the Honey Bee' (1853). His scholarly papers on antiquities in Pisa, Ravenna, Syracuse, Assisi, Whitehall or Westminster, fill out the pages of *Archaeologia*.[27] Neo-Norman, Early English, Decorated, Perpendicular, Lombardic, Early Renaissance, High Renaissance, Tudor, Jacobean – anything but Baroque – each style he mastered in turn and reproduced with few personal variations, competently and almost anonymously. Not surprisingly, his best Gothic works were restorations: the reconstruction of York Minster and the Temple Church. Temperamentally, he was a born classicist. He could handle classical elements with considerable finesse. But when it came to formulating theories of design he had nothing to add to Renaissance tradition. His lectures at the Royal Academy were a disappointing performance – predictably empty and predictably popular. Precisely for those reasons, they are certainly worth re-reading. The quality-scale of Victorian architecture was so immense – sublime, mediocre and ridiculous – that to understand it properly we must occasionally soil out fingers. Dullness makes its own demands on the historian. We learn more about the generality of mid-Victorian architecture by studying the leaders of the profession – men like T. L. Donaldson, Sydney Smirke and Sir William Tite, orthodox and often dull – than by analysing the eccentricities of rogue elephants like E. Buckton Lamb and J. Basset Keeling. To get a balanced picture we must look at the insiders as well as the outsiders.

As an ecclesiastical architect Sydney Smirke belonged to the same generation as Butterfield, Carpenter and Scott. Just to name all four in the same breath is to indicate the discrepancy between them. Sydney Smirke's Gothic designs are archaeological not ecclesiological, and seldom exhibit either originality or ingenuity. But he had a true architect's eye for scale and balance, and these qualities often mitigate mechanical detailing. His bleak, yellow-brick church of St John the Baptist, Loughton, Essex (1846), in emasculated Neo-Norman, received short shrift from contemporary critics. Yet Goodhart-Rendel commends its 'effect of great massiveness and of everything being larger than life'.[28] The *Ecclesiologist* noted that in his design for Christ Church, Folkestone, Kent (1850), 'the wide departure from ecclesiological precedent' was 'painfully conspicuous'. Yet considering the limited budget, it was (before bombing) a satisfactory essay in

51

'early Decorated'.[29] His Frewen Turner mausoleum at St Mary, Northiam, Sussex (1844–46), is an attractive late Gothic addition, executed with care and restraint.[30] His work at Holy Trinity, Penrhos, Montgomeryshire (1844),[31] and Holy Trinity, Leicester (1838, remodelled by Teulon),[32] is unimportant. But at St Mary the Virgin, Andover, Hampshire (1840–46), both the scale of the design and the fluency of its Early English detail are equally remarkable – so much so that Goodhart-Rendel even doubted Sydney Smirke's contribution and suggested Edward Garbett. In fact Sydney Smirke's responsibility for the whole of the tower and much of the remainder is well documented. Anyway, a country church with details inspired by Salisbury was hardly beyond the capacity of the man who restored York Minster.[33]

In 1829–32 Sir Robert Smirke had restored the choir of York Minster after its destruction by a lunatic incendiary named Jonathon Martin.[34] When the south-west tower and the roof of the nave were accidentally destroyed by another fire in 1840 Sir Robert was again commissioned. But this time he handed over the job to his younger brother. The result was perhaps the most extensive piece of church restoration in the early Victorian period. The cost soared to some £90,000. The materials included 670 tons of Huddlestone stone and 218 tons of Graseby stone, quantities of Memel oak and lead for the external roof of the nave, and large supplies of cast-iron trusses and lead or copper coverings for the roofs of the south aisle, north transept and central tower. The work involved local craftsmanship of high quality. Ribs and bosses in the nave were meticulously carved by John Wolstenholme from drawings of the originals previously made by John Browne. Wailes's stained glass in the nave was none too happy, but the pier capitals and carving at the west end, restored by Robert Bradley and Thomas Temple, were particularly well done. Over the design and execution of all these operations Sydney Smirke kept tight control. He was, for example, personally responsible for the design of the great west doors, with their rich Decorated mouldings. The carving was executed in Newcastle by J. Wallace and R. J. Scott. Sydney Smirke disapproved of their performance and ordered them to renew it. This they did on the lower part, but refused to do so on the upper portion. The work was therefore turned over to Wolstenholme and Coates, and with it went the contract for the new doors of the north-west tower. As soon as all this had been completed a well-timed bequest from a local physician made possible the restoration of the Chapter House. Here the ceiling was given a polychromatic finish by Willement; the floor was patterned with encaustic tiles by Minton; and highly competent glazing was supplied by a local artist, J. J. Barnett. The work was executed with great skill and care. On the whole the *Builder* was enthusiastic and the *Ecclesiologist* cautious.[35] Verdicts were similarly divided over the restoration of the Temple Church in London (1840–43). But there the *odium ecclesiologicum* was aggravated by a first-class professional quarrel when James Savage was dismissed and Sydney Smirke took over the bulk of the unfinished work.[36] Sydney Smirke never really satisfied the rigid standards of the Camden Society. Reconstruction was his forte rather than restoration: for example, the refurbishing of the Savoy Chapel, London, after successive fires in 1842 and 1864. On the second occasion he had at his command equally reliable subordinates in the shape of White, Blore and Forsyth. 'Needless to say,' remarked the *Builder*, the architect 'has done his duty well.'[37] All things considered, it was perhaps just as well that although he began the restoration of Lichfield Cathedral in 1853, he was soon superseded by Sir George Gilbert Scott.[38]

Sydney Smirke's secular Gothic work aroused less criticism – for here he was largely outside the range of the Camdenians. He can never have been very happy

52

52   *York Chapter House. Vault restored by Smirke, with decoration by Willement*

about his essays in Jacobean. Neither King Edward's School, Witley, Surrey (1867),[39] nor The Rocks, Uckfield, Sussex (1838),[40] could possibly be described as exciting. And his extension (1847–48) of Paper Buildings in the Inner Temple is memorable only for its nickname: to distinguish it from Sir Robert Smirke's monochrome work of 1838, waspish lawyers christened Sydney Smirke's (now truncated) bricky turrets 'Blotting-Paper Buildings'.[41] Nearby, however, there stood until the Blitz one of Sydney Smirke's more successful Gothic designs, the Inner Temple Hall (1867–70). Unlike Hardwick's new hall at Lincoln's Inn (1843), it marked no new stylistic development. It was, nevertheless, a thoroughly competent performance, with elaborate Perpendicular tracery, buttresses, battlements and pinnacles, and a full-blown hammerbeam roof.[42] In 1834–37 he had been responsible for a careful restoration of Westminster Hall, faithfully reported in academic journals.[43] Perhaps this gave him a penchant for the Great Hall as a feature of secular design, for in 1862 he went out of his way to incorporate a massive new hall, modelled on Hampton Court, in his reconstruction of Lambton Castle. During the 1930s the whole building was judiciously pruned, and Sydney Smirke's hall, with its timbered roof and great Perpendicular windows, disappeared. Its attached arcade, modelled on that of St James's Palace, shrunk into a *porte-cochère*. Only his panelled library and dining room survive. Lofty and sombre, their scale is undeniably impressive—even though their details display, in Christopher Hussey's words, 'an ugliness . . . better imagined than illustrated'.[44]

  Almost from the start Sydney Smirke's classical designs abandoned the austerity of the Greek Revival for the richer Italianate usually associated with Sir Charles Barry. His début at the Oxford Street Pantheon (1833–34) was something of a

53   SMIRKE. *Pantheon Bazaar, London*
54   SMIRKE. *Oakley Park. Entrance portico*

triumph for the Cinquecento style. Since the 1770s Wyatt's Winter Ranelagh – 'Baalbec in all its glory', as Horace Walpole called it – had been once burnt and thrice rebuilt before Sydney Smirke was called in to turn it into a grandiose covered market. He added a cast-iron portico to Wyatt's Oxford Street frontage, replaced the roof with a light-weight, timber-framed structure, and transformed the interior into a great basilican bazaar 330 ft long. The Roman arcades of its barrel-vaulted nave were decked out with papier mâché mouldings by Charles Bielefeld and arabesques designed by C. J. Richardson, executed in oil on canvas by Lambalette. Viewed from gallery-level, the sale-counters below were said to form 'a complete parterre or labyrinth'. At the Marlborough Street entrance visitors passed through a conservatory and aviary, cool with fountains and thick with potted plants, roofed over with cast iron and glass, and decorated with 'some unique ornaments of painting . . . in the Persian style' by C. J. Richardson. The work was carried through at great speed and expense: £40,000 was spent in six months. At first all went well. Traders willingly surrendered ten per cent of their takings in return for the privilege of such a fashionable address. But within thirty years the project had ceased to be commercially viable. The building was converted into Gilbey's Wine Cellars in 1867 and demolished in 1937 to make way for Marks and Spencer.[45] At Exeter Change in the Strand (1843–44), another shopping arcade, smaller and even more ephemeral, Sydney Smirke again introduced some Cinquecento decoration, executed this time in distemper by Collman. On this occasion, however, the exterior was masked with Jacobean brickwork and the interior was less remarkable for its polychromy than for the ingenuity of its plan: an oblique-angled central aisle, coved and glazed, 60 ft by 12 ft by 20 ft high, its obliquity disguised by ante-chambers at either end, one heptagonal, the other hexagonal.[46] Sydney Smirke certainly knew how to exploit the potentialities of this new form of commercial architecture. A retail market was really a multi-tenanted shopping centre under one roof. It required a fresh architectural approach, more intimate, less austere than – for example – Charles Fowler's covered markets for the wholesale trade. The Burlington Arcade was more popular, the Royal Opera Arcade and the Lowther Arcade were architecturally more distinguished, but the Pantheon remained the grandest supermarket in Victorian London, and Exeter Change the cleverest.

53

55 SMIRKE. *Oxford and Cambridge Club, London*
56 SMIRKE. *Conservative Club, London. Staircase*

It was not until the second half of his career that Sydney Smirke developed the rich palazzo style for which he is best remembered. Several of his earlier classical works share the simplicity and restraint of his elder brother's designs. His four custom houses at Shoreham (1830), Gloucester (*c.* 1830), Bristol (1836) and Newcastle (*c.* 1840, incorporating earlier work), are wholly Regency in feeling, with round-arched windows, plain cornices, Tuscan porches and shallow rustication.[47] His reconstruction of Luton Hoo, Bedfordshire, after the fire of 1843, seems to have added little in the way of enrichment to the work of Robert Adam and Sir Robert Smirke.[48] At Bury, Lancashire (1846–47), his multiple design for assembly rooms, hotel and athenaeum made good use of a prominent corner site but scarcely began to exploit the rich variety of Graeco-Roman forms already fashionable by that date. It was essentially an economical design: the athenaeum section cost no more than £4,000.[49] Sydney Smirke's additions to Bethlehem Hospital (1838–46) fall into the same category of plainness. But there the boldness of the scale more than makes up for any decorative deficiencies. James Lewis's building of 1812–15 had itself been large, costing some quarter of a million pounds. To this Sydney Smirke added a central portico and dome and double extensions to the wings at either end, front and rear, fireproof and centrally heated throughout. The frontage was thus elongated to no less than 697 ft. The centrepiece is still impressive – some 150 ft from ground to summit. A portico of six giant unfluted Ionic columns leads the eye upwards to the great dome. The dome itself rises from an octagon set upon a square base, the octagon being punctuated by Corinthian pilasters and circular lunettes. Inside the dome Sydney Smirke installed the hospital chapel. Originally Bedlam inmates had been denied the consolation of religion: many of them already suffered from religious mania. Some services had been belatedly provided in the shallow cupola of Lewis's building. Sydney Smirke turned the 37 ft drum of his new dome into an ingenious little chapel, lofty, slender and octagonal in shape. Galleries supported on cast-iron stanchions were placed round five of the eight sides. The vestry was tucked away in the apex of the pediment. In recent years the old Bedlam building has become the Imperial War Museum. Sydney Smirke's extra wings have been removed and for some time his chapel housed an assortment of books, papers and military bric-à-brac. In their new setting – a municipal garden – his great portico and dome have become a familiar part of London's landscape. 'Everyone knows the dome,' wrote C. H. Reilly, 'in silhouette against the sky from many a train window . . . a simple, solid piece of work, very typical of the best side of Victorian culture.'[50]

It was of course in Sydney Smirke's series of London club houses that his penchant for the Renaissance found full expression. However, two country houses, designed early in his career, indicate his gradual progress towards that stylistic goal. At Gunnersbury Park, near Ealing, Middlesex (1834), his emancipation from the Greek Revival had scarcely begun. The bow windows, the banded rustication, the round-arched fenestration arranged in triplets, the pilastered orangery, even the triumphal arch, are all treated with Regency restraint.[51] But at Oakley Park, near Eye, Suffolk (*c.* 1830), Neo-Classical proportions are combined with a decorative scheme which in its strength of colour and boldness of contour can only be described as Early Victorian. Until its demolition during the 1930s, Oakley Park seemed almost a Pall Mall palazzo which had strayed into the Suffolk countryside. It was basically a drastic remodelling of an eighteenth-century building, Hoxne Hall. Some of the older chimney-pieces and plastered ceilings were incorporated in the new work, thus encouraging the architect to make use of Palladian rather than Grecian forms. Greek antae still appear as window jambs. But the controlling order is a bold Corinthian, and an accumulation of minor details contribute to an overall sense of rich texture and bold projection – the scagliola columns raised on pedestals in the top-lit central hall, the paired columns of the grand portico, the balustrades and urns ranged up and down the terraces, the scrolly stable cupola, the bold keystones and massy brackets.[52]

Similar tendencies are visible in the design of the Oxford and Cambridge Club. This building marked a watershed in Sydney Smirke's career. It was Sir Robert Smirke who advised upon the choice of site in 1834, negotiated a lease from the Commissioners of Woods and Forests and was commissioned by the club committee in 1835. It was he who superintended the laying of the foundations and the raising of the superstructure. The accounts were his responsibility, and the architect's five per cent commission of £1,254 was paid in his name. Sydney Smirke's assistance appears to have been confined to the drawing board. But he seems to have been responsible at least for the façade, and it is not unreasonable to attribute to his influence the richness of effect produced by an accumulation of features unusual in a design from Sir Robert's pen. Contemporary journals gave most of the credit to the younger man; on completion of the club in 1838 both brothers were elected to honorary membership. Despite the irregularity of the site the plan is both regular and functional. The staircase hall (altered by Blomfield, 1907) is approached from the vestibule by a steep flight of steps flanked by square Doric pilasters. Together these rooms neatly bisect the ground floor. Before the addition of Blomfield's attic storey, the Pall Mall façade consisted of two storeys plus mezzanine and basement. Corinthian columns and a stucco entablature mark the central entrance, flanked on each side by three round-headed windows separated by stucco piers. Above the balcony seven rectangular windows are flanked by Doric pilasters and divided by piers coursed with chamfered joints. Panels above each of these windows contain bas-reliefs by W. G. Nicholl modelled on designs by Robert Smirke Sr, illustrating 'the exalted labours of the mind'. The composition is crowned by an anthemion frieze, a dentilled cornice decorated with scroll-modillions and an interrupted balustrade. This façade was praised at the time for its 'air of monumental grandeur', and its 'highly intellectual character'. Produced by the united talents of three members of the Smirke family, the Oxford and Cambridge Club effectually marks the limits to which the Grecian style could be stretched before its eclipse by Renaissance forms.[53]

54

55

Sydney Smirke's rejected design for the Reform Club (1837),[54] entered from the west side by a grand Corinthian portico, must have echoed Oakley Park in several ways. Like the Oxford and Cambridge it marked a transitional stage in the development of full-blooded Renaissance forms. During the 1840s, however, the Tory party commissioned two London club houses specifically designed to eclipse Barry's Whig palazzo in Pall Mall – the Conservative Club[55] and the new Carlton Club.[56] Both commissions went to Sydney Smirke, but in both cases by a somewhat devious process. Founded as a back-bench organization in 1840, the Conservative Club at first employed Decimus Burton to negotiate for the site of the old Thatched House Tavern in St James's Street. Burton was thought to be 'very ill used' when in 1842 the committee dispensed with his services and invited four new architects to submit designs: George Basevi, Sydney Smirke, Thomas Hopper and William Railton. After twice balloting, with and without proxy votes, the committee reached deadlock and eventually chose the first two names as *joint* architects. Three years later, on the completion of the building, both men became honorary members.

Meanwhile the competition for the new Carlton Club was in full swing. Founded in 1832, the first of the political clubs and very much a front-bench organization, the Carlton clearly felt outclassed by the architectural competition from its next-door neighbour, the Reform. Sir Robert Smirke's original building (1833–36) had been small, dignified and plainly Grecian. It was a competent piece of work, but out of date almost as soon as it was finished. The committee therefore decided to double the size of their premises by buying up adjoining property and by rebuilding the whole structure in the palazzo manner in two successive stages. The competition became a *cause célèbre*. In 1844 the selection committee – Lord Salisbury, Henry Hope and Gally Knight – invited no less than fifteen architects to submit designs. Charles Barry, Philip Hardwick, C. R. Cockerell, Decimus Burton, A. W. N. Pugin, Edward Blore, Matthew Wyatt and Ambrose Poynter all declined, although Cockerell privately produced some splendidly Baroque sketches. Sydney Smirke, Basevi, Messrs Lee and Bury, Railton, Salvin and Hopper all accepted. The result was disastrous. The committee ruled out Salvin's rambling Elizabethan design as impossible, only to find that it was precisely that design which the majority of club members preferred, along with Hopper's adaptation of Inigo Jones's Banqueting House. A fresh competition was therefore set on foot in May 1845; members were asked to vote again, this time not for a design but for any architect of their choice. Sydney Smirke and Basevi decided to unite their supporters by sending in a joint nomination. Peel made known his approval, and the combination triumphed. Nine architects scored no more than a handful of votes, namely Roberts, Nelson, Beazley, Blore, Hardwick, Railton, Burn and Cockerell. Hopper scored 57, Salvin 89, Barry 210 and Basevi and Sydney Smirke 220. One defeated contestant described such competitions, in which architects were 'kicked about like footballs', as 'mere farces – flimsy blinds to screen some intended favouritism'. But the result was smoothly ratified by the club committee. And when in October Basevi fell to his death from the roof of Ely Cathedral, Sydney Smirke found himself in sole possession of one of the key commissions of the 1840s.

Sydney Smirke thus became chiefly responsible for both Tory answers to Barry's Whiggish palazzo. The first answer was Palladian, the second Venetian. Both marked significant steps towards the richness and plasticity of High Victorian classicism. The Conservative Club was hailed immediately as a veritable 'King of Clubs' – even its kitchens outshone the Reform. Its staircase hall (recently gutted) was bedizened with Raphaelesque arabesques in Sang's encaustic polychromy, and

56

57 SMIRKE. *Carlton Club, London*

seemed almost to 'baffle description'. The two architects co-operated to produce
the façade, the ground-floor rooms being credited to Basevi and the first-floor
rooms to Sydney Smirke. But the relationship between the decoration of the
staircase hall and the decoration of the Pantheon was clear enough. And thanks to
the accident of Basevi's death, Sydney Smirke emerged with most of the credit. The
only criticism, then and since, relates to the lower half of the St James's Street
façade—it lacks the boldness and rich modulation of a truly Renaissance podium.
57 By contrast the Carlton Club was sufficiently bold and richly modulated to satisfy
even the most jaded palate. As the *Athenaeum* noted in 1847, it 'marks the triumph
of Italianism over Greekism'. Strolling down the 'sweet shady side of Pall Mall'
towards the end of the 1840s, visitors were left in no doubt as to the way in which
English secular architecture had progressed during the previous twenty
years – Decimus Burton's Athenaeum (1828–30), mitigating Grecian severity with
Roman Doric columns and flat rustication, Barry's Travellers' Club (1829–32)
calmly Raphaelesque at the front, in the manner of the Pandolfini Palace in
Florence, and mildly Venetian at the rear, then the Reform Club (1837–41),
Barry's dramatic adaptation of San Gallo's Farnese Palace in Rome, and finally the
new Carlton Club, exchanging Barry's sombre Roman Cinquecento for the
opulence and colour of sixteenth-century Venice. And on the other side of
London's 'street of palaces' the same spectator would certainly have been struck by
an even lusher specimen of Italianate – stemming directly from the
Carlton – Parnell and Smith's Army and Navy Club (1848–51). The 'triumph of
Italianism' was indeed complete. At the Carlton Club Sydney Smirke took up the
theme of Sansovino's Library of St Mark, and adapted this Venetian precedent to a
metropolitan setting. The layout of rooms around a central *cortile* echoed that of
the Reform. But in richness of decoration it quite eclipsed its rival. Its florid
cornice and figured spandrels, boldly sculptured in high relief, struck the keynote
for a whole range of commercial architecture throughout the 1850s and 1860s.
60 And its use – apparently for the first time in London – of polished columns in pink
and green granite, set a precedent which proved only too popular. At the time

58 *Burlington House, London, showing the top storey added by Smirke*

doubts were voiced as to the weathering qualities of such materials. During the next three-quarters of a century the Aberdeen and Peterhead granite merely lost its patina; but the mass of Caen stone mouldings crumbled away completely and had to be wholly replaced in 1923. It was therefore Sir Reginald Blomfield's rusticated façade – not Sydney Smirke's – which finally fell victim to the Blitz.

If Pall Mall saw the origins of High Victorian classicism in London, the Burlington House complex saw its culmination. Here again Sydney Smirke had a crucial part to play. Right from the start of his career he had been moving away from the reticent conventions of the Regency. Just before he set out on his architectural Grand Tour, C. R. Cockerell had advised him to shake off the influence of Sir Robert Smirke by studying the Renaissance classicism of north Italy. Cockerell added, a little wryly, that only after 'seven years' freedom and travel' had he himself escaped from the same 'master's spell'.[57] Sydney Smirke's escape was easier. Even as late as 1856, however, at 20 Irish Street, Whitehaven, he combined a boldly rusticated palazzo façade with a strangely old-fashioned Regency bow window.[58] Perhaps in the provinces he could afford to be nostalgic. But in London, in the same year, he submitted a design in the Foreign Office competition which was thoroughly, monumentally Palladian.[59] That commission went to Gilbert Scott. But with Burlington House – the *locus classicus* of Palladianism – Sydney Smirke had the chance of a lifetime to establish an independent reputation as a classicist. At best he only partly succeeded. His transformation of Lord Burlington's private palace was certainly thorough – Pevsner calls it an operation of 'High Victorian cruelty'.[60] But the cruelty was not entirely of his own making. In 1859 the Royal Academy nominated Sir Charles Barry as architect of their new premises in Piccadilly, and Barry prepared a grandiose scheme to redevelop the whole area in conjunction with his assistants R. R. Banks and Charles Barry Jr. A few months later Barry died and the Royal Academy turned to Sydney Smirke, Cockerell's newly appointed successor as Professor of Architecture. He was directed to add an extra storey to Burlington House, plus galleries and schools along its garden frontage. The

58

government, however, retained Messrs Banks and Barry as architects of a new quadrangle fronting Piccadilly, designed to house the various learned societies. At the same time James Pennethorne, architect to the Office of Works, was commissioned to add a new administrative centre for London University along the Burlington Gardens section of the site. Responsibility for the whole project was thus initially shared between four architects. Sydney Smirke's Academy Schools and Exhibition Galleries were erected in 1867–68. Pennethorne's London University building followed in 1869. In 1872 Sydney Smirke's second storey was begun. And in 1873–74 Banks and Barry completed the new courtyard with its accommodation for the Society of Antiquaries, the Geological Society, the Astronomical Society etc. Just as these buildings were finished, Sydney Smirke resigned, leaving his interior work to be completed by G. E. Street and E. M. Barry. Even then the roster of architects was not complete – Norman Shaw added a restaurant and other rooms in 1885, and Sir T. G. Jackson redesigned the entrance hall in 1899. Sydney Smirke must therefore share the credit – and the blame – for what was done. On the credit side Pennethorne scores full marks for his striking façade in Burlington Gardens, E. M. Barry and Norman Shaw for their regal adaptation of Isaac Ware's grand staircase. On the debit side, the destruction of Gibbs's courtyard colonnade by Banks and Barry seems to have been largely due to governmental pressure. Sydney Smirke wished to avoid such a catastrophe and produced a number of alternative suggestions – in fact several of his variant schemes are a good deal more attractive than his final compromise with the necessity for extra space. Nevertheless his final treatment of Campbell's work only just fell short of complete success. The Exhibition Galleries are dignified and well lit – the Octagon even has a ponderous touch of drama. And the top storey of Burlington House is a bravura exercise in Cinquecento vein, boldly modelled with columns of tinted granite and emblematic sculpture by Weekes, Calder Marshall and Durham. But there is too much of it: Campbell's easy proportions have been squeezed away by such an over-mighty attic and the whole façade has been thrown off balance by the rusticated arcade below. As for the Piccadilly front by Banks and Barry, its richness of effect is undeniable – too rich, it seems, for Goodhart-Rendel's palate, but much to the liking of Sir Albert Richardson.[61]

Burlington House was Sydney Smirke's last major work. But three more commissions remain to be considered. During the latter part of his career he was engaged on three projects which certainly testify to the diversity of his practice: the Round Reading Room of the British Museum, the Horticultural Society's Galleries in Kensington and Brookwood Cemetery. All three – library, botanical exhibition and cemetery – illuminate central themes of Victorian culture: the prestige of learning, the cult of nature and the obsession with death.

During the second quarter of the nineteenth century the laying-out of cemeteries became first a necessity and then an art. Walker's *Gatherings from Graveyards* (1839) and Chadwick's *Practice of Interment in Towns* (1843) gruesomely exposed the inadequacies of London's old parochial burial grounds. Each year it was reckoned that more than 44,000 bodies were crammed into the 218 acres of London's available space; and each year's load of corpses was said to emit more than 2,500,000 cubic feet of obnoxious gases into the fetid air of the metropolis. Such grisly arithmetic was unanswerable – the romantic mist of an eighteenth-century churchyard turned out to be mephitic vapour. Rather belatedly (Père Lachaise dates from 1765), London dealt with the problem in characteristically British fashion – joint-stock companies were set up to bury the dead. Cemeteries appeared at Kensal Green (1833), Norwood (1838), Highgate (1839), Abney Park, Nunhead and Brompton (1840). This stage was completed by legislation in 1847

59 SMIRKE. *Gardens of the Royal Horticultural Society*

and 1852, placing them under the Burial Authority for the Metropolis. Brookwood Cemetery belongs to the next stage – the decentralization of metropolitan interments. In 1855 the London Necropolis Co. bought 2,100 acres near Woking – enough, it was hoped, for five or six centuries – a massive burial ground linked to its source of supply by twenty-four miles of the new South-Western Railway. Sydney Smirke and Sir William Tite were called in to design the necessary accoutrements. Sydney Smirke designed the private departure platform at Waterloo Station, complete with Neo-Norman carriage entrance, steam-powered lifts for coffins and mourners' waiting rooms divided into three classes. Tite designed two Gothic cemetery stations at Woking, one in consecrated and one in unconsecrated ground; plus two cemetery chapels of brick and timber, cruciform in shape, with towers and slated spires. The cost of a first-class railway funeral was apparently £21 14s 2d 'all in'. George Godwin, editor of the *Builder*, considered the whole project vital to 'the all-important Burial Question'. He seemed to think it almost the duty of all good Londoners to find themselves 'some quite resting-place in the dry sand of a Woking grave'. In one respect at least Brookwood fulfilled the optimism of its share-holders – more than one hundred years after its foundation the cemetery has all the evergreen luxuriance of a landscape by J. C. Loudon.[62]

Architecturally speaking, the development of the South Kensington area – 'Albertopolis' as it was called – was a triumph for High Victorian polychromy. This was a subject on which Sydney Smirke held strong views. Unlike Ruskin he believed that colour should emphasize structural qualities, not ignore them. 'Zebra stripes' he condemned as 'one of those eccentricities of the past which scarcely deserve to be disinterred'. Unlike Butterfield he disliked 'chequering over the exterior of a church with bits of bright coloured materials'. If the 'intense polychromatism' of the 1850s was not to degenerate into random indulgence it must be governed by a sense of harmony and propriety. With such principles in mind Sydney Smirke designed his architectural setting for the specimens of the Horticultural Society. Prince Albert had secured the Society a large, sloping site to the south of the present Albert Hall. Under the direction of the Department of Science and Art redevelopment proceeded sporadically between 1859 and 1862. W. A. Nesfield laid out a geometrical garden studded with fountains and sprinkled with walks of coloured gravel. Captain Francis Fowke RE was responsible for two key buildings which temporarily dominated the site – a spacious conservatory to the north, and the giant 1862 Exhibition building to the south, and Sydney Smirke contributed a series of open cloisters to the north, east and west of the Society's terraced gardens. Like Fowke's arcade on the southern

59

side – modelled on the cloisters of St John Lateran at Rome – these open walks were designed as an architectural backcloth to the Society's exotic botanical exhibits. Polychromy was *de rigueur*. In fact Sydney Smirke displayed part of his design in Fowke's adjacent Exhibition palace under the following title: 'A Study in Polychromy, showing how coloured marbles and terracottas may be ornamentally used in external architecture.' His northern arcade, 600 ft long, 23 ft wide and 26 ft high, derived from the arcade of the Villa Albani at Rome. His eastern and western arcades, each 630 ft long, 20 ft high and 24 ft wide, followed fifteenth-century Milanese precedents at the Ospedale Maggiore. Minton tiles, yellow brick, red brick and terracotta were the dominant materials. The terracotta enrichments – capitals, spandrels and friezes, modelled by Stevens's pupil Godfrey Sykes and manufactured by Blanchard of Blackfriars – were supposed to combine 'the smoothness of stone and the sharpness of metal'. Certainly the scale of the thing was impressive – the covered promenades alone measured no less than three-quarters of a mile. Prince Albert hailed the whole project as 'a valuable attempt to reunite the science and art of gardening to the sister Arts of Architecture, Sculpture and Painting'. Pevsner's dictum on Matthew Digby Wyatt's 1862 work is perhaps more appropriate: he calls it an 'odd combination of the festive with the turgid'. Either way the sculpture remained incomplete, the trees never reached full height and most of the buildings were soon demolished. Today all that remains of the Horticultural Society's campus is the memorial to the 1851 Exhibition – by Durham and Smirke – standing a little sadly in the shadow of the Albert Hall.[63]

Polychromy bulked large in Sydney Smirke's Royal Academy lectures.[64] But so did the spectre of cast iron and the search for a new style. In 1851 he had admired Paxton's Great Exhibition building, but only as a vast greenhouse.[65] From 1857 onwards his professional opinions on such knotty questions were retailed to students and widely reported in the press. They sum up only too well the hazy viewpoint of uncommitted architects in the 1860s, and justify detailed quotation. He begins by denying the equation of utility and beauty:

Why . . . should Architecture be forbidden to indulge, moderately and wisely, in some *graceful inutilities?* . . . Ornament begins where utility ends . . . [For] ornament [is] . . . something intended to give pleasure to the eye, without offending the dominant sense of usefulness . . . The mere dry, unimpassioned beauty resulting from the quality of fitness, however it may satisfy the engineer, will hardly suffice to meet the aspirations of the architect [for] as artists . . . we desire something more.

Style is thus merely a regularized system of expressive ornament, 'the language of architecture'. Neither the classic tradition nor the Gothic tradition has a monopoly of excellence; the structural premises of both are now outdated, and their purpose is now primarily evocative and disciplinary. Style is the product of circumstance, not the invention of individuals. The circumstances have changed and yet no new style has emerged. 'It is useless to deny that aesthetics generally have not kept pace either with physics or with the exact sciences . . . [Architecture] has not kept pace with time.' There is a crisis of confidence in the profession. What can be done?

Were I disposed to encourage the search after *a new style* (a search which I am very far indeed from encouraging you to prosecute) I would say to you, seek it in the application of some *material,* or in the invention of some new *system of construction.*

But such technical details lie outside his terms of reference: 'architecture as a *fine art*.' Royal Academy lectures exist merely 'to form the taste of the students and to instruct them in the laws and principles of composition'. In this sphere,

as . . . in morals, . . . it *may* be that no new important principles remain to be discovered . . . [Therefore] seek rather for that which is *good*, than for that which is *new*, and in this search you may perchance fall in with something *new* which is *good* . . . The modern tendency to repeat and perpetuate old forms . . . to live . . . upon the wits of our predecessors . . . to feed upon the réchauffées of the past, is . . . mischievous.

Look to the past for principles, not details. Select the useful, reject the irrelevant.

This doctrine is stigmatised as eclectic or latitudinarian, and as an encouragement to an indulgence in all manner of fantastic excesses . . . [But] let us . . . hold fast to that which presents itself to our minds as good and right, allowing no superstitious prejudice to warp our judgement, be it *Greek* or *Gothic*, and I think we may rest assured that such a course would afford us the best chance of ultimately arriving – it may be after a long purgatorial period of folly and excess, yet ultimately arriving – at a sound, consistent and original style, worthy of the genius and civilisation of the nineteenth century.

Such indecision, such confused optimism – endemic among mid–Victorian architects[66] – is clearly visible in Sydney Smirke's most significant design, the Reading Room of the British Museum.[67] When Sir Robert Smirke retired in 1846 51 his great quadrangular museum was almost finished. Designed as early as 1823, his giant Ionic colonnade had at least been built. It merely remained for Sydney Smirke to add on a few minor exhibition rooms and to finish the forecourt – in the process designing the splendid entrance railings, cast at York by John Walker and Co. But scarcely had the forecourt been completed when, in 1854, work began on a new circular reading room in the centre of the original quadrangle. Ever since its foundation the museum had been short of space. Various schemes for making use of the quadrangle had been proposed during the 1840s and 1850s. Several of these involved circular reading rooms. In 1852 Sir Anthony Panizzi, 'the Napoleon of Librarians', made up his mind that a Round Reading Room there should be, and from then on it was just a matter of convincing the Treasury. Panizzi's was the energy behind the scheme, but the design belonged to Sydney Smirke. 'Every aesthetic merit,' he wrote, 'that the reading room may possess, I claim as literally and exclusively my own.' When it was opened in 1857 Sydney Smirke's reputation was made – his award of the RIBA Gold Medal followed naturally in 1860.[68] First of all, the sheer size of the structure seemed stupendous; the dome was 140 ft in diameter, larger than both St Peter's and St Paul's and second only to the Pantheon; its building, together with the adjacent stacks, involved 2,000 tons of iron and provided 25 miles of shelving for 1,300,000 books. Secondly, as an exercise in the architectural use of cast iron the Reading Room seemed a massive portent of the shape of things to come. 'Cast iron,' wrote Sydney Smirke, 'perfectly satisfies me of its excellence as a building material.'

Yes, but what about style? The giant ribs of the dome dictated their own symmetry. The formalized pattern of the galleries – happily echoing the chequering of the great oculus – had the right metallic formation. The only weakness of the whole design lay at the points where it compromised the logic of its construction – the Lombardic fenestration of the clerestory, the interpenetration of drum and dome, the false bookcase masking each rib at lower level. Such compromises might occasionally be carried off with panache. After all, even the peaks of High Victorian achievement were sometimes shot through with compromise. But in the hands of lesser architects compromise hovered on the brink of platitude. The sheer bulk of Victorian architecture made whole quantities of platitude well-nigh inevitable – all the more reason for lowering our historical sights now and then, and studying a man like Professor Sydney Smirke, RA, a first–class second–rate architect.

IV

John Loughborough Pearson
noble seriousness

DAVID LLOYD

John Loughborough Pearson was born in 1817, the youngest son of a watercolour painter of the city of Durham, where Pearson lived till he was twenty-five. The place is important: Durham Cathedral must have had a profound effect on the young Pearson, and made itself felt in his later rather than his earlier works – not the actual style of the cathedral, but its form and proportions, its superb relationship of structure and space. In Durham width is ample but height is emphasized by the upward thrust of the shafts between alternate bays, from which the ribs of the vaulting spring – how poignant that Pearson was brought up in the place where (as far as is known) the first ribbed vaults were wrought. Length, at Durham, is not excessive in relation to width, and the transepts, though important parts of the spatial composition, do not create a strong cross-axis to counteract the effect of the main axis. Vaulting heights are even in nave, choir and transepts; the crossing arches provide punctuation but not strong breaks in the continuity of the roofline, so that the whole of the main part of the building forms a single great space. The climax is the delicate altar screen, above, beside and even through which are glimpses into lesser, more intricate and more compressed spaces which add mysterious complexity to the clarity of the main spatial creation. Anyone who knows Pearson's great later churches will appreciate how the influence of Durham permeated his vision, although his earlier creations were more often inspired by French precedent.

At the age of fourteen, Pearson was articled to Ignatius Bonomi,[1] the son of the Late Georgian architect Joseph Bonomi. Ignatius Bonomi lived and practised in Durham, where he was also County Surveyor – a post which made him responsible to the County Quarter Sessions for the maintenance of bridges and the design and upkeep of county buildings. Bonomi's private work is scattered over the north-eastern counties, and is found in country houses as well as churches, eclectically in classical, Gothic or even Romanesque styles, as was the work of so many architects of the second quarter of the nineteenth century. Pearson left Bonomi's office in 1842, and after a short period with W. G. Pickering, a Sunderland architect,[2] moved to London to work with Anthony Salvin (himself of a County Durham family)[3] for six months. Late in 1842 he joined Philip Hardwick as assistant, and under him supervised the building of the Tudor-Gothic Hall and Library at Lincoln's Inn.[4] Finally, Pearson set up on his own as architect in 1843.

Pearson's first three churches are in the East Riding of Yorkshire, confusingly called Ellerker (1843), Elloughton (1844–46)[5] and Ellerton (1846–47). They are minor works. North Ferriby (1846–47), also in the East Riding, is more considerable. It is a typical 'Middle Pointed' church, very much according to the precepts of the Camden (later Ecclesiological) Society, whose influence was then near its peak, but with an unmistakable punch and quality which lift it above the ordinary. This is especially true of the steeple where the buttresses are stepped out just below the belfry stage, which it leaves clear and foursquare; the broach spire has sharply gabled lights above the break from square to octagon – features which are prophetic of later works. Concurrently at Weybridge in Surrey (1846–48) Pearson designed a somewhat similar church with a grander, but less subtle, spire

66

60 JOHN LOUGHBOROUGH PEARSON. *Portrait by W. W. Ouless*

61 PEARSON. *St Augustine, Kilburn, London*

added in 1855.[6] Neither North Ferriby nor Weybridge owes anything specific to the architectural traditions of the region in which it is set; both are modelled on the typical high medieval church of the east or south Midlands which the ecclesiologists of the time idealized, and so was the now vanished Holy Trinity, Bessborough Gardens, Pimlico (1848–50), Pearson's first church in London, cruciform with a central spire.

Pearson travelled widely in France between about 1849 and 1855, visiting and sketching innumerable churches. He designed no new buildings during that period but undertook some church restorations, most notably at the magnificent Saxon-Norman cruciform church of Stow in north Lincolnshire. This was then wood-roofed throughout, but Pearson discovered evidence, scant but convincing, that the late twelfth-century chancel had been vaulted. He set himself the task of recreating the vault – a formidable task since the chancel is 26 ft wide and very few Gothic stone vaults of any size had been attempted since the seventeenth century. The chancel walls have very shallow buttresses, like pilasters, which had clearly been sufficient to stand the thrusts of the original vaults, so Pearson sought to design his new vault in such a way as to avoid the need for additional buttressing. After much experimentation he devised a rib vault with infillings of small flat stones set so as to transmit the load as much as possible downward rather than outward. The construction of this vault was a triumph for Pearson, and a major landmark in the Gothic Revival, even though the next substantial vault, at St Peter, Vauxhall, was not designed until several years later.[7]

The small church at Eastoft on the Yorkshire-Lincolnshire border (1855) shows emerging self-assurance; the design is not based on an ecclesiological model, but it is assertive in a personal way, with its steep and thrusting gables, tall lancets and elegant open bellcote over the east nave gable, with stepped-in sides and gabled top. Catherston Leweston, near Charmouth in Dorset (1857–58), is another small but very sophisticated church, with wide string course near the base of the chancel, passing round the buttresses; tiny pinnacles on the gable ends, and another subtly shaped bellcote to the west.[8]

62 In 1858 came Pearson's first really major work, Dalton Holme in the East Riding (sometimes called South Dalton), with one of the most beautiful spires in the country. Coming from Beverley, the effect is unforgettable. The spire first appears to rise over a fold in the chalklands. Then, down in the centre of the village, tower and spire suddenly appear to their full height, unbelievably slender, and unerringly proportioned. The base of the tower up to about nave roof level is solid, with little detailing; the buttresses are minimal, dying into the wall surfaces low down; a few thin string courses provide horizontal incidents. Then, at the base of the belfry stage, the steeple breaks into Gothic exuberance, with three tall and slender gable-topped lights, recessed on each face between octagonal angular buttresses, which continue as sharp spirelets above the springing of the spire.

The church itself is designed with complete self-assurance. It is not very large – an aisleless nave, chancel, transepts, with small side chapel and ancillary structures. It is very carefully related to the ground – a plinth is subtly stepped back twice, string courses define the sill level, the windows rise, relatively tall, in exuberant Gothic tracery, the buttresses, restrained but firm, die into the walls below the eaves. A strongly balustraded stepway leads up into the richly detailed porch. Different parts are gabled at different angles, making a carefully contrived irregular composition culminating in the soaring spire, the whole effect being one of uplift from solid earth to heaven. In few relatively small churches is this symbolic effect so well contrived. Inside, too, one is uplifted by architectural

68 means. The wall surfaces are plain to above head-level, where there is a strong

62 PEARSON. *St Mary, Dalton Holme*

string course, with corbels from which shafts rise between the deeply recessed and delicately traceried windows to a lacy but boldly projecting cornice, from which spring the arched wooden beams of the roof. The chancel is treated in a similar way, but more lavishly than the nave, and a double arch, iron-screened, allows a glimpse into the side chapel. This last effect is prophetic of the complicated cross-vistas into flanking spaces which Pearson so delighted to create in his later churches.[9]

Contemporary with Dalton Holme is Scorborough (1857–59), a few miles away. This is a smaller church – indeed a simple rectangle – but treated as a major work. There is a similar careful progression from ground towards heaven in the

63, 64

69

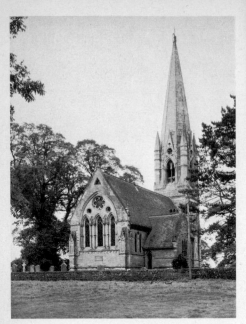

63, 64   PEARSON. *St Leonard, Scorborough. Exterior and detail of chancel*

massing of plinths, buttresses, gables and western steeple (which is much more massive than Dalton Holme), to an ingenious design based on French precedent. The belfry is in the lowest stage of the spire, its lights surmounted by steep gables and flanked by tall sharp pinnacles; the spire itself has a marked entasis. Inside, the windows are deeply recessed behind shafted openings, so giving (as at Dalton) something of the spatial depth otherwise lacking in aisleless churches, and the roof rises from a lavish corbel table much like Dalton Holme. The space under the spire at Scorborough, like the porch at Dalton Holme, is vaulted.

67   Daylesford, Gloucestershire (1859–61), is another French-inspired church set in a very English estate village, with dark surrounding trees which emphasize its smooth solidity. It is cruciform, the emphatic central tower having single deeply recessed belfry lights and a blunt but assertive spire surfaced with scale patterning. Everything builds up, once again, from solid earth to spire. Inside, the treatment of the nave is simple; the central space is emphasized by strongly moulded, marble-shafted arches with luxuriant capitals, and beyond this is the climax of the short vaulted chancel, lit by a trio of lancets behind traceried frames. Here again a small church is given grandeur by skilful massing, sure proportions and careful concentration of rich detailing.

65   In 1863 Pearson married Jemima Christian. Their son Frank was born in 1864, and Jemima died the following year. Appleton-le-Moors (1863–66) is the church whose building spans Pearson's brief married life. It is possibly the most intense of his designs. Set in a dour, dignified village on the southern flanks of the north Yorkshire moors, it is as exotic to its surroundings as any of his creations, thoroughly French in inspiration, and local only in the rough (though regularly coursed) stone of the external wall surfaces. It is quite a small church, with nave and aisles under one sweeping steep-pitched roof, apsidal chancel and flanking south tower and spire in a variant of the Scorborough-Daylesford theme. The entrance to the church is in a deeply recessed doorway set within a low projection of the

66   western wall between two bold buttresses. Inside, the first surprising impression is

70   that of the rich and varied colouring. Pearson never tried to emulate Butterfield in

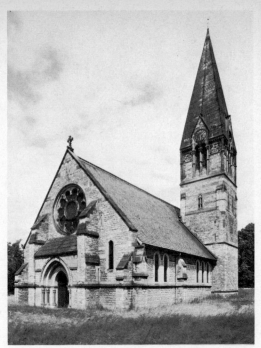

65, 66 PEARSON. *Christ Church, Appleton-le-Moors. Exterior and chancel*

polychromy, but in some of his churches of the later 1850s – Dalton Holme, Catherston Leweston, Daylesford and especially Scorborough – he contrived modest colour contrasts, usually by bands of stone in tones significantly lighter or darker than the adjoining wall surfaces. Appleton's interior has stonework in two tones, near-black and brown, forming extraordinary geometrical patterns against the smooth cream colour of most of the wall surfaces. Capitals are heavily luxuriant, and marble shafts provide further contrasts. Round the apse is a band of sgraffito decoration in white against red. The spatial composition is basically simple; a main rectangular round-ended space, unbroken structurally between nave and chancel, its roofline defined by a bold continuous cornice (as at Scorborough), but its roof quite a simple carpenter's job. Spatial complexity is given (in a way which was later to be typical of Pearson) by the tiny north chapel, compressedly rich, open to the chancel through a much moulded and shafted double arch with open quatrefoil, and entered through a very narrow double arch at the end of the aisle. The chapel has a miniature vault, and is lit by richly treated windows with more sgraffito decoration. Altogether this church is more frenziedly rich than any other of Pearson's creations.

If Appleton-le-Moors is a tempestuous building, Sutton Veny, Wiltshire, suggests an after-storm calm. In some ways it harks back to Pearson's earliest churches like North Ferriby, Weybridge, or the vanished Holy Trinity, Pimlico, with its fairly conventional Neo-Decorated external details and its plain but well-proportioned central tower and spire. But inside it is prophetic of Pearson's future, with the vaulted space under the tower and the rib-vaulted chancel – restful yet uplifting. The vaults themselves are composed of thin stones laid horizontally near the base, changing subtly to a diagonal pattern farther up, with wider bands of darker (and presumably stronger) stone at intervals, creating a mild polychromatic effect. In this vaulting Pearson was clearly following the lesson in construction he had learned over ten years earlier at Stow; this is indeed one of his first considerable vaults after Stow.

But not the first. In this largely chronological sequence of Pearson's churches

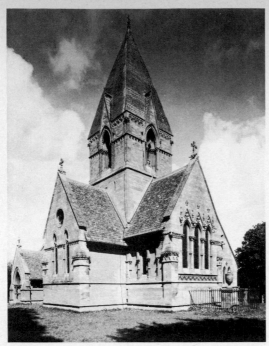

67   PEARSON. *St Peter, Daylesford*
68   PEARSON. *St Peter, Vauxhall, London*

one has so far been omitted – St Peter's at Vauxhall, London (1860–65), which is in several ways different from those already described. Almost all of Pearson's earlier works are in villages or on country estates where there was not the need to accommodate large congregations, but where in most cases there was plenty of money. Vauxhall, on the other hand, was a crowded urban area with few resident rich, and in great need of church accommodation as well as spiritual uplift. Pearson provided a church built largely of brick, relatively cheap for its size and grandeur – a building of the same material as the humble houses around but far excelling them in scale and beauty.[10]

Vauxhall was the first of Pearson's churches to be wholly vaulted – indeed one of the first in the whole Gothic Revival, since James Savage's St Luke's, Chelsea (as surprisingly early as 1820–24), had so far had few followers. Apart from Stow, Pearson himself had hitherto attempted only very small vaulted spaces – the chancel at Daylesford, the chapel at Appleton, the porch at Dalton Holme, the towerspace at Scorborough. All these were of stone – Vauxhall's vaults are of brick with stone ribs.

68   In its design Vauxhall was, in many ways, a prototype for some of Pearson's later grand churches. The main space is tall for its width but the arcades and aisles are relatively low; above the arcades are blank stretches of wall and above that the tall clerestory (with French-type Geometrical windows). The vaulting over the main space is in a straightforward Neo-medieval rib pattern; over the aisles it is stylistically a little more inventive, since the transverse arches are of brick and unmoulded, dying into the side walls, while the diagonal ribs are of stone. Nave and chancel form essentially one unified space, broken only by a chancel arch which is hardly thicker than a transverse rib between vaulting bays. The chancel ends in an apse, without recession in breadth or height, with the eastern windows – tall lancets – closely ranged in the semi-circle above the altar. The vault radiates, within the apse, in a semi-stellar pattern. The intricately patterned stained glass (originally by Clayton and Bell, Pearson's favourite glass artists) and the painted frieze round the apse below the windows (also by Clayton and Bell, somewhat faded) bring the chief colour variations to the otherwise austere interior,

largely faced in rough brick. To the north of the chancel in a pseudo-transeptal position is a widely vaulted Lady Chapel, into which are fascinating, very Pearsonic, cross-vistas. In certain respects – the relative heaviness of the arcades, their elaborate capitals, the Neo-French clerestory windows – the church has affinities with Pearson's work of the late 1850s and the nearly contemporary Appleton-le-Moors. In its elevational form, its spatial side-effects and its vaulting it is a forerunner of some of his subsequent achievements.

Externally, Vauxhall has more in common with works to come than those that went before. It has a tall impressive west front with high Geometrical windows between boldly projecting buttresses, strong angle pinnacles, a high-pitched even roofline, a fleche over the east end of the nave and, notably, no buttresses against the clerestory wall except one on each side of the chancel arch. Clearly most of the thrust of the roof is transmitted, thanks to Pearson's still little-tried skill in vault construction, downward on to the arcades, and out through the narrow, thick vaulted aisles which themselves act as buttresses.[11]

Pearson did little important work in the late 1860s. Apart from Sutton Veny the best church of this phase is Freeland in Oxfordshire (1868–69), quite small, and more in his early style with its vaulted apsidal chancel and relatively simple nave with Geometrical windows. The saddle-backed tower has a counterpart at Over Wallop in Hampshire where he restored the church in 1863–64 and rebuilt the chancel in flint with bands of stone – one of his very few churches in this combination of materials. At Freeland is one of Pearson's few memorable pieces of domestic architecture,[12] a beautifully complex vicarage with rough stone walls, artfully designed buttresses, irregularly arranged windows and, most significantly, a jutting piece of half-timbering on the first floor, oddly gabled over the attic above. Perhaps only here does Pearson rival G. E. Street in the design of parsonages; the Freeland vicarage has a subtly contrived picturesque beauty which would be worthy of Norman Shaw and Lutyens. Other parsonages by Pearson, such as that at Appleton-le-Moors, are far less interesting (although at Appleton he did design an attractive school in 1870 with a dash of half-timbering, recalling Freeland).

69

69   PEARSON. *St Mary, Freeland, and Vicarage*

In 1871 Pearson began his finest work, St Augustine's at Kilburn in London (completed *c.* 1877; tower and spire finished in 1898).[13] Many consider this to be the finest parish church of any date in London. The arrangement of the body of the church is without parallel in England. There are comparatively low double aisles to the nave, each vaulted, and above the inner aisle is a gallery, like an upper storey aisle, taller than the aisle proper and open to the nave by an upper arcade. The gallery is a series of shallow vaulted bays, interconnected by small arches to enable it to be used as a processional way, bridging the entrances to the transepts and altogether helping to create an effect of astonishing spatial complexity. Internal wall surfaces, where not painted, are mostly of brick with fine stone dressings; the nave vault is of brick with stone ribs, but the aisle vaults are wholly of stone. Windows are mainly big lancets. The nave vault is almost continuous with that of the chancel, the chancel arch bringing only a slight pause in the continuity. The presence of the transepts is not expressed in the bay arrangement, which simply continues, with the upper galleries forming bridges, over the transept entrances. A stone rood-screen[14] (an unusual feature for Pearson) links with the galleries but does not provide a very strong structural barrier between the nave and chancel, which essentially form a single space. The east end is squared and northern-monastic in inspiration, with two tiers of tall lancets, the outer two of the top tier disappearing behind the arch of the end bay of the vaulting – a motif which always gives a slight but effective feeling of space. What makes the church quite unforgettable is the endlessly varying series of vistas through interconnected spaces – through the arches at both levels into the intricately high-vaulted transepts, lengthwise along the low vaulted aisles with oblique glimpses into the second aisles, diagonally into the exquisite Lady Chapel south of the chancel (a composition in itself with one broad vaulted bay and intricate apsidal sanctuary with radiating vault), and above all the unparalleled effects obtained from a perambulation of the galleries. Yet for all this intricacy, the main space is clear and definite like that at Durham: the intricacy of the lesser spaces serves to emphasize the clarity of the main space.

Externally, Kilburn has a general form and outline of a type which was varied and refined in churches to come – sharply spired corner turrets, a west front with a rose window and range of lancets recessed in a great arch, a central fleche, long even roofline to the main mass, tall lancets lighting what is, outside, apparently the clerestory (actually the outer wall of the gallery), and no visible buttressing at high level. The walling is in deep red brick, with stone dressings. Above all, Kilburn has its spire – one of the regrettably few of Pearson's intended spires to have been built – rising gracefully and soaringly from a slender tower, set off by tall corner pinnacles and intermediate belfry lights – a thing of beauty but lacking the ethereal quality of the steeple at Dalton Holme, which Pearson never excelled.

Kilburn marks the beginning of a series of churches, mainly in towns, which are large to medium in size and grand in scale. It seems that in the late 1860s and early 70s Pearson's genius finally reached maturity. His varied and brilliant earlier churches – Dalton Holme, Scorborough, Vauxhall, Appleton-le-Moors, Sutton Veny – were all the expressions of a youthful genius experimenting with structure, space and embellishment towards the attainment of ideal forms of Gothic architecture to suit the requirements and aspirations of nineteenth-century Anglicanism.[15]

After Kilburn the vision seems to have been more clear and consistent – between 1875 and 1891 Pearson designed five churches which are basically similar in form, though varying in details and degree of inspiration. They are St Michael's, Croydon; St Alban's, Birmingham; St Stephen's, Bournemouth; St Agnes', Sefton Park, Liverpool; and Holy Trinity, Friern Barnet. Another, St John's, Norwood, differs from the others mainly in the treatment of the east end; St Michael's, Headingley, Leeds, is a simplified variant. All Saints', Hove, is rather different; St John's, Red Lion Square, London (now destroyed), was another brilliant variant. All these are urban churches; Wentworth, Yorkshire, and Cullercoats, Northumberland, are churches for essentially rural parishes where there was less need for space but as much call for grandeur. Thurstaston, Cheshire, is a small village church where internal grandeur is achieved without abandoning intimacy. At the same time Pearson carried out restorations of various cathedrals, Westminster Abbey and Hall, and a large number of parish churches, most notably the abbey church at Shrewsbury, Hythe in Kent and Lastingham in Yorkshire.

In this later phase of Pearson's career much of his inspiration clearly came from the great medieval churches of the north-east of England – churches in the tradition of Beverley and Rievaulx, Whitby and Tynemouth, Hexham and the choir of Southwell (an outlier in this tradition), and great parish churches like Darlington and Hartlepool. With many of these he would have been familiar in youth; others, like Beverley, he must have come to know early in his career. In these and other churches of the early medieval northern British tradition (which influenced Scottish churches as well) there is a marked emphasis on height in relation to width; details are firm but seldom lavish and are, usually, directly related to the structure; windows are often tall lancets, sometimes tiered in ranges; vaulting, where it exists, is usually in basic ribbed form. Such characteristics are very typical of Pearson's post-1870 churches. At the same time the French influence, so predominant in his churches of the late 1850s and early 60s, is still strongly felt – especially in the complicated apses, often with ambulatories, the emphasis on height (as characteristic of the French as of the northern British tradition), the liking for hard geometrical tracery patterns in windows wider than lancets and, most especially, in the general external massing of his churches, which often have a complicated and diffuse skyline punctuated by turrets and frequently a fleche. St Agnes', Liverpool, was rightly called by Sir Nikolaus Pevsner 'English with French touches, combined to achieve perfect unity'.[16]

A field in which Pearson supremely excelled was in the design of spires – for which he was clearly influenced by both English and French precedents. One of his most beautiful steeples, after Dalton Holme, is at Wentworth in Yorkshire, where a new village church (serving Wentworth Woodhouse) was built by Earl Fitzwilliam in 1872–73. The spire rises from a central tower (in the tradition of

Sutton Veny and the earlier lost Holy Trinity, Pimlico, but grander than either) on a broadening base and (if the eye is not deceived) with a delicate entasis. Inside, Wentworth has a fairly low vaulted nave with aisles, leading up to the tall-arched space under the lantern tower, beyond which the chancel, although it rises no higher than the nave, has greater vertical emphasis. Space is revealed not laterally but upward, first in the lantern and then in the vaulted heights of the chancel, which are not fully revealed until one is near or under the crossing.

Three of Pearson's great later churches were designed and started in the late seventies – St John's, Norwood (1875–87),[17] St Alban's, Birmingham (1879–81), and St Michael's, Croydon (1876–85).[18] Croydon is the most nearly perfect. Outside it is of red brick, with stone dressings; inside, the walls and vaults are of London stock brick, with the framework (arches, shafts, ribs) in stone. The interior is primarily one great space, tall for its width, ending in an apse; the chancel arch, as elsewhere, is only just perceptibly thicker than the other transverse arches in the main vaulted space. The transepts are as tall as the main body of the church, but do not create a significant cross-axis. Nave arcades are conventionally moulded, shafts rise between the bays to support the springing of the vault ribs – more than any other feature these shafts emphasize the verticality of the church. There are string courses over the arcades and below the clerestory, between which are sections of bare wall space where a triforium might be. The clerestory is fairly tall and consists of single lancets, one in each bay. The vaulting is straightforward quadripartite, with slender ribs. Aisles are low in relation to the main space and vaulted; they too are lit by lancets. The one main bay of the chancel is like those of the nave; beyond it is a compressed bay and the apse, with radiating vaulting, tall lancets at clerestory level, and semi-circular arcade opening into an ambulatory, which is lit by narrow lancets. There is no proper chancel screen, only a stone stump wall.

If that were all, St Michael's would merely be a superbly proportioned, essentially single-space church. What makes the church romantic are the subsidiary spaces, especially the south-eastern Lady Chapel. This is entered through a triple arch from the transept, the central arch wider than the others; it consists of one rectangular vaulted space with a tiny sanctuary behind, entered through another arch of beautifully slender form and with crowded, complicated vaulting. This is an exquisite space in itself, and the views into it from the main body of the church are enthralling, the Lady Chapel's delicate complexity contrasting with the clarity of the main space. Externally St Michael's masses impressively in a way more French than English, with varying rooflines, a complex eastern termination and a skyline with pairs of eastern turrets and a central fleche. The tall lancets in the transepts are more of northern English than French derivation. One feature detracts: the stump of the tower is tall enough to be prominent but, in its incomplete form, is terribly ungainly. St Michael's is the paradigm of Pearson's later churches (even to the unfinished steeple) against which other late churches can be assessed.

Norwood differs from Croydon mainly in its eastern termination – squared with two tiers of lancets in the northern monastic tradition – and it has a simpler Lady Chapel – a single apsed space, but still very effective in sideways glimpses. St Alban's, Birmingham, has an apse with ambulatory; the Lady Chapel is mainly a single-space vaulted chamber with a tripartite west end, integrated with the entrance to the ambulatory. The west front has a wheel window with a row of lancets above; the transept façades have tall groups of lancets. The tower was completed to a new design with a saddleback top instead of a spire by Frank Pearson long after his father's death.

70

70 PEARSON. *St Michael, Croydon*

Slightly earlier than these three great buildings is the small country church of Chute Forest in Wiltshire (1874–75). It is utterly simple – brick-faced within but given complexity and lengthwise scale by transverse arches in nave and chancel and an eastern trio of lancets. Almost no embellishment – all the effect is due to form and proportions.

In 1879 Pearson began one of his most interesting restorations, at Lastingham, a venerable church close to Appleton-le-Moors. The church has an early Norman vaulted crypt; the main body, Norman in origin, had long lost its original vault and been overlaid by restoration work in the early nineteenth century. Pearson constructed an intersecting groin vault without any ribs, starkly beautiful in its rough stone.

Between 1880 and 1885 five major churches were built or started – St Stephen's, Bournemouth (1881–98),[19] St Agnes', Sefton Park, Liverpool (1882–85), All Saints', Hove (1889–1901), Cullercoats, Northumberland (1882–84), and St Michael's, Headingley, Leeds (1883–84).

St Stephen's at Bournemouth is like Croydon in many ways but has individual features – notably a closing in of the width of the nave towards its eastern end (a spatial trick inspired no doubt by Canterbury choir, which Pearson did not try elsewhere). It also has double aisles giving a specially splendid variety of vistas, and its Lady Chapel is, unusually, on the northern side. The chancel is apsed, and there is an ambulatory. Here the steeple was built to the tower top, impressive enough, but Bournemouth is all the poorer for the absence of the intended spire soaring above the pines.

St Agnes' in Liverpool has a gallery above the aisles slightly reminiscent of Kilburn, but elaborated by traceried balustrades within the arches to the nave, giving the effect of a series of balconies. Apse and ambulatory are on the pattern of Croydon, and a Lady Chapel is in a similar position, entered through a trio of arches of which one is in fact the entrance to the ambulatory, as at Norwood. The chapel is a miniature vaulted space flanked by two bay arcades with their central piers beautifully slender, and ending in a short square-ended sanctuary. Each of the differing subdivisions of this small space is vaulted, so that the total effect – in enthralling contrast to the main space of the church – is of closely-spaced piers of varying girth and tight-compressed vaults of varying pitch – as marvellous a piece of miniature Gothic as Pearson or anybody attempted in the nineteenth century.

St Agnes' has the unusual feature of western transepts, similar in general form to the main transepts, and these help to give the exterior, in its deep red brick (the interior is of stone), special complexity in its massing, with characteristic angle turrets and central fleche making a more than usually varied skyline; the church was never intended to have a spire.

All Saints', Hove, is in its spatial form fundamentally different from the churches in the Croydon-Liverpool group. Externally it suffers, like Croydon, from having the all too prominent stump of an unfinished steeple, and the rest of the exterior does not make so immediately compelling a composition as Liverpool or Bournemouth.[20] Inside, there is one great space without any important subsidiary space. It is unusually wide – too wide for even Pearson to have attempted a vault, but the space is articulated by transverse arches at each bay. The subtlety of the internal effect is due not to any cross-vistas but to this articulation. The last bay of the nave is open to the transepts, and wider, but the two main bays of the chancel are narrower than those of the nave. The sanctuary is a shallow space, behind a final transverse arch of significantly less width than the others, with a trio of tall two-light Geometrical windows over an elaborate reredos. The spatial drama is tremendous; looking east the space is first drawn out, then telescoped, and the climax is very definite.

Cullercoats looks like a great model on its seashore site, the apse and the flanking spired tower soaring above the low sandy cliff. It is a straightforward design – lofty vaulted nave with low aisles, chancel of the same height, no significant subsidiary spaces or cross-vistas, internally all in smooth uniform ashlar such as Pearson almost invariably used (except in his brick-faced churches) during his later years.

St Michael's, Headingley, is a suburban church not quite so grand as Hove, Liverpool or Bournemouth but achieving moderate splendour with, obviously, a smaller budget than any of those three. Headingley is not vaulted, but articulation is obtained by transverse arches across the main space, as at Hove, and also across the aisles[21] (following the medieval precedent probably familiar to Pearson at Hartlepool, County Durham). The east end is northern-monastic, with two tiers of lancets, and there is an elaborate and delicate iron chancel screen imparting more intricacy. There are transepts, and a Lady Chapel opening characteristically off the south transept. The spatial effect – from the south aisle into the higher transept and then into the Lady Chapel – is splendidly Pearsonic. Headingley is lucky to have its spire, slender and commanding, and there is another fine Pearson spire a few miles away at St Margaret's, Horsforth (1877–83), a church which is not otherwise among Pearson's best.

71

71 PEARSON. *All Saints, Hove*

In 1885–87 Pearson designed a small village church at Thurstaston in the Wirral, Cheshire. It is not especially notable outside except for the fairly modest central spire, but it has a superb interior, achieving grandeur on a small scale. The aisleless nave has three vaulted bays with shafts beginning from corbels at string-course level (a hark-back to Dalton Holme and Scorborough). There is a vaulted space under the central tower, mostly hidden from the nave by the western tower arch, across which is an openwork stone screen. Similarly the high chancel vault is not fully revealed until one is under the crossing. There is thus an upward unfolding of space as one proceeds east.[22] Something of the intensity of Pearson's mid-career village churches seems to be recaptured here, although the forms are largely those of his mature phase.

In the late 1880s Pearson undertook four important restorations. At the abbey church of Shrewsbury he added a square-ended vaulted choir (1886–87) to the surviving Norman nave. At Hythe in Kent he added vaulting which had long been lost to the magnificent thirteenth-century chancel (1886–87).[23] In Bristol he restored the superb Lord Mayor's Chapel, originally a small monastic church which had been heavily overlaid by picturesque accretions. Pearson removed these and restored the building to what he thought was its pristine beauty. He renewed or restored the nave windows to a simple triple-lancet design for which there was sufficient authentic evidence, and replaced a lost transept, recreating a rich thirteenth-century arch of which some remains had survived (1887–90).[24] At St Margaret's, Westminster, in 1889, he added the fine tripartite porch across the west front.

72 PEARSON. *Truro Cathedral*

St Hilda's, Darlington (1887–88), Pearson's only church in his native county, is a simple, cheap church of brick which has something of the nobility of his larger churches – tall clerestory lancets emphasizing the height of the main space, low aisles, and an asymmetrical Lady Chapel (north) introducing spatial complexity. Another simple late church was St Bartholomew's at Nottingham (1895–1902), now demolished, showing what an impressive effect could be achieved with simple means through good proportions. The tall severe lancets of the clerestory and, especially, the west wall set the scale for the whole building. One of Pearson's last sizable churches was St John's, Friern Barnet, London (1889–1902 and later), which has the same basic form as Croydon and its related churches – tall nave, low aisles, apsidal sanctuary with ambulatory, side Lady Chapel, unfinished steeple – but strangely lacks inspiration; the spark in him was then dim. Like St Bartholomew's, Nottingham, and other churches, the church was not finished until after Pearson's death.

72   Space does not permit more than a mention of Pearson's extensive work on cathedrals. Truro was his largest work, though not his greatest. It was designed in 1880 but finished under his son long after his death in 1910. In its outline it has more than a suggestion of Durham, but its architecture is Gothic and unmistakably North British-French, with more of the emphasis on French than usual in his later works. He did substantial and usually conservative work at Lincoln,[25] Norwich,[26] Rochester,[27] Chichester[28] and the choir of Bristol.[29] At Westminster Abbey, he took over from Scott as architect to the fabric, and completed the restoration of the north transept – the elaborate portal is Scott's, the rest Pearson's (apart from what

73 PEARSON. *Design for proposed central spire to Peterborough Cathedral*
74 PEARSON. *Drawing for restoration of Westminster Hall*

remains of the medieval original).[30] Pearson's ideas on restoration are well illustrated by the story of his work at Peterborough. He was first called in to advise on the central tower in 1883; it was in such a tottering condition that it had to be entirely rebuilt. Pearson recommended that the two Norman crossing arches (north and south) be rebuilt in replica, but that the east and west arches, which had been altered in the fourteenth century, be recreated in Norman form so as to restore the crossing to its original purity. He would then have recreated the vanished Norman lantern storey (demolished in the fourteenth century but of which enough fragments survived, re-used in the existing fabric, to convince Pearson of its appearance), and placed above it a replica of the existing fourteenth-century tower, crowned by a beautiful spire of his own creation. After much controversy the tower and crossing were rebuilt under Pearson's direction exactly as they had been before, without the spire which would have been one of his most memorable monuments.[31] The controversy over the west front, on which Pearson reported in 1895, reveals the depth of feelings on the whole subject of restoration at the time when the ideas of William Morris had fully taken root.[32] The west front was in a terrible condition, leaning outwards in places. Pearson advocated demolition of much of the upper structure, including the gables, the stones being numbered and re-used in the same places wherever possible, defective ones being replaced by new ones which would deliberately not be made to look anything other than new. The great arches, distorted through unequal stresses, would have been partly reconstructed on similar principles, so as to regain their proper shape. The Morrisites, led by the SPAB and the Society of Antiquaries, with the public support of W. R. Lethaby, Detmar Blow, Philip Webb, T. J. Micklethwaite, E. S. Prior, Halsey Ricardo, Mervyn Macartney. T. Morley Horder, Henry Wilson, Ernest Newton, E. Guy Dawber, C. R. Ashbee and J. J. Stevenson,[33] advocated preservation of the weathered façade with all the irregularities and distortions occasioned through time, using hidden structural means such as pouring cement or other binding material in the gaps behind the leaning front to secure it for ever in its existing position. Pearson, supported publicly by Butterfield, Blomfield and Waterhouse (very much the 'old guard'), had his way in the end. There had earlier been controversy over Pearson's restoration of Westminster Hall, from 1883 onwards.[34] This followed the demolition of Sir John Soane's Law Courts of the 1820s which had abutted on to the west side of the Hall and which had become redundant with the completion of G. E. Street's new Law Courts in the Strand in 1882. The demolition revealed the medieval west wall of the Hall, with stonework from the time of William II (1097–99) and from the great reconstruction under

73

Henry Yevele (1394–1402).[35] The Norman stonework would have quickly deteriorated if it had been exposed to the weather, and substantial restoration, and part renewal, of Yevele's massive buttresses were seen to be imperative. Pearson was called in to prepare a scheme for the new treatment of the west side of the Hall. He found that there had, in the Middle Ages, been structural work between Yevele's buttresses and abutting on to the Norman wall; traces of foundations and marks on the stonework and buttresses indicated the general outline of this work, but gave hardly any clue as to its detailed form. Pearson prepared a scheme for a two-storey range between the buttresses following the evident medieval outline, with a cloister on the lower storey and small rooms above. Inevitably this was largely conjecture but Pearson claimed, in effect, that it was as authentic as his knowledge of medieval architecture, and his scrupulous desire for historical correctness, could lead him to make. This gave rise to furious controversy about the propriety of such a 'restoration', but it was difficult for the opponents of the scheme to offer any constructive suggestions for alternative treatment. Several of the leading architects of the day[36] spoke publicly for Pearson, whose final scheme was carried out; the low two-storeyed structures between the restored buttresses on the façade of Westminster Hall as seen from St Margaret Street are Pearson's. So is the wing projecting westwards from the north end of Westminster Hall towards St Margaret Street, also on part of the site of Soane's demolished Law Courts. Its dimensions are those of a vanished medieval building whose foundations were discovered but, again, its design is based simply on conjecture as to what the medieval building looked like.

Pearson restored the north (entrance) façade of Westminster Hall to accord with Barry's adjoining buildings. Here his work was never completed, since he intended to add one further storey to the two towers which flank the north façade but which now end below the rooflines. The upper storeys were to have pinnacled parapets and thrusting corner turrets with long spirelets, rather like some of the medieval towers of the Bristol region.[37] These additions to the skyline would probably have accorded well with Barry's and Pugin's architecture and given Westminster Hall slightly greater prominence, in relation to their buildings, than it has today. Like the spire of Peterborough Cathedral and those intended for numerous Pearson parish churches they are among the might-have-beens of architecture whose absence one regrets. Even so, no post-medieval architect, other than Barry and Pugin, contributed to the collective architectural effect of the heart of Westminster more than Pearson, with the restoration of the north transept and other parts of the Abbey, the west porch of St Margaret's and the substantial renewal, externally, of the west and north sides of Westminster Hall.

Pearson died, fully active and creative, in 1897, leaving his son to finish off great and small works, including Truro Cathedral. It is a matter of opinion whether he was a greater Gothic architect than Street or Butterfield, or even Bodley, but in one respect – the creation of superb Gothic spaces – he was unsurpassed. His works are not generally interesting for their detailing (apart from a few in what might be called the 'Appleton phase' of his career, overlapping, as it happens, with his short married life); in his best later churches the structural details were simple but refined – not interesting in themselves but as parts of the whole. With a few exceptions his designs for altars, reredoses, organ cases and stalls were curiously uninspired. The textural and colour effects of materials did not seem to have interested him (except, again, in his 'Appleton phase'), but he was obviously a perfectionist in respect of the quality of stonework – smooth, carefully laid and jointed, and uniform in colour and texture. He nearly always produced a similarly uniform colour and textural pattern in brickwork whether the bricks were smoothly finished or rough.

He had no evident self-conscious feeling for local character; his buildings are inspired by medieval models, but not necessarily those of the region in which they are set: he placed hard Midland churches in picturesque Surrey, a very French church on the Yorkshire moors, a cathedral in Cornwall which owes nothing to the distinctive far western traditions. Vaulting was his great speciality; he taught himself at Stow how to vault a space without visually obtrusive buttressing, and followed that example in so many other places. His vaults are always aesthetically perfect, usually straightforwardly simple in their outward form (however painstakingly devised in their inner constructional details), except where they are related to complicated spaces, such as apses, ambulatories, or those deliciously complicated Lady Chapels like those at Croydon and Liverpool which, in themselves and in relation to the greater spaces with which they are interconnected, are among the masterpieces of miniature Gothic creation. In restoration work Pearson was exceedingly conscientious; in his *Builder* obituary it is stated that his intention was

as a rule, to confine himself to removing decayed material and replacing it with new; isolated stones were removed one by one; disintegrated masses were taken down and replaced stone for stone; mouldings and ornaments were copied from the old ones, unless there was nothing left to copy . . . when the designs were frankly new, with the same mixture and in the same style as the old, but such as no one, certainly no architect, could mistake for the old ones themselves.

In other words his aim was the recreation of an old building to its perfection, using old materials where possible, but, failing that, using new ones which were obviously so, and not hesitating to recreate original features which had been lost, correctly if the evidence was there, using his imagination scrupulously if it was not. That did not happen to be the attitude towards restoration of the Arts and Crafts architects at the time of Pearson's death, but objectivity gained through passage of time leads one to suggest that Pearson's theory of restoration was just as tenable as that of the early followers of William Morris.

This chapter includes only the barest biographical details of Pearson's life. That is wholly appropriate – Pearson as a man, if not a creator of architecture, was self-effacing. He was pleasant and likable to friend and acquaintance, seldom if ever effusive or provocative in his manner. He shunned publicity, tried to avoid controversy (although this raged around his restoration work towards the end of his life), and expressed himself wholly through his works. He must have been a convinced Christian, but he is not known to have favoured any particular form of Christianity other than the normal 'middle-of-the-road' Anglicanism of the Anglican Church in its heyday – and for this he provided splendidly. His son carried on his practice after his death, perhaps rather disappointingly, but inspiration must have been passed on to his pupil W. D. Caroë, an architect of uneven achievement who, at his best, could achieve internal effects worthy of Pearson.

V

George Frederick Bodley
climax of the Gothic Revival

DAVID VEREY

If it be true that the Tractarian Movement and the Gothic Revival went hand in hand, then Sir Ninian Comper when describing the hierarchy is right in saying, 'After Pugin and Butterfield comes George Frederick Bodley'.[1]

Like many another High Churchman, Sir Gilbert Scott, however, desired to tread the *via media*[2] and it was to Scott that Bodley was first sent as a pupil. Scott's brother had married Bodley's sister. The Bodleys' father was a doctor who was practising in Hull when George Frederick was born there on 14 March 1827. He claimed descent from the founder of the Bodleian Library at Oxford, and the right to use his coat of arms, and finally achieved Harley Street status. Meanwhile during the son's youth the family had moved to Brighton, and Bodley has described how he came to take up architecture.

Just previously I had been reading H. M. Bloxham's 'Principles of Gothic Architecture elucidated by question and answer', 1829, and had become bitten with a curiosity about the history and the art. My father arranged at my wish that I should be with Gilbert Scott, and in 1845 I went and lived with Mr and Mrs Scott in Avenue Road, Regent's Park. I had not drawn at all before. The only sketch I remember making was one of the sea at Brighton when the moon made a broad path of light that led to mystery and darkness. I remember showing it to Scott, who said it was not architecture – which it certainly was not.[3]

Bodley served a five-year apprenticeship, and afterwards declared it had been a dreary time, anyway to begin with. He subsequently reacted against Scott's brand of Gothic. The publication of *The Seven Lamps of Architecture* by Ruskin in 1849, followed by *The Stones of Venice* in 1851–53, must have been crucial. Until the end of his life he was permeated by Ruskinism. He would mutter to himself, 'I wonder what Ruskin would make of that,' as he designed, and his two published papers maintain the principles of *The Seven Lamps*. Another influence, because they had much opportunity to discuss their theories together, was that of George Edmund Street. They (and William White) were in Scott's office at the same time, and shared the same religious views. Their early works reflect their mutual influence, though they diverged afterwards. Eastlake thought that generally ecclesiastical architecture was scarcely affected by the new doctrines of taste, and that Ruskin's first influence was on secular architecture; however, he went on to say that 'a certain number of younger men, including Street, Woodyer, White and Bodley showed an early inclination to strike out in a new line for themselves'.[4] Street, who was three years older, set up on his own in 1849, and got Bodley to help him when he was hard pressed. He went on a tour in France in 1850, followed by one in Italy in 1853, which resulted in the publication two years later of *Brick and Marble Architecture of North Italy*, an important book in connection with Bodley's early work. Bodley was also a friend of Butterfield, for whom he had an unqualified admiration.

One of Bodley's first clients appears to have been the Rev. Thomas Keble, brother of the more famous John, and equally Tractarian. He was Vicar of Bisley in Gloucestershire, and had several lesser parishes in his care, one of which was Bussage, where J. P. Harrison had built a church in 1846, paid for largely by a group

84

76 BODLEY. *St Augustine, Pendlebury. Nave looking east*

of Oxford undergraduates. To this church in 1854 Bodley added a south aisle, and afterwards declared, 'What works I carried out for some time I could trace to this added aisle at Bussage'. Bodley's buttresses have gables with bosky corbels; the arches of his arcade die into their responds, and have hood-mould stops of carved leaves between which are lifelike lilies in high relief. The breakaway from Scott has hardly begun but the influence of Ruskin is there. Bodley's design for Long Grove Church in Herefordshire was completed by March, 1854. A charming little church

85

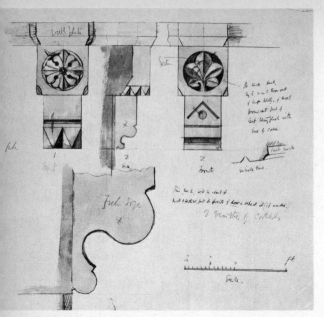

77, 78   *Details from St John the Baptist, France Lynch. Left: drawings for corbels by Bodley. Right: sculpture designed by Bodley and executed by Thomas Earp*

and not at all dull, it nevertheless pales before France Lynch, which is a masterpiece. By July 1854, Bodley, who still lived in Brighton, and was now aged twenty-seven, had written the specification for a brand new church for Tom Keble to be built at France Lynch. It was consecrated in September 1857, and had cost £2,738. It is perhaps worth while to note Bodley's method of procedure. Apart from the original set of drawings which were sent with the specification, Bodley drew out

77   quarter-size details which were folded up and posted in the form of a letter. Bodley was to become notorious for his unbusiness-like ways, and it was said that he would make drawings on his cheque-book. When he first started business he worked without assistance, practically without an office, and later when he lived with his mother in Harley Street his brother William, a priest, took his affairs in hand, and would make out his accounts for him. This did not, however, prevent him from paying attention to every detail of design. On 21 March 1857 he wrote to Keble,

Will you be so good as to tell Gregory that the plaster for the walls is to have a sandy surface, or as he calls it a 'grit on the face', not one, however, of too great roughness. The plaster for walls should be a shade darker than the stone colour – one does not want an exact match. The stucco for roofs I should like coloured a warm buff colour, darker than the walls. With regard to the glazing I have had an estimate made by a man in town (N. W. Lavers) for filling all the nave and one chancel window, with quarry glass of a very pleasing though simple kind.[5]

78   Thomas Earp was employed to do all the ornamental carving *in situ*. The chancel shows that from the very beginning Bodley raised his sanctuary on many steps, and the effect of elevation given to the altar here with six steps is remarkable. The marble inlay of the sanctuary and reredos, and the use of lapis lazuli and malachite in the low choir-screen and pulpit, is very sensitively done, and would have been approved by Ruskin. The high and sparsely placed two- and three-light windows give the nave a special character. At the west end there is a pair of two-light windows set wide apart, with French Gothic tracery; but afterwards, in this

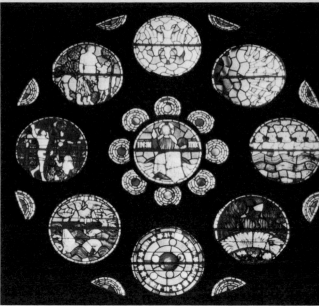

79   BODLEY. *St Michael and All Angels, Brighton (the large addition by Burges is on the left)*
80   PHILIP WEBB. *West window of Bodley's All Saints, Selsley*

early period, he always put a single rose window in this position. Externally the sloping site and Bodley's gift for massing result in a beautiful church, 'young man's church' though it may be. From the £102 10s which he was paid for all his work he generously deducted £16 towards the cost of the reredos. Bodley at this time also designed the school at Bisley for Keble, and a school in Cheltenham, now part of St Paul's College; both show a close study of Butterfield's secular work.[6] Bodley's first big job was St Michael and All Angels, Brighton. The *Ecclesiologist* approved of him from the beginning, and as early as 1855 had said of France Lynch, 'The whole design shows great merit, and we hope to see many future works from the same hand'. Of St Michael's they said in 1859 that 'they had to notice a remarkably good design, obtained by scale and constructional colour with simplicity of detail'. St Michael's is perhaps closer to Street than to Butterfield; but in this period some of Bodley's proportions, and detailing such as his roofs and his magnificent tiled pavements are distinctly Butterfieldian. In later years Bodley, was to refer to St Michael's as a 'boyish effort, even antagonistic'. Bodley's church is now only the south aisle of the existing church which was greatly enlarged by   79 Burges, and the original nave has consequently lost its north arcade. It is built of brick with stone dressings. There are no mouldings to the arches of the arcade, which have black brick edges to the stone voussoirs and spring from rather dumpy cylindrical columns with carved stiff-leaf capitals similar to those at France Lynch. The windows have plate tracery, and the west end resembles the exactly contemporary church Bodley built at Selsley in Gloucestershire, both designed in 1858, and both built 1861–62.

It is possible, but unlikely, that Bodley's impressive saddleback tower at Selsley was inspired by Sir Samuel Marling's wish to have a church based on that of his namesake in the Tyrol. In 1859 Bodley designed the tough plain saddleback tower he added to Christchurch, Pendlebury, and after making a Streetian broach spire design in 1861 for Scarborough, he altered it to a saddleback. He reversed the process at Haywards Heath; here it was an intended saddleback which was discarded in favour of a pyramid roof.   87

81   BODLEY. *St John, Tue Brook, Liverpool. Interior looking east*

Bodley had made friends with the Pre-Raphaelite Brotherhood in 1858 and
gave William Morris his first chance of making ecclesiastical stained glass[7] at
Brighton, Selsley and Scarborough. At Brighton the roundels of the rose window
have angels by Burne-Jones; the similar window at Selsley has the story of the
80   Creation designed by Philip Webb. Other windows at Brighton have Morris glass
too; particularly charming is the small Baptism window by Madox Brown in the
west of the south aisle, given by Bodley in memory of his father. The chancel roof
was painted by Morris, Webb and Faulkner with their own hands.

At St Martin-on-the-Hill at Scarborough, besides finding employment for the
Pre-Raphaelite glass-painters, Bodley also decorated the walls and ceilings. Any
flat surface could be painted, and with his impeccable sense of colour and immense
talent for decorative design Bodley's achievement in this field must be pre-eminent
above all other architects. It is not surprising therefore that he was the first architect
to employ William Morris, perhaps the greatest of all pattern-makers. At
Scarborough Morris and Webb painted the chancel roof, and Bodley painted
above the chancel arch. The tempera colours used have not lasted at all well, and so
it is impossible for this generation to see a Bodley church as it was unless it has been
restored. The pulpit is typical of several of this period, and depends entirely on the
painted scenes in the panels like most Pre-Raphaelite furniture; in this case there is
an Annunciation by Rossetti with other figures by Morris and Campfield.

The arcades at Scarborough have alternating octagonal and cylindrical piers
with pointed arches. Bodley no longer uses carved capitals – they have given way
to simple mouldings, and the arches are chamfered. This was repeated in his next
church, St Wilfrid's at Haywards Heath (1863–65). Here is the beginning of a
88   return to a style with more English antecedents. The glass is still by William

Morris, who himself appears as St Peter in the west window of the baptistery.

Two designs for All Saints, Jesus Lane, Cambridge, were published in the *Ecclesiologist* in 1861 and 1863. The second was chosen and part of the church was built in conformity to it; but the general form was modified when it was completed in 1870. Bodley justified his design by its function; he planned a spacious nave and narrow aisle because 'the area of the nave is more valuable than that of the aisles'. Architecturally it is a turning point in so far as his first plans showed much of the French Gothic detail he had used before, including a rose window in the west wall, and a saddleback tower. However it is said that the powerful Dr Whewell suggested changes which overwhelmed Bodley, normally antagonistic to outside interference. His second design is remarkable for its reversion to English, early-Decorated forms preferred by Pugin, and some so 'late' as to suggest the still forbidden Perpendicular. The *Ecclesiologist* noted 'with some satisfaction that Mr Bodley has restricted himself to pure English forms', and it observed that 'the time for a reaction from exclusively French or Italian types has at length arrived'. It is a building both simple and direct, yet showing great subtlety of mass and materials, built of handmade brick and faced in ashlar of Northamptonshire oolite, with a lofty nave and steeply pitched roofs to both nave and aisle. The most beautiful feature is the tower of three stages with a tall spire, having bell-openings with pointed gables, and even ogee arches with which we shall become very familiar later on. The tower is supported upon two acutely pointed arches over the chancel. It is one of the major buildings of the Gothic revival, with an east window by Morris, and painted surfaces by Kempe, Hughes and Bodley himself. Butterfield said it was one of the few churches in which he could worship.

Almost every inch of its internal surface glows with stencilled patterns; the lower panels with dark yellow and damask green canopies and crowns, the upper with pink and blue *planta genista* pods and flowers, and above is the free sweep of the ceiling designs.[8]

Although this is an up-to-date description, to other eyes this church appears sombre.[9] The reason is simply that Bodley's wall-paintings have not lasted well. The effect of restoration by Stephen Dykes Bower can be seen in Queens' College Hall, which was decorated by Morris & Co. for Bodley in 1875.

Bodley's influence on Morris at this time can hardly be over-emphasized, though Morris later developed a far greater freedom of design in his secular wall-papers and textiles. Edward Warren, Bodley's pupil, says that Bodley himself actually designed one or two of Morris's early wallpapers.[10] Bodley's great strength as a church-decorator was that he saw an interior as a whole and kept a tight control on everything between floor and ceiling, including, preferably, even the altar vessels and vestments. Tiled floors were suited to bold patterns; a fine example at Cambridge is the floor of the crossing in Jesus College Chapel. Almost without exception his later chancels had patterned black and white marble floors. He much preferred to board in his roofs so that there would be a flat or tunnelled ceiling to paint on; this became so important that chancel arches causing a division between nave and chancel were soon to be omitted altogether. In many cases Bodley continued to supply furnishings long after the fabric had been completed and the church opened for services.

St Salvator's, Dundee, was begun in 1865. Bodley's splendid interior comprises a gilded wrought-iron screen, dark woodwork, much-diapered walls, and a magnificent carved wooden reredos, painted and gilded. This was followed by St John the Baptist's, Tue Brook, Liverpool (1868–70), the last complete church

82   BODLEY. *Vicarage of St Martin, Scarborough*

designed before his partnership with Garner, which began in 1869, and showing
his total acceptance of English precedent. Like All Saints it has a tall spire and the
window tracery is Geometrical Decorated. There is a chancel arch, and the arcades
have octagonal columns and moulded capitals supporting pointed arches. The
roofs have open wooden trusses painted with sacred monograms and roses, in fact
everything is painted from the marvellous diapered walls to the pulpit, screen and
reredos. The painting was the first of many commissions given to C. E. Kempe,
who had been trained by Clayton and Bell. It has recently been restored to all its
glory by Campbell, Smith & Co. under the direction of Stephen Dykes Bower,
Bodley's principal – indeed only – successor at the present time ; in its restored form
the interior is in the most breathtaking contrast to this rather poor part of
Liverpool. No longer can it be described as looking like a 'much worn Persian
carpet'.[11] Most of the windows have clear glass diamond panes, with splendid
ferramenta ; but there are some by the Pre-Raphaelite Brotherhood and in the
Lady Chapel one perhaps by Burlison and Grylls, a firm which Bodley and Garner
(together with G. G. Scott Jr) helped to found in about 1870, and which they were
to design for, and employ in a lot of their later work. A most memorable example
is the great rose window in the south transept of Westminster Abbey.

The parsonages of the 1860s at Burrington and Valley End are quite
Butterfieldian. Bodley would never allow Gothic for domestic use. The Vicarage
at St Martin's, Scarborough, was built of brick with slightly projecting bays
having pairs of sash windows under brick pediments, with a steeper pediment over
the door. It looks as if it could have been done by Philip Webb, and it was to Webb
that Bodley turned for help when he was ill with blood-poisoning in 1869. The job
in hand was the finishing of the houses in Ranelagh Road, Malvern Link. They
could be called Queen Anne and are brick-built with sash windows and shutters,
and white-painted weather-boarding round the bay windows. Bodley writes

They have given leave for some papering in the largest house. What will be
best? The stone colour ground Trellis for saloon and staircase, the white fruit

81

82

83, 84   BODLEY. *St Augustine, Pendlebury and (left) watercolour showing the unexecuted tower*

pattern for the Indigo coloured wood in the little morning room . . . some bedrooms – the daisy pattern – dark and light, and the Venetian?[12]

These were all early Morris wallpapers. Five days later, on 29 August, he thanks Webb for visiting Malvern and asks him to draw out the plan for a proposed alteration. 'If you had left out the word "stupid" as applied to my clients I should have been glad, as I should have forwarded your note to them.' Bodley was always well known for his courtesy. If he found a letter difficult to reply to, he did not answer it. In a P.S. he says 'I will let you know about the Welsh house; there will be no hurry for that'. This must refer to Cefn Bryntalch, Llandyssil, near Welshpool, which he was building in 1869. In another letter he says, 'I am getting on a little, but am so lame I am fit for but little'. (The lameness was to plague him for the rest of his life.) 'You have not sent me your account.' Webb was never good at doing this. 'I cannot let you do work for me for nothing . . . I hope it may not be long before I can get to town. I am heartily sick of Brighton. I think I shall write to ask you if you could go to Manchester (Pendlebury) and to Welshpool for me bye and bye. I want to see if I can manage it myself.' This illness may have forced him to realize the need to take Garner into partnership. Webb's friendship ceased; on Bodley's death he wrote: 'He was a man of some taste and discrimination and for a while I had pleasure in his company. It died away under the "Restoration", his respectability increasing, and mine going.'

Bodley's reputation, at the time of the formation of his partnership with Thomas Garner, was already secure. All Bodley could remember was that the 'Parsonage house at Pendlebury came before Garner'.

It was begun in 1869, and has now been demolished. St Augustine's Church, Pendlebury, remains, surely Bodley's greatest achievement and, as Pevsner says, 'one of the English churches of all time. Its sheer brick exterior and the majestic *sursum* of its interior have never been surpassed in Victorian church building'. It was designed before Garner's influence became very apparent, so great is the difference between Pendlebury and Hoar Cross, which was begun in 1872. The   91 building of Pendlebury begun in 1870, or after, went on till 1874, and was financed by E. S. Heywood, who gave £50,000; but even so it was not finished, in so far as **83** the detached tower that Bodley designed for it was never built. Drawings by Bodley and Garner showing the tower were exhibited in the RA in 1875. It looks **84** nowadays from the outside like the hulk of an enormous ship washed up on a forlorn beach. According to the *Builder* (vol. XXXV, 1877, p. 639), the exterior was deliberately kept relatively austere because of the nearby mills. The slums by which it was later surrounded have been demolished. Bodley's two-storey vestry – he often hitherto seems to have insisted on two storeys in his vestries – is quite dwarfed by the enormous height of the nave roof. Edward Warren's description cannot be bettered.[13]

Its walls are of brick, and stone is used for the dressed work of doors and windows, for columns, arches, and the decorative bands that add to the distinctive character of the exterior. The plan is a long parallelogram, embracing nave and chancel, without any structural division between them. The aisles are mere passages pierced through the deep internal buttresses that resist the thrust of the waggon-vaulted **76** timber roof. The church is long and spacious and lofty. The succession of tall piers with their slender engaged shafts, bearing softly moulded and finely proportioned arches, is most effective in the rhythmic sense of vertical emphasis which it gives. The noble sweep of the high roof, with its repeated interspacings of light ribs, the perfect proportions and skilful placing of the great eastern window, the refined dexterity of the furnishing – screen, font, pulpit, and stalls – complete the intense impressiveness of an interior splendid in simplicity and inspiring in the stately lift of its noble lines. And if the form is fine, so is the ordered scheme of colouring, both constructive and applied; which is essentially characteristic of its authorship. The gently contrasted browns, greys, and creamy whites of the piers and arches, the soft rich tones of blue, green, and gold of the panelled wainscot of the aisles, the diapered painting of the chancel walls, and the arched roof, the deep browns of the oakwork, and the mellow translucency of the stained glass (Burlison & Grylls), all contribute to a sum-total of decorative harmony which is as impressive as it is impossible of description . . . . A striking feature of the chancel is the convergence inwards of the north and south walls, which accounts for the termination of the passage aisles. This was, I believe, the first modern instance in England of the use of the pierced internal buttress.

We must now have a look at Thomas Garner. He was born in 1839, the son of a Warwickshire farmer who brought him up to country pursuits including riding. He entered Scott's office in 1856, which of course was several years after Bodley had left it. Garner afterwards worked in Warwickshire on his own account or as assistant to Scott, who designed Walton Hall (1856–62), only a few miles from Garner's home at Wasperton, and All Saints, Sherbourne (1862–64), where possibly Garner may have had dealings with Farmer and Brindley, the stone carvers. Garner became Bodley's partner at the end of 1869, but there was never any legal deed of partnership, and it was their practice to give separate attention to separate works. Garner was a happily married man; Bodley followed his example, though not so happily, and in 1872 married Minna Reaveley of Kinnersley Castle, Herefordshire.

Unlike Bodley, who did not produce very brilliant finished drawings, Garner was an exceptionally good and rapid draughtsman. He worked at home amongst books of all kinds, and Mrs Garner – we are told by Comper – read to him while he drew. His results were much more attractive on paper than Bodley's, 'but we knew they would not materialize so well,' adds Comper. He goes on to say that 'when the partnership was finally severed it was Garner's work which most **92** betrayed it'. This took place in 1897, when Garner was received into the Roman

85, 86   BODLEY. *Holy Angels, Hoar Cross. Choir and exterior*

Catholic Church, and he thought, quite rightly, that his action would harm Bodley's practice. Comper tells us, however, that 'for a good many years before this they increasingly gave up the close collaboration of the earlier days,' in which he also insists Canon Frederick Sutton played an important part. Sutton was specially interested in organ cases and 'it was in them that his hand particularly appeared'. He designed the great organ case at St Augustine's, Pendlebury, and his experience was of extreme assistance to Bodley. It is probable that they first met in 1864 when Bodley designed a case for an extension to the organ in Jesus College Chapel, Cambridge, which had originally been built by the Canon's eldest brother, Sir John Sutton, a founder member of the Cambridge Camden Society. In 1872 Frederick Sutton published a book *Church Organs, their Position and Construction*. His designs are strongly influenced by Pugin who had been employed by the Sutton family at West Tofts, and designed the organ case there with medieval German examples in mind.

Bodley's close collaboration with Sutton, however, dates from the building of Holy Angels, Hoar Cross, where Sutton planned the organ and designed the painted case, a magnificent example of late Gothic work towering to the height of the vault on the north side of the choir, and an integral part of the faultless decoration of the church. Sutton became rector of Brant Broughton in 1873, where he found time to paint glass, and train the blacksmith in wrought-iron work and his butler in embroidery. Bodley and Garner rebuilt the chancel for him, and he painted the glass helped by Kempe. Bodley's meticulously designed reredos was carved by Rattee and Kett.

The Church of the Holy Angels at Hoar Cross, near Lichfield, was built at the expense of Mrs Meynell Ingram, a daughter of Lord Halifax, in memory of her husband who died in 1871. From that moment to the day of her death in 1904 it was the all-absorbing thought of her life, and to it she devoted her considerable wealth. Such a client – both extremely High Church, and very rich – presented Bodley and Garner with an almost limitless opportunity. It is said that she spent so much that she took pains to prevent anyone knowing how much, and destroyed the accounts. After the church had been built once it was decided that it was not large enough, and so the west end was taken down and rebuilt with an extra bay. Many years later Bodley visited the church and found it locked. This was by order

93

of the Bishop, who was endeavouring to reduce the High Church practices, in spite of attempts to hide them with such things as a dual-purpose confessional which could be made to look perfectly innocent when not in use. Bodley was so annoyed that he built on a narthex from which the public could gaze into the church from the west through a wrought-iron screen. In the narthex Bodley and Garner were later to be commemorated in a memorial tablet; other reminders are Bodley's portrait in a stained glass window in the sacristy, and Garner's head on a buttress of the south transept. The church is now looked after by the Community of the Glorious Ascension, and receives many visitors, some of whom no doubt would be amazed if they realized that the church is only a hundred years old, so perfectly medieval does it seem to be.

85, 86   It is built of a mellow sandstone and has a very strong looking rectangular tower at the crossing, with deep triple recessions on each face and vertical emphasis, a lofty chancel and less lofty nave. It is the ideal product of Bodley's mature fourteenth-century style; English architecture carried on, as it were, after the Black Death of 1349 to a perfection it never actually achieved in medieval times. All contemporaries agree that it is difficult to judge exactly what was Bodley's and what Garner's contribution, so close was their collaboration. Warren, however, has stated that the chancel, together with Mr Meynell Ingram's tomb, were chiefly Garner's work, and these are the parts which have been given the greatest elaboration of sculpture. The chancel walls are covered with images under nodding ogee canopies, or standing on concave moulded brackets between the windows, and in the central mullions of the windows which branch out into arches. The ogee arch is ever present, with ogee foils and rose-tipped cusps, trailing vines, leaves and flowers, but all disciplined and controlled. The window tracery is a mixture of flowing and Perpendicular lines; the windows pointed inside and square-headed outside. The reredos, with two rows of images, is raised on six steps. All the glass is by Burlison and Grylls, to Garner's designs; mostly single figures of saints rather than pictorial scenes. Both chancel and crossing are stone-vaulted, and the floor has elaborate black and white marble patterns and heraldry. The nave, lower and very dark, has one of Bodley's wooden tunnel roofs, and the windows have straight heads and Decorated tracery with ogee shapes; an atmosphere of religious twilight was deliberately created. The electric light fittings were designed by Bodley in 1897. The Lady Chapel was added in 1892, and All Souls Chapel in 1898. They show clearly how Bodley's later work tended to become more and more refined.

In 1886 Bodley told the students of the Royal Academy, in a paper entitled 'English Architecture in the Middle Ages', that the golden age in England was the fourteenth century.

Its style is especially an English style. It is not too much to say of it that, at its best, it is quite unsurpassed by any other Gothic work in the world. Tired of the geometry of the earlier manner, the architects of this time invented the grace of the ogee line in their traceries. It was, I make no doubt, the culminating point in the history of Gothic Art.

This shows how Bodley himself had progressed from plate tracery to the ogee line. He goes on to talk about stone.

In Gothic buildings you can suit your details with great freedom to the stone with which you have to build. In using a fine stone your mouldings may be, no doubt, very delicate. In using a rougher stone they should be broader and simpler, never, however, without refinement. For example, a large 'wave' mould as it is called is well fitted for a sandstone, but it is one of the most refined of mouldings, or may be so. Here then you have in Gothic a style in which you can deal with your building material with great freedom, making your detail to suit it. It may be a stone that soon turns grey, but it will show light and almost silvery in effect . . . it will as it were but re-echo the silvery gleam of the cold English sky hanging over the dark hill-side.

He then goes on to say that of course the inside of a building is more important than the outside, and discusses the use of colour.

For an interior there was no thought of any rude roughness of surface. [This was very necessary with so many ignorant scrapers in the profession.] It was either of smooth ashlar or of smooth plaster, and either case and in all ages such surfaces received colour . . . rich and magnificent diapers in the later fourteenth and fifteenth centuries. . . . An architect has perhaps the most interesting and delightful profession a man can have. In England he has the finest Gothic to study. It will be our own fault if we are not the best Gothic architects in the world.

Comper wrote:

The truest and best memory of Bodley is in those churches of his middle period, and in his less known writings which explain their principles. His lecture at the Royal Academy in 1885 is an epitome of all that is greatest in his art. Amongst principles he puts *Refinement* first. 'Nature, our great guide, never stops in her refinement. We cannot gauge the infinite delicacy of nature, nor her redundance of life and its variety. Now it is in refinement for architectural work, that this expression of life is chiefly shown. True refinement denotes restrained power.' Other principles listed are the *True Use of Detail*. 'It is a great error to suppose that by boldness of detail you make your building look large. The reverse is eminently the case.' *Contrast*. 'Breadth of surface contrasted with delicate detail.' *Avoidance of Extravagance of Manner*. Under *Symmetry* and *Suitability* are two remarks too characteristic of Bodley to be omitted. 'Symmetry of design denotes care and pains on the part of the designer. It is a courteous manner and has much to recommend it.' And, 'One sees examples of what we must call bad manners, when the surroundings have been ignored'. *Work founded on that of the Past*. 'The more extensive your acquaintance is with the works of those who have excelled, the more extensive will be your powers of invention; and what may appear still more like a paradox, the more original will be your conceptions . . . . It is thus Art hands on the tradition of Art, the spirit of which is immortal.[3]

Referring to the principle of Truth, Bodley admits he has little to add to what has already been said by Ruskin, nevertheless he elaborates the fallacy. 'What are many of our new street fronts but examples of most untruthful architecture. Iron columns and iron girders are concealed by stone columns and thin stone friezes and like deceptions.' Finally Bodley insists that architecture should be animated by religion, or civil dignity, domestic feeling, or honour to the departed. 'For art should be delighted in, not for itself alone, but as the expression, in a lasting way, that can perpetuate the feeling expressed.'

An earlier paper, read at the Church Congress in 1881, is more distinctly ecclesiological. Its salient point is 'that the highest Art has had its spring in Religion'. He produces a hopeful argument against the demolition of redundant City of London churches. 'In a more religious age these churches, if allowed to remain, may be turned to better use.' Pleading as usual for Gothic he says, 'When I enter St Paul's I feel how great is man, but when I enter Westminster Abbey I feel how small man is.' He then argues in favour of building bigger Gothic churches, and quotes Ruskin as saying we build like pigmies.

In former days in our land, and now in many places abroad, the churches were and are the very homes of the devout poor. What a change and repose for them after their cramped and squalid houses, and the noise and hardness of the day's work to find privacy and dignity in the great silent darkening church, and there pour out their hearts to God. Let us build and adorn our churches for God and His poor.

In Bodley's writings and work Comper thought there was a slight trace of preciousness, 'an affinity perhaps with Pater, or a more delicate expression of the aesthetic side of William Morris and the Pre-Raphaelites'. Garner on the other hand and G. G. Scott Jr were free from it. All three were neighbours in Church Row, Hampstead, and they influenced each other's work. They founded the firm called Watts & Co. (What's in a name?) in order to produce church furnishings to their own designs. Garner in his partnership with Bodley in the 1880s would seem to have had most to do with the domestic and therefore classical or Renaissance work, such as Hewell Grange and the St Paul's reredos, now destroyed. Hewell Grange, Worcestershire (1884–91), is built of sandstone with five shaped Flemish gables, and chimneys with concave-moulded sides and capitals, a huge porch with an oriel window above the arched *porte-cochère* and a central cupola. It is symmetrical, and is based on Elizabethan examples like Montacute. Inside all is Italian Renaissance in coloured marbles. Bodley's own excursions in a parallel field were more questionable. He had a predilection for transforming and decorating existing houses. This seems to have begun in 1877 when Mrs Meynell Ingram persuaded him to convert the Georgian library at Temple Newsam into a private chapel. Spirals of gold leaves were applied to the Corinthian columns, while the frieze was garnished with gilt stars and texts.[14] Wimborne St Giles is another example, though his displacement in the house of Adam's simpler work by greater elaboration has since been corrected. At the Fishmongers' Hall he scornfully swept away much of the fine redecorating done by Owen Jones thirty years before. In the great hall he suggested 'suitable inscriptions in gold letters'. Goodhart Rendel removed as much of Bodley's work as possible. Another house built chiefly by Garner (1876–79) is The River House, on the corner of Chelsea Embankment and Tite Street. This has Queen Anne brick curvilinear gables ending in pediments, with narrow sash windows with segmental pediments, stairs with twisted balusters and a central dome. There was also the head office of the London School Board on the Embankment near the Temple, inspired by the French Renaissance and afterwards enlarged by Robson. St Swithun's Buildings, Magdalen College, Oxford (1880–84), was another large project in which Garner played an important if not the major part. Bodley and Garner appear self-effacing in Oxford where they received a considerable number of commissions. Their work fits in so well, even when they built in famous much visited places such as Christ Church, that it is, in some instances, difficult to distinguish from the historical style they were matching. Most of the Oxford work was done during the period of the partnership, except that for the Cowley Fathers. This was later, by Bodley alone, and suffers less from historicism. Comper became a pupil in 1883, and among other buildings going on at this time were St Michael's, Folkestone (1873–83), and the beautiful St German's Church, Roath, Cardiff (1883–84).

St Michael's, Camden Town, just finished, was a great influence on Bodley's pupils. To Comper it was the revelation, he says, which turned him to architecture. A man's pupils are strictly those articled to him, but in a wider sense they may include his employees, like his assistant Walter Tapper, who probably brought to the office at 7 Gray's Inn Square what business qualities it possessed. If he dealt a little roughly with Bodley, he was so suave with neglected clients that he protected him from their wrath. In after years Tapper was President of the RIBA and was knighted, thereby outstripping Bodley who shared with him only the honour of

being appointed Associate of the Royal Academy, given Bodley in 1882. Bodley was not a member of the RIBA and the Gray's Inn pupils of that time never heard mention of it; but much later Bodley relented and accepted the gold medal. Other assistants were Vaughan, Bucknall, Cleverley, Eden and Hare, and his pupils included Edward Warren, Henry Skipworth, Frederick Simpson, C. R. Ashbee, F. Inigo Thomas, A. G. Humphry, Bernard-Smith, and some who never worked under him may be included, such as Giles Gilbert Scott, Bodley's godson. Bodley had the greatest courtesy in speech, and a slight stammer or hesitation only added to the impressiveness and charm of his manner. He was a great whist player, and took half-crowns from his pupils. An even greater fault in the eyes of most of them, however, was that he would turn up at noon on Saturdays with the silent appeal for someone to stay on with him. He did all his drawing at Gray's Inn, and Comper says he never saw him draw a moulding without the full sizes before him of Bowman's fourteenth-century examples. Pugin's *Examples and Specimens* he also had at hand, and one solitary sketch book of his own. 'From these, and not without them, he hammered out in the roughest pencil what we all knew would turn out so well in reality.'

The east window of St Michael's, Camden Town, is by Charles Eamer Kempe (1837–1907). Bodley's association with this great stained-glass artist was fruitful and many of his churches have Kempe glass. Kempe was an ardent Anglo-Catholic, and it is said he always conducted Compline himself in the chapel of his house in Sussex, even though there might be distinguished clergymen among his guests. He had a very bad stammer, and was a confirmed bachelor. To the end he made out the designs himself, but they became more mannered and the glass settled down to a greenish tinge all over. Like Bodley, Kempe was responsible for much wall and ceiling decoration; but for some reason or other their personal friendship became strained, ending for a time in complete estrangement.

The year 1886 brought Bodley another opportunity similar to that of Hoar Cross. This was Clumber Church for the Duke of Newcastle, externally rather plainer with less emphasis on the vertical line, but conveying an even greater sense of easy security and instinctive proportion. Bodley considered that Clumber and Eccleston were his best works. The former was built when the partnership had practically ceased, and the latter in 1899 well after Garner's departure.

The mansion at Clumber is now demolished, and so Bodley's chapel no longer fulfils its original function, and is preserved by the National Trust. The setting is

88, 89   BODLEY. *St Mary, Clumber Park. Exterior and nave looking east*

unforgettable, standing as it does on the edge of what was Sherwood Forest, with a great sward of grass to the south, cropped close by flocks of Canada geese from the
88   ornamental lake. It is built of a white stone, which, in Bodley's own words, 're-echoes the silvery gleam of the cold English sky', contrasting with the warm dark red Runcorn sandstone of tower and dressings. The central crossing divides a chancel and nave of equal lengths and almost equal heights, though the chancel is slightly the higher. The square, buttressed tower is surmounted by an octagon with crocketed pinnacles and flying buttresses, and above that a spire; a wonderfully subtle outline with nothing unnecessary. The window tracery is curvilinear Decorated, and only the transept window is Perpendicular over a very small main entrance, like the human figure, giving scale to the composition.

89   The interior of warm red Runcorn stone gives the impression of total harmony and perfect proportion. There are no windows at a low level. The narrow verticality of the nave and chancel is produced by bowtell mouldings from the floor to the springing of the stone vaulted roofs. The horizontal division is achieved by a narrow triforium passage with ogee-headed openings, really piercings in internal buttresses. The crossing has short transepts, and a rood screen separates the chancel which is elaborate with choir stalls and many images of saints and prophets carved in lime wood. On the south of the choir is a stone screen with curvilinear ogee quatrefoils and embattled cornice, refined delicacy contrasting with bolder mouldings, and iron-work grills with small patterns. The sanctuary is luxurious with 'Bodley' materials; lush stamped velvet dossal, ridel curtains, and sedilia, lit by clear glass windows either side, and a Kempe east window high above.

The quintessence of ecclesiastical perfection is so persuasive that most visitors think in some miraculous way they have stepped right back into the Middle Ages. It certainly looks more medieval than most medieval churches because it has suffered from no iconoclasts. The niches are filled with images, the windows have complete stories in stained glass, and there is rich colour and gilding on the bosses in the vaults, on the harps of the angels, and on the many monograms of the Sacred Name. *Dum festa colit anima suspiret ad perpetua.*

90   St Mary's, Eccleston, built for the Duke of Westminster, is most characteristic of his later manner. 'Less inspired and therefore less inspiring' than Pendlebury, Hoar
98   Cross or Clumber; 'stiffer and more formal of line, colder of aspect . . . . It still

shows, however, vigorous and proportionate planning, and the high perfection of skilful detail'.[15] All Bodley's characteristics have been brought to an almost mechanical perfection. It is so symmetrical, so effortless, so much the work of a master hand, one feels that when Bodley said it was a pity he had to go to sleep just when he was beginning to know something, he could have gone on designing churches like this for all eternity, provided of course there were enough dukes to pay for them.

Bodley's chief churches of his later period, in more or less chronological order, were: St Mary of Eton, at Hackney Wick (1880); St Saviour's, Roath (1887–88); Queens' College Chapel, Cambridge (1890–91); Holy Innocents, Norwood (1894–95); All Saints, Danehill (1892); Horbury Junction (1892–93); St Matthew's, Chapel Allerton (1897–98); St Edward's, Holbeck, Leeds (1903–04); St Aidan's, Bristol (1903–04); the Chapel for the Sisters of Charity, Knowle, Bristol (1900); Holy Trinity, Prince Consort Road, Kensington (1902–06); St Faith's, Brentford (1907); St Bride's, Kelvinside, Glasgow (1903–07); and All Souls, Leicester (1904–06).

The Church of St John the Evangelist, Cowley (1894–1902), however, stands alone in treatment and intention. It is a monastic church, and one that Bodley was well suited to design. The Cowley Fathers wanted a long chancel, screened from the relatively short nave. The austere dignity and ordered reticence of its high white interior give it a calm distinction of its own, though all the characteristics we have come to expect from Bodley are present—the beautiful mouldings of the arches, dying off into their responds or supported on exquisitely keeled and capped shafts, the continuous painted waggon roof with only an indication of a chancel arch and the elaborate wooden screen.

The tower at St Chad, Burton-on-Trent, is a masterpiece and on the way out of historicism. Designed in 1903, it was completed after Bodley's death by Cecil Hare in 1910. The reredos in the north chapel is as typical of Bodley as the tower, yet the grandeur of the tower and the busy-ness of the reredos do not easily make up into one personality. Hoar Cross, large, sensitively detailed, lavishly decorated, a *chef d'oeuvre*, a *tour de force*, as Sir Nikolaus Pevsner says, has nothing of the masculine, wholly architectural power of Bodley's only slightly earlier Pendlebury. This repeated dichotomy of character, which cannot be entirely due to Garner, makes Bodley all the more intriguing as an architect. St Chad's tower is a most brilliant invention, separated by a rib-vaulted corridor from the north aisle and thus standing tall and erect, almost on its own.

90　BODLEY. *St Mary, Eccleston*

Bodley was frequently called upon to design furnishings for existing churches, particularly screens, organ cases, and reredoses (probably carried out by Farmer and Brindley). The firm's plate was mainly designed by Bodley: its execution was for two decades entrusted to Barkentin and Krall. The standard Bodley design for a chalice is based on late fifteenth- and early sixteenth-century prototypes from the Low Countries and Germany with its compressed knot and prominent bosses.[16] Micklethwaite said of him, 'Bodley is the only man I know who can and does make a silk purse out of a sow's ear'. To take only examples in London: he designed the screen, pulpit, sounding board, organ grille, lectern and stalls at St Paul's, Knightsbridge, besides plate, vestments and several altar frontals. He designed the screen and floor at St Matthew's, Westminster, and the reredos, ceiling and ironworks at St Barnabas, Pimlico, the most fashionable Anglo-Catholic church in the nineteenth century.

He wielded greater influence on church architecture after the death of Street than any other architect during the last years of the nineteenth and beginning of the twentieth centuries. Architects not directly associated with him reflected his influence – R. J. Johnson of Newcastle, for example, also captured his refinement of detail and texture but lacked his powerful constructional ability and the subtlety with which he integrated his masses. Bodley's name has been given to the Buildings he designed for King's College, Cambridge, towards the end of his life. They are built of buff-coloured Ketton stone, with an open quadrangle facing the Backs. The style is well-mannered Tudor with the slightest hint of classicism on the corner nearest to the Gibbs Building.

The final episode of all is strange. He had been very disappointed at his failure in the Truro Cathedral competition in 1878, although he and Garner were successful at Hobart Cathedral, Tasmania (1868–94), and he had been consulting architect to the Dean and Chapter of York since 1882.[17] In 1906, however, he was not only commissioned to design the cathedral for Washington in conjunction with his former assistant, Henry Vaughan of Boston, but also one at San Francisco. Bodley and Vaughan were commissioned together for Washington, the Bishop having been told that Bodley was the foremost Gothic architect, and the Chapter feeling strongly that an American architect must be used. In the autumn of that year Bodley travelled to America with Cecil Hare, described in his will as his secretary. On his return, and while employed upon yet another remote cathedral in India, he began the designs for the American cathedrals, particularly for the National Cathedral in Washington. He found himself in exactly the same mind as Henry Vaughan (1845–1917) who was in his office from about 1867 to 1881, when, having risen to be head draughtsman, he went to America to do a convent chapel. He stayed, as Bodley had urged him to 'spread the English Gothic message', and designed some important buildings which were instrumental in initiating the last phase of the Gothic Revival in America.[18] At Washington Cathedral they are not given due credit. Vaughan is responsible for the Bethlehem Chapel underneath the sanctuary and the east end above it, and perhaps part of the choir. The rest of the cathedral was changed over the years by P. H. Frohman, so that the best parts of Vaughan and Bodley were homogenized, and the whole thing now looks like white confectioner's sugar.

Bodley lived at Bridgefoot House, Iver, from c. 1895–1905, and then at the Manor House, Water Eaton, Oxfordshire. The east window of the chapel adjacent to the house has glass in Bodley's memory and shows him kneeling at the bottom. He died aged eighty on 21 October 1907, and was buried in the churchyard at Kinnersley, his wife's old home in Herefordshire, and near the church, the nave and chancel of which he himself had decorated with a rich diaper of colour many years before. His grave is such as he, the designer of the memorial ledger stone to G. E. Street in Westminster Abbey, would have approved. The arms of Bodley impaling Reaveley lean against a low tomb-chest upon which is carved a floreated cross in high relief enriched with lilies.

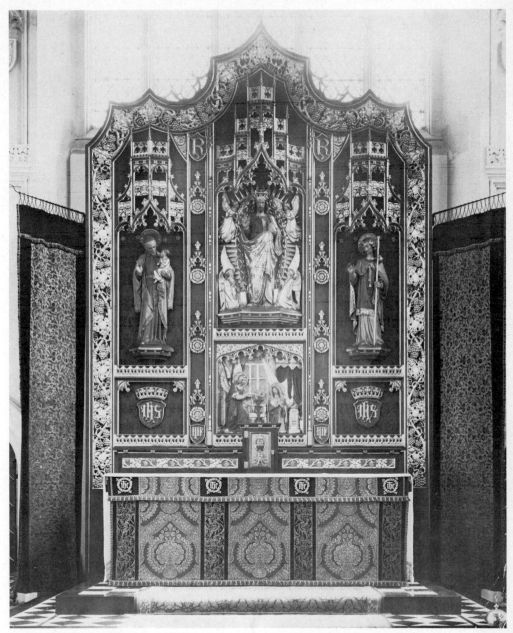

91   BODLEY. *Reredos in the Chapel of the Sisters of Charity, Knowle, Bristol*

VI

Alfred Waterhouse
civic grandeur

STUART ALLEN SMITH

Alfred Waterhouse was born on 19 July 1830, at Aigburth near Liverpool. He was the first of eight children born to Alfred Waterhouse and his wife Mary, both prominent members of the Society of Friends.

To the age of eighteen his contacts were exclusively Quaker, within a family that was intelligent and literate without being scholarly. He had very early shown an aptitude for and love of painting and drawing, but it was not conceivable within the limitations of the Quaker milieu to approve of a career in something quite so impractical. A family compromise was reached by which the boy would follow an architectural career. It was reasoned that there would be scope for his artistic talents, but they would be employed in an undeniably practical and business-like occupation.

Waterhouse was bound to Richard Lane of Manchester for a period of five years commencing 9 March 1848. It may safely be assumed that he did not learn much from the years with Lane. In later years Waterhouse, who was normally generous in assigning credit for help or influence, never mentioned his early teacher and, of the various works in progress during the time he was in the office, he saw fit only to keep a personal record of some alterations to his uncle's house.

To judge from his notebook[1] of the period 1851–52, Waterhouse was well in the Gothic camp. He copied Ruskin's illustrations of the Campanile of Florence Cathedral and, by his own later accounts, Pugin, Scott and Ruskin were his early mentors. At the same time he was looking, as he was always to look, at the buildings around him. Far more than books, and far more than personalities or theories, the great source of inspiration was the careful study of the buildings he encountered on his travels.

Already by 1852 he was fairly well travelled in England. Sketches recorded in the pocket sketch books he began to keep in 1851 show that he travelled extensively in the Midlands, in Scotland, to London and the south-west. Being *hors de combat* of the theological and stylistically restrictive Anglo-Catholic attitudes of the Camden Society, his eye was free to be caught by interesting house plans, by Edmund Sharpe's terracotta church at Rusholme,[2] warehouses, hotels and the working man's cottage at the Great Exhibition of 1851.

On 7 June 1853, having completed his five years with Richard Lane, Waterhouse set off for an extended continental trip. As travelling companion he took a school friend, Thomas Hodgkin, at the time recuperating from a severe bout of undiagnosed convulsive illness.

The two set out amid misgivings expressed by Mrs Waterhouse that her 'precious Alfred'[3] would be alone in Europe if Hodgkin returned, as he planned, after six months. They travelled to Paris via Dieppe and Rouen, pausing to examine the late Gothic work in both cities, and paid particular attention to the 94(b) Palais de Justice in Rouen. They were in Switzerland by the end of June, arriving in Rome towards the end of November. Hodgkin left at Christmas 1853, and Waterhouse apparently spent January in Constantinople where he sketched Santa Sophia and the Mosque of Sultan Suliman. In the spring he made his way along the 102 94(d) Riviera to Arles and then north to Brittany and home.

THE·MANCHESTER ASSIZE·COURTS

ALFRED ARCH'T

WATERHOUSE 1862

93   WATERHOUSE. *Manchester Assize Courts. Entrance Hall*   103

94(a)
94(c)

To judge from the preserved portions of his sketch book,[4] his interests were encyclopaedic, ranging from the Greek remains at Paestum to the staircase of the Palazzo Barberini. His appetite was voracious; he seems to have sketched every major building that caught his eye, and if not the whole building then details that seemed to sum up the spirit of the work – staircases, windows, buttressing or, more importantly, constructional methods or quirks of composition.

He seems, from the beginning, to have been able to sum up the essential lines and mass of a building in a few quick strokes of the pencil. Economical in their detail, the sketches were enough to jog his astonishingly accurate visual memory when he later looked over them. Thus armed, Waterhouse returned to Manchester and, having taken offices in Cross Street Chambers, began his career as Alfred Waterhouse, architect.

The earliest recorded design[5] to have emerged from Cross Street Chambers is for a plain brick block of stables in Liverpool, its plan dated 2 August 1854. Commissioned by his father, the job could as easily have been given directly to a builder, and the loss must be mourned for sentimental rather than architectural reasons.

Of greater interest is the house built for Miss E. H. Head, Rothay Holme[6] at Ambleside, which dates from the same year and, happily, survives. Its plan is of interest in that it organizes the main rooms around a central stair hall with the domestic portion in a tail to the rear. This hall arrangement was one that he was to use consistently in all his houses, the scale modified to suit conditions but always present or intended.

The design of the exterior, although not without charm, was destined to be more ephemeral. Inspired, no doubt, by the mountainous locality and the current enthusiasm for things Swiss, it presents a curious blending of the Tyrol and domestic Gothic. There is no specific source for the Tyrolean detail, and it is intended to be evocative rather than descriptive.

More specifically derivative, and yet at the same time an imaginative and practical design, was the Binyon and Fryer Warehouse of 1855.[7] Quite frankly a reworking of the Doge's Palace in Venice, its closed façade had considerable merit of application for a sugar warehouse. The use of exposed iron columns to support the ground-floor arcade remained unique in his work, as was the extent of Ruskin's influence. The Binyon and Fryer Warehouse is the only borrowing of a complete idea in Waterhouse's early career and must be put down to the combination of Ruskin's publication of *The Stones of Venice* (1851–53) and Waterhouse's recent European travels.

In September 1855, Waterhouse set out in company with his brother, Theodore, and two uncles to visit the Paris Exhibition. Stopping overnight at Amiens, they fell in with other tourists and discussed the relative merits of Beauvais and Chartres[8] until late at night. The next day, while walking through Amiens, Waterhouse noted, 'much struck with the way that brick and stone are alternated horizontally in some houses'.[9] Most significant for the future is the comment noted in a margin 'much struck by the terracotta work – red brick being occasionally in bands and arches for colour's sake'.[10] The same interest in contrasts of texture can be deduced from his examination of Gau's St Clotilde in Paris, which he criticized because the building, although possessing 'many pretty parts . . . loses its effect being built entirely of polished work'.[11]

He concluded the entries for his trip on the twenty-seventh with the carefully printed note: 'returned home much disgusted with English architecture. We want size, light, and shade, and colour in our buildings – and in ourselves more good humour and good manners – cost of journey £11.6.1½'.[12]

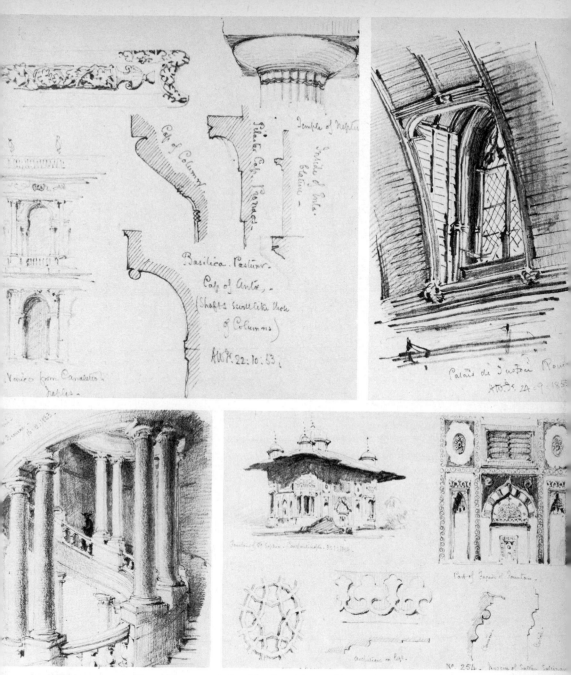

94   WATERHOUSE. *Pages from travel sketchbooks: (a) Mouldings and detail from the temples of Paestum; (b) Window of the Palais de Justice, Rouen; (c) Staircase of Palazzo Barberini, Rome; (d) Fountain of St Sophia and mouldings of the Mosque of Sultan Suliman, Istanbul*

95   WATERHOUSE. *Hinderton*

Despite his earnest hopes for size, his practice, following his return to Manchester, was to consist of the expected repairs, survey work and alterations. But among some small house commissions was one published in the *Builder*,[13] bringing him his first more than local notice.

95   Hinderton, begun for Christopher Bushnell in 1856,[14] has fortunately survived, but in a somewhat altered form. Although not a large house (the main block is some 50 ft by 70 ft), Hinderton was Waterhouse's first opportunity to produce a full-fledged, two-storey entrance hall.[15] The organization of the reception rooms around it in a loose yet logical and convenient way, together with the above-ground kitchens in the service wing to the left (south), put it in a sequential development that includes Butterfield's earlier parsonage work and the future activities of Philip Webb, but its publication in the *Builder* must make it more important than its less impressive exterior would indicate.

Professor Hitchcock believes that the 'agglutinative' plan derives from the forced asymmetry of the picturesque and received its first significant use in Pugin's house at Ramsgate (1841–43). However, he feels that Webb's use of it in Benfleet Hall, Cobham (1859), is most significant for future development. The fact that Waterhouse had three years previously designed Hinderton on these principles is treated by Professor Hitchcock as an isolated and virtually coincidental happening. The fact of the matter is that Hinderton represents the culmination of several years' work beginning with Rothay Holme, a development that continues to be further refined with the large house commissions of the late 1860s and early 70s, all of which received considerable publicity.

It would be pure speculation at this stage to do anything more than point out that Philip Webb's Benfleet Hall is based on the identical layout and follows publication of Hinderton by a year.

In its exterior treatment Hinderton is less original, its consistent use of deep-set, square-headed windows and its smooth wall surfaces owing much to the example of house designs of S. S. Teulon so extensively published in the *Builder* in the early 1850s.

A stylistic exercise of a very different order was the Bradford Old Bank of 1857.[16] Waterhouse's building originally provided banking chambers and offices on two floors. The rusticated ground floor was pierced by seven round arches filled with Palladian windows and the upper floor consisted of the same number of

WEST ELEVATION   scale ⅛ to I'0"

96 WATERHOUSE. *Barcombe Cottage. West elevation*

round-arched windows set in aedicules of flanking columns and segmental pediments. This use of sixteenth-century Venetian forms was not unique. There had been a considerable vogue for it in Manchester beginning in the late 1840s, and the example of its use for banking purposes could be attributed to a number of buildings.

Where the Bradford Bank differs from the earlier examples is in the use of heavier, more robust forms and an equal increase in texture to provide for a greater play of light and shade across the façade. It was to emphasize this latter aspect that Waterhouse introduced the contrasting colours in the ground floor.

The additions of 1881 have robbed the original design of much of its clarity and strength by crowding the first-floor fenestration and altering its proportions through the blocking up of the lower part of the windows, but even before these changes it was obvious that Waterhouse had not intended an archaeologically exact use of a Venetian design.

Unless he was engaged in a specifically designated restoration or replacement, Waterhouse did not copy forms exactly nor did he borrow textural and rhythmical values. In the case of the Bradford Old Bank he took recognizable Venetian forms sanctioned by site and previous use and reissued them in a new context. He knew Venetian architecture; he had studied it sympathetically and intelligently, but he felt no obligation to it.

It seems that in his early years Waterhouse viewed historic styles in the same way as associative values. It was possible to have a building that could summon up the atmosphere of a bygone age just as it was legitimate to dress up a functionally sound warehouse as a Venetian palace, but neither style nor associative values were central to the basic task of architecture.

In the same year (1858) Waterhouse built Barcombe Cottage for himself in   96 anticipation of his marriage to Elizabeth Hodgkin. Barcombe Cottage draws on previously explored territory in that it contains elements of Swiss, domestic Gothic and Italian work. Within its romantic outline the details were crisp and straightforward, each elevation in itself symmetrical and separate from the others. The principal gable to the garden was conceived as a two-storey arcade tied together horizontally by the cornice between the floors and the boldly outlined colour bands on the upper floor. The entrance court used the same window openings but spaced them wider apart and then framed them with a wide   107 shouldered overhang standing on a mid-level cornice continued around from the garden façade.

The organization of Barcombe Cottage, with each principal façade a separate composition, was sophisticated and highly successful, yet the constituent elements were without an equivalent interest. The ground-floor windows were square-headed and grouped in threes with heavy stone frames. The upper-floor windows might be called Tudor, but at the same time it would have to be admitted that the specific curve was the only identifiable manifestation of that style. Each element in the building was solid and carefully placed but, in itself, lifeless and mechanical in appearance.

The combination of stylistic sources in the early buildings did not prove long-lasting but the design sense as revealed by them was to be constant. Within an exuberant and highly sophisticated outline, the detail would be historically derived but mechanically conceived, rigid in its distribution and hard in effect without being consciously aggressive.

93, 97   It would be difficult to overestimate the importance of the Manchester Assize Courts building in the future career of the young architect. Not only did it bring him national attention, it brought him almost universal praise. Even well into the period when revived Gothic was anathema to the critics, the building was held to be a model of sound and imaginative planning. It stood throughout Waterhouse's lifetime as evidence of his fidelity to his client, his thoroughness in design matters and his obvious ability to produce a workable and practical structure. In short, it stood as proof that here was a capable, reliable man able to deal confidently yet sympathetically with men of business singly or in groups. It was to be his passport to a career as an architect to the expanding world of business. It was, at the same time, the direct cause of his receiving commissions at Oxford and Cambridge and an undoubted reason for his other large government commissions.

In deciding on Gothic for the Assize Courts, Waterhouse was prompted not by anything he read but by actual examples of Gothic civic work sought out and studied.[18] This search confirmed that Gothic architecture was applicable to modern requirements. The form that Gothic architecture was to take in his hands was equally characteristic.

The key to his attitude on the use of historic sources was contained in an address to members of his profession.

The mouldings and details are thirteenth century in their general character. But wherever I thought that the particular object in view could not be best obtained by a strict obedience to precedent I took the liberty of departing from it.[19]

The departure from precedent was more than occasional, since later in the same address, while paying tribute to the builder for his co-operation, he said of the detail work:

I believe there was hardly one that was carried out in the way in which it was originally intended. During the progress of the work it became evident that many things which I thought had been carefully considered beforehand would bear modification with improvement, and especially this was the case with mouldings and matters of detail.[20]

Waterhouse's attitude towards style was established before the Manchester Assize Courts competition, and had been consistently demonstrated in several interesting if minor buildings. It was not the result of sudden revelation but rather the slow sorting out and modifying of many current theories.

    Pugin had died during Waterhouse's last year of pupilage under Lane, but his

97 WATERHOUSE. *Manchester Assize Courts. Original project*

established reputation and the reissuing of *The True Principles* the next year ensured
that his ideas and programme were well known, and Waterhouse visited Alton
Towers in October 1856, filling five pages with sketches. Impressive as Pugin's
accomplishments were, and Waterhouse in later years acknowledged their power
many times, they could not at first hand have had application to the younger man's
work. Pugin's restrictive approach, the codification of aesthetic values into law,
could not be acceptable to the independent Quaker mind. It was the attitude of
mind rather than the Catholic commitment in itself that made it impossible to
accept the revival of architecture on Pugin's lines. It was from specific examples of
building on Pugin's principles rather than through the principles themselves that
Waterhouse came to a belief in revived Gothic architecture.

The impact of Ruskin at mid-century was enormous, and his attempt to fuse the
ethical, social and artistic components of life into a harmonious whole without
being specifically sectarian seemed at first to succeed. In a way that Pugin could
not, Ruskin raised the dignity of architecture and widened its appeal, making it
seem important to the layman to an extent that has not been equalled since. *The
Seven Lamps of Architecture* and *The Stones of Venice* were both read by Waterhouse
at the time of their publication and they had the same effect they had for other
readers. The fullness and richness of Ruskin's language, the almost overwhelming
force and weight of it, swept them all along in a wave of enthusiasm. But where
Pugin was specifically archaeological and restrictive, Ruskin was the very opposite.

Ruskin was a moralist, forwarding a post-Rousseau belief in nature as a source of
revelation and an enthusiasm for historic architecture as part of that nature. In this
prophetic role he was compatible with the basic Quaker approach of individual
thought and interpretation, but as a teacher of architecture he had little to
recommend him. Ruskin's chief function for Waterhouse was to confirm his
painter's eye in compositional effects and to authorize the use of continental models
and styles that Pugin did not permit.

As had been the case with Pugin, the writings of Ruskin in their more extreme
aspects could not be totally accepted by Waterhouse, and it is from other architects
working along Ruskinian lines that his message was principally absorbed.

109

Having accepted a direction from Ruskin, the men of Waterhouse's generation required specific information and this they obtained either from their own travels or from books like Street's *Brick and Marble in the Middle Ages*. At the time he wrote (1855) Street was opposed to any mixture of styles and the continuing emphasis in his book is on the correctness of usage, even in those practices of which he did not approve. It was on that point of eclecticism that he parted company with Gilbert Scott.

As early as 1849, Scott had introduced French elements in his work,[21] but he disclaimed any great influence in transmitting them to general use in England. This fashion he attributed to the results of the Burges and Clutton triumph in the Lille Cathedral competition of 1856. He had visited Italy in 1851, travelling with Benjamin Ferrey, and while in Venice met Ruskin. At first Scott was not impressed with Venetian architecture, perhaps due to Ferrey's muttering 'Batty Langley'[22] at every Gothic building they saw, but we are told he gradually came to an appreciation of it. His conclusion was very much what Street's was to be:

I was convinced that Italian Gothic, as such, must not be used in England, but I was equally convinced and am so still, that the study of it is necessary to the perfecting of our revival.[23]

In the end it was Scott's eclectic attitude supported by the editorial position of the professional press[24] that dominated architectural thinking when Waterhouse came to design his first major commission, and it was to the architecture of Scott in particular that he was attracted for ideas and detail. To be worthy a building would have to be Gothic and ideally English in inspiration, but suitable detail from foreign examples could be included if it enhanced the effect. This was in essence Scott's attitude and it became Waterhouse's. With one or two exceptions there would be no archaeological purity nor complete commitment to nationality, instead an eclectic Gothic suited 'to modern needs'.

The competition prize forced changes which were to have a strong influence on his career. The need for a large staff to handle the multitude of detail drawings and endless tracings forced an immediate expansion of the office and, in large part, determined the basis on which that office was to function throughout his career. The design was solely his and had been arrived at by decisions made alone. He had then an immediate need for capable professional draughtsmen, men who could quickly and directly transfer his sketches and ideas into working drawings, and they are precisely what he looked out for. This preference for the working draughtsman prevented the creation of the collaborate atmosphere which can only be engendered by a group of equals. While Waterhouse's draughtsmen more and more came to determine detail within a building, they seldom went on to produce buildings in their own right. The students who did pass through his office received a sound training in office routine and did a great deal of work on the buildings under construction, but they had little or no contact with the actual design process or the generation of the plan, and so had no group characteristics or repertoire of recognizable decorative peculiarities to take away with them.

Waterhouse's success with the Manchester Assize Courts gave him a nation-wide reputation. He established a London office in 1864 with at least three draughtsmen, and from that year the London practice grew to such an extent that he eventually closed the Manchester office altogether.

The second half of the 1860s saw him engaged on three major projects. One of them, the new Law Courts in London, he lost to Street, though he was a prime contender. The other two, the London Natural History Museum and Manchester Town Hall, occupied him simultaneously from 1867 onwards.

98   WATERHOUSE. *Natural History Museum, London*

Waterhouse was approached to execute the designs of Captain Fowke for both the Museum of Natural History and the Museum of Patents and Inventions on 23 February 1866. He prepared estimates of superficial and cubic footage and investigated the Fowke proposals to the point where detailed cost estimates could be given. As late as January 1868, however, he had still not been given a clear go-ahead for construction as it was necessary for him on 9 January to state the proposed terms of his employment to the First Commissioner of Works.

In May 1868 Waterhouse submitted plans and elevations of his proposal. They were more than a development of the Fowke plans and incorporated ideas expressed by the professional staff of the Museum.

The final version of the Museum was accepted on 20 January 1872, but alterations to the towers were made in 1876. There had been two earlier versions submitted – the first in 1868 and the second in 1871. Both early versions employed a central dome and circular entrance hall, and the first had domed towers at either end of the façade.

With the exception of the iron framework and extensive use of glass, it was Waterhouse's intention that the building be entirely of terracotta. But there is a brick core to the walls and the stairs are of Craigleath stone. The exterior walls are structural, but the interior is carried completely on a steel frame as are all the floors and the roof. All steelwork except the exposed beams of the entrance hall is encased in terracotta.

The choice of terracotta as a building material for the Natural History Museum,   98
as Waterhouse acknowledged, had originally been made by Captain Fowke, although it is unlikely that he intended to use it exclusively. There was already a considerable amount of terracotta in the new South Kensington buildings through the previous activities of Fowke and General Scott – enough to justify Waterhouse's decision to retain it – and he was further reassured by the rising professional interest in the material.

The employment of terracotta in South Kensington, however, had been chiefly in Renaissance forms, and these were not suited to the decorative problem that faced Waterhouse. From the outset, Professor Owen of the Museum had been anxious to unite contents and architectural decoration. He therefore proposed, and it was accepted by Waterhouse, that extensive use be made of plant, mineral and animal forms as sculpture. This was clearly not possible within any Renaissance context, and inevitably Romanesque forms were the answer for both the material and the decorative scheme. It was typical of Waterhouse that the choice of Romanesque was determined by the nature of the problem at hand, and it seems not to have mattered to him that the building would, as a result, be outside the mainstream of fashion.

Having decided on Romanesque in a characteristically straightforward and logical way, the form that it took was equally typical. Waterhouse's travels had provided him with an overwhelming variety of examples, for he had made four trips to Germany from 1857 to 1871, five trips to Italy in the same period and seven to France.

The splayed entrance arch of the Natural History Museum contains eight pairs of patterned shafts carrying round arches. Is this a conscious reworking of the Gnadenpforte of Bamberg Cathedral[25] or is it an entrance designed by a man who had as thorough a knowledge of the style as did a Romanesque builder? The logic and symmetry of fenestration, its setting within a recessed frame, is in keeping with Romanesque precedent. Again one may ask, is he consciously copying a specific example such as Andernach,[26] or is it a characteristic observed in many French and German examples and subsequently absorbed into his own Romanesque vocabulary? The polychrome techniques have Romanesque precedents, notably at Le Puy,[27] as does the rigidity and clarity of the composition, and the towers are similar to those in the Calvados district of Normandy. The use of animal sculpture on the façade has Romanesque precedent, most spectacularly at Worms[28] and St Jacob's Church, Regensburg.[29]

Did Waterhouse actually copy? No. He was thoroughly at home with the characteristics of the style. Nor was it a rigidly nationalistic knowledge that he drew on, for, as he had in the 1850s, Waterhouse felt free to pick and choose, to cross national and stylistic boundaries at will. He had immense respect for history but it did not bind him in his own work.

Goodhart-Rendel called the Natural History Museum 'a development of Romanesque',[30] and that is precisely what it is. The building can be called Romanesque because its design sense is Romanesque. It is successful because it is complete and perfectly suited to the purpose for which it was built. It is original because the forms employed, while they are based on precedent, are entirely of their author's devising.

Even more important for Waterhouse's career and fame was the commission for the new Town Hall in Manchester. The competitions[31] for this were hard and bitterly fought contests. There was much at stake; for it was obviously the biggest civic commission of the decade and the resulting publicity would bring the winning architect as much again in new work.

Waterhouse responded immediately to the first open competition announced on 12 March 1867. A second competition was called on 17 September 1867, with final date for submissions being 14 February 1868. The eight[32] invited competitors were not bound by their drawings in the previous round and there were no new conditions save those of specifying portions of the building for specific purposes and stating that the mezzanine floors in any part of the building were undesirable.

The General Purpose Committee met to view the completed submissions and on 27 February appealed to T. L. Donaldson and G. E. Street for a professional assessment. Waterhouse's chief rivals at this stage were Speakman, Charlesworth, Scott and Worthington. The identity of the competitors was given token protection by the retention of the competition mottoes although it would be difficult to imagine that they were unknown to the Committee or to the interested public.

The judges elaborated on their valuation in the process of nominating Waterhouse as overall winner:

The architectural character of this design is, as we have said, not quite so good as some of the others; but the plan has such great merits, is so admirably and simply disposed, and so well lighted that we cannot but feel that it is thoroughly entitled to

99　WATERHOUSE. *Manchester Town Hall*

the first place. The general disposition of the masses of the elevation is very
picturesque; and there is much dignity about the treatment of the principal storey
towards Albert Square. We are bound to say that in some respects the design
appears to us to require additional study and modifications of which it admits
without difficulty.[33]

The nature of the report was bound to cause dissension and the *Guardian*
carried in the same issue a letter calling for the public viewing of the plans and
objecting to the selection of 'an imperfect piece of architecture'.

There was, from the first public viewing of Waterhouse's proposal, no shortage
of advice on how to improve it. However, the basic plan was not significantly
altered[34] from its inception prior to the first competition. Its clarity, simplicity and
obvious functional perfection was nothing less than astonishing to contemporary
architects. If, as Le Corbusier has said, 'To make a plan is to determine and fix ideas.
It is to have had ideas,'[35] then Waterhouse has here determined and fixed on an
architectural idea that is ordered, logical and grand in its effect.

The building was designed completely to occupy its triangular site with two
wedge-shaped areas left open on either side of the public hall in the centre. The
exterior generated by the plan went through modifications in its final design stages

100, 101   *Eaton Hall. East front and plan: A Private wing; B Service wing;*
C Chapel; D Dining room; E Drawing room; F Great Hall; G Grand staircase

and during the early construction period. There was, however, nothing near the tremendous adjustment and change of detail that marked the early stages of the Assize Courts project.

99   The chief structural change came in the main tower to Albert Square. The competition design provided an octagonal clock face above the tall square-based belfry storey, and this arrangement had been criticized by the *Guardian* amongst others. In the final version this was altered to a square clock face with octagonal tower and spire above. This additional height had been suggested by Donaldson and Street and repeated publicly by the *Guardian*.

Each of the four elevations is a different length and is seen under different conditions, the main elevation to Albert Square being the only one seen face on at any distance. Each façade employs Waterhouse's characteristic composition of a prominent central bay flanked by balanced but not symmetrical arms with terminal accents.

Both Waterhouse's and Worthington's designs read best from a distance and depended on general outline, on the silhouette, for their principal effect. Within that, both worked the surface on a scale suited to the overall size of the building. Within the silhouette, Waterhouse was more active, each elevation adjusting its organization to the street situation and carrying a greater amount of surface enrichment. Worthington's design was much less active and would have required a distant view on all sides to be completely effective. Neither employed colour or the play of light and shade and, in Waterhouse's case, this is now evident, thanks to the recent cleaning, to an extent that was not obvious within the last ninety-five years.

For Waterhouse those qualities were deliberately and carefully developed. In the late 60s he was aiming at elevations that were picturesque and elaborate in outline. As he said when advising young architects on the process of design,

Then again he may devote himself to the details of his composition while neglecting its outline when seen against the sky. This in our somewhat murky atmosphere, is a fatal flaw.[36]

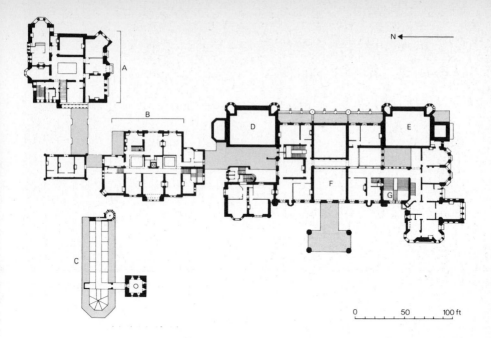

Attention to the silhouette, however, was never to be at the cost of the plan His advice to young architects while President of the RIBA was clear and unmistakable on that point, and established his priorities.

First find out exactly what is wanted; never think about elevations of your building until you have ascertained this and embodied it in your plans as fully and perfectly as you can.[37]

Within that first stage there was a factor that played an important part in the design.

The real architect will not fail to appreciate the peculiarities of the site on which he is called upon to build. He will make his work grow so naturally out of it as to seem and to be the inevitable building for the spot.[38]

His lack of archaeological commitment was a stated source of dismay to critics, such as the *Building News,* in his early years, just as his conservatism was to be in his late years. He would gradually become almost indifferent to style; as he said to the students of the RIBA:

When I was young we were hoping that the Gothic of about 1200 would be met with general approbation. Of late years a free treatment of the Renaissance has found more favour. The style will no doubt answer well if you will but stick to it while it grows under your fostering care.[39]

His concept of growth made it essential that he retain the control over his detail to the extent of refusing to copy from selected sources, and the direction of growth from plan outwards made it difficult to transfer solutions from one building to another.

Waterhouse was to design many other public buildings, banks, offices, hospitals and colleges, but his style was now mature and remained essentially consistent for the rest of his life. One area, however, remains to be described: the country house. And one example must serve to illustrate all the rest: Eaton Hall, Cheshire.

When Hugh Lupus Grosvenor became Marquis of Westminster in 1869, he

102 WATERHOUSE. *Eaton Hall. Stable and coach house*

determined to rebuild Eaton Hall as drastically as it had been rebuilt in 1803. He called in Waterhouse who, between the 23 May 1870 and the end of 1897, signed certificates for a total of £603,103 6s 11d.

101 As Porden had done before him, Waterhouse preserved the seventeenth-century arrangement of dining and drawing rooms with their ante-rooms. In general lines he kept the main corridor disposition and much of the interior partitioning in less important areas of the main block. The south wing was completely removed and a new library placed along the south side. The north wing built by Gummow to house the chapel and state apartments became the kitchen and general domestic area with servants' quarters above, unchanged in overall size. The new private wing could be entered from the service wing, which also gave access to the stable yard or the garden. Both these entrances opened on a central hall lit by a skylight, with the principal rooms opening off it. The chapel was entered through the ante-chapel or porch along its eastern end. This ante-chapel was approached either from a southern entrance or from the corridor which connected its northern side with the main block.

The disposition of the plan was faultless on a purely functional and practical basis. Given the requirements and situations of the day it was, for all its size, manageable, comfortable and efficient and continued to be so until shortly before the Second World War. The house was able to function efficiently on the two levels of public and private life because the necessary services, kitchens etc., were in fact the core of the plan. It was no farther from stove to table when the Duke and Duchess dined alone in the private wing than when they sat down to dinner with sixty house-guests in the main dining room.

In the matter of giving physical expression to his plan, Waterhouse could not escape his age, and that age demanded that a building both be picturesque and, however freely interpreted, possess recognizable stylistic characteristics.

The Porden house had been the work of a draughtsman. Its detail, its very shape, was a creation of line, not volume. Waterhouse came to his task as a sculptor, modelling and raising the mass and volume of the existing building.

To unify the entire complex accumulation of buildings into a well-composed whole required great visual skill. Much like his client, Waterhouse was at home working on a large scale, and Eaton Hall must be considered his triumph as a

103 WATERHOUSE. *St Elisabeth, Reddish. Choir and choir screen*

practitioner of the picturesque. The house was seen from three principal vantage
points: the east or garden front, the main entrance façade, and the stable yard. The
first two were inherited with the Porden house, but in both there is a complete
mastery of composition through a balance of vertical and horizontal and forward
and recessive elements. The garden front was perhaps the most difficult problem,   101
for the symmetrical disposition of its parts tends to separate it from the rest.
Waterhouse overcame this by emphasizing the verticals of the corner towers and
pavilions, the chapel tower and the pavilioned gable of the private wing to give the
group a definite unity, yet at the same time preserving the intentional recession and
broken skyline to the right.

   The main entrance appears as a three-storey block dominated by a low spire at
the far right. The viewer's eye moves down and back from right to left only to rise
quickly again and end with the massive vertical of the chapel. The result is perfect
repose through a balanced but complex and ingenious arrangement of major and
minor motifs.

   The stable entrance had no match in England. If picturesque architecture is   102
intended to charm and delight the eye that chooses to see reality in its most

romantic aspect, then what a joy the view from the stable yard must have been. Its low black and white buildings, overshadowed by the chapel and its tower, with, off to the left, the towers and pinnacles of the main block, appearing for all the world like a medieval town, were however not the result of happy chance but of a carefully and thoroughly prepared presentation.

During the twenty years before he retired in 1901, Waterhouse was for the most part content to follow the path that he had already mapped out, and one can perhaps detect a falling off in freshness of invention. An exception is his only major essay in church architecture, St Elisabeth's, Reddish. Built in 1882–83, in red brick with stone dressings, it combines Norman with Continental Romanesque in a vigorous style which is entirely in keeping with his principles but which he never actually tried to repeat.

103

What, finally, can we define as Waterhouse's particular contribution to the architecture of nineteenth-century England? He is always considered to have been, at least in the early years of his career, one of the major Gothic Revival architects. Yet what is precisely Gothic in his work and his attitude towards it is seldom considered. The structural basis of his buildings is not Gothic. From his earliest commissions[40] he employed structural iron, and it was the systematic logic of the rolled-iron beam, not the pointed arch, that determined the exterior rhythm of his structures.

Waterhouse began his career as a nominally Gothic architect because he was impressed by the intensity, seriousness and dedication of its proponents, but he saw the revival only as the means to an end. In later years, speaking for his own generation, he told students that 'they hoped the Gothic revival would be more than a mere revival – that it would turn from a revival into a growth'.[41] To say of Waterhouse's work, as Ralph Dutton has said of Blackmoor, which Waterhouse built in 1869, 'Doubtless all the detail was copied with a scrupulous correctness',[42] is to misunderstand both Waterhouse's intention and his work.

That intention was stated simply and clearly in 1878 on the occasion of his being presented with the RIBA gold medal.

I accept this medal at your hands as a proof that you are willing to recognize one who would put in a plea for architecture to be considered, on some occasions at any rate, as distinct from style and archaeology.[43]

The alienation and dislocation felt by painters in the nineteenth century, with their accompanying changes in social status and patronage, were reflected in the architectural profession. The situation was further complicated by an inherited conflict between engineering and architecture. There was a continuing reliance on exterior cladding to give a sense of integrity to a design that did not arise naturally from the plan, but even more, there was, in England at least, a failure to accept new materials in the complete sense. Iron was used, concrete was used, but the implications of the extensive use of these materials in design and their aesthetic impact was never fully accepted. It was in the face of the post-Ruskin aesthetic confusion and his own long-standing independence that Waterhouse more and more chose to reduce his stylistic commitment.

The clearest reflection of the attitude expressed in his RIBA gold medal speech can be seen in those works of the late 1870s where the combination of red brick and red terracotta becomes the consistently preferred material. The preference for terracotta is partially the outcome of Waterhouse's theory that colour contrasts kill form, partly its durability, but most important its ideal suitability to a manufacturing process. From the mid-1870s it is to be expected that in a Waterhouse building all the detail will be both manufactured and standardized.

104   WATERHOUSE. *Prudential Insurance Building, London. Inner courtyard*

The window frames of the Hove Town Hall and the casements and shafts of the   104
Prudential Building in London are but two examples.

The preferred forms continue to be Gothic and of the simplified non-archaeological type already preferred by Waterhouse. In order for a standardized unit to be easily manufactured and capable of widespread application, it was necessary for it to be smoothly finished and simple enough to be appropriate to most situations. Waterhouse sincerely believed that an over-developed regard for history was the chief obstacle to a dynamic nineteenth-century architecture. As part of an attempt to overcome that, he was determined to move away from hand work, with its implications of recognizable style and period.

The Liverpool Royal Infirmary of 1886 was a source of much dismay to Professor Reilly[44] when he came to teach architecture at Liverpool University in 1904. He found it hard, ugly, built to no plan, and was even more unhappy to hear that an eighteenth-century building had been demolished to make way for it. Professor Reilly was right in his opinion that the building lacked charm, but plan it had. And it was a hardheaded efficient plan of the sort Reilly was incapable of in his own practice. The basic problem in hospital planning, then as now, was to achieve efficiency for both the practice of medicine and administration, while recognizing that what serves the former may not serve the latter. Waterhouse provided here a central administrative and specialized treatment block from which all shared services flowed. In the six ward wings specialized or routine treatment could be facilitated by grouping related illnesses in units that were virtually self-sufficient. The increase in the use of specialized staff and equipment over generalized wards is obvious, as is the protection against the spread of infection. For this reason each ward provided its own doctors' and nurses' offices, dining and convalescent room and scullery, but for administrative reasons the cooking was done in a central kitchen on the fourth floor of the central block and sent along a tram-line to lifts at the head of each ward.

When it came to giving external expression to this plan Waterhouse was committed to basic principles of design rather than to an historic style as such. In accordance with his principle of repetition and lessening of detail on large structures, the decorative elements are restricted to terracotta panels between the second and third floors with pilasters at that level terminating in plain finials. String courses run between the floors, and occasional relieving arches appear over the square-headed windows. The main block and the wards are each organized with a central emphasis and terminal bays. There is in it all exactly what he wanted – a hardness of material, uniform repetition of simple elements, and their subsequent employment in a logical, almost necessary, unit.

'His work is wholly devoid of charm, and looks as if it were conceived, and almost if it were constructed, in cast iron rather than in stone.'[45] What the unnamed critic in the *British Architect* was witnessing without being aware of it was the dying moments of historicism in architecture. The new mechanical, machine-orientated aesthetic was uncomfortably crammed into an older style, just as Stuart architecture presents a new architecture through the introduction of foreign elements in an older style, and as in Stuart work, there exists a strong but uncomfortable logic.

The Quaker sense of social separateness and the necessity of constant individual moral and social decisions produced in Waterhouse, as it did in all Quaker businessmen, an astonishing self-confidence in the world of business, together with a tenacity of opinion suitable to men who were prepared to stand alone on Judgment Day. No Quaker ever believed in a governing church body as the final arbiter of conscience, and the young Waterhouse inescapably applied that principle to his profession. This is not to say that he would ever be a rebel. He extended the same respect and consideration to the members of his profession as he had given and received within his religious community. The only honours he accepted or valued in his lifetime were those granted by the architectural profession, and in his late years it was the withdrawal of that respect that was so cruel a blow to him.

The application of this Quaker sense of individuality to his architecture can be seen clearly in his attitude to the competition for the Manchester Assize Courts where, despite the fact that he had read Pugin, Ruskin and Scott and was allied to the Gothic Revival, he found it necessary to visit the Flemish town halls to test that style at first hand. Late in his career the Quaker rationale can be seen in the University College Hospital in London. The building begins with a plan that is sound and suited to its purpose, and its exterior is selected to suit the plan, not the surrounding area. The building preserves its individual integrity and the resulting separation from its neighbours could not be considered a fault by its Quaker author.

Waterhouse had perhaps as good a knowledge of historic styles as any architect of his day, yet he would not copy formulas from the past. His plans are a functional

105 WATERHOUSE. *University College Hospital, London*

solution to problems presented. Having logically solved the needs of client and site in a plan, he then produced an elevation to suit it. When he assessed his plan in terms of the materials, the site and the public function, it inevitably suggested some historic precedent. In the use of that historic precedent, he would accept only its most important parts and then draw up the elevations in a personal design. This method of selecting style on a functional basis makes any purely aesthetic assessment of his work a very difficult process as there seems to be no carry-over from one building to the next. That this approach to architecture was the result of a thought process and not style-mongering can be proved by his adherence to it through gradually increasing unpopularity, as the logic of his attitude forced him to reject more and more stylistic precedent and to rely on his own aesthetic sense.

When he ceased practice in 1901, Waterhouse was a very wealthy man.[46] He had, in his years of practice, left his mark on English architecture, yet the public admiration for his buildings was gone. He was, however, left with a high personal reputation based on those qualities that gave him his start. He was an honest upright man of the sort that Vitruvius looked back on with such high regard, and the generation that was his severest critic also passed what must remain for some time yet the final summation of his abilities:

Whatever his defects of taste, a man who had such capacity and readiness in planning and designing buildings on a large scale, and who seemed able to grasp and deal with every practical problem in building, as soon as it was presented to him, was essentially a great architect.[47]

Edwin Lutyens
the last High Victorian

RODERICK GRADIDGE

During the last years of the life of Edwin Lutyens[1] most people considered him another Wren. Even the man in the street knew his name – a very rare, if not unique, compliment for an architect in this country. But the more doctrinaire generation that followed him consistently denigrated his work; of his honest yet sophisticated Surrey houses they find that 'like a dream they are unreal, like a dream they have left nothing behind';[2] a serious historian calls New Delhi and the Viceroy's House 'a series of grandiose barracks incorporating classical and Mughal motifs without synthesis or sympathy';[3] in the view of others his designs have displayed 'naughtiness or wilful originality'.[4]

At the same time, anyone not entirely blinded by didactic and unarchitectural ideas has had to admit that Lutyens's architecture, *as Architecture*, is superb. Even Robert Furneaux Jordan, most doctrinaire of critics, has said, 'I once worshipped Lutyens only this side of idolatry and certainly came into architecture because Lutyens had existed'.[5] However, later generations, with perhaps a better understanding of Victorian architecture, see Lutyens in a less extreme way:[6] for Paul Thompson he is 'most easily explained as an exceptional survival of the best of the Victorian period'.[7] Indeed Lutyens could not have produced his very fine work without this Victorian background; it is this High Victorian quality which makes Lutyens's work so much more interesting than that of his many talented contemporaries. Throughout his career this High Victorian skeleton was never far from his drawing board.

Lutyens was almost untrained, perhaps untrainable; as Sir Herbert Baker remembered him 'he seemed to know by intuition'.[8] But the decade in which he was born enabled him to take advantage of the revolution in English architecture that had been brewed in avant-garde architects' offices some fifty years earlier; and he happened to be the finest artist born in that decade. Since Lutyens was self-taught, watching building in the builders' yards and on the sites by his home at Thursley in Surrey, right from the start he imbibed the natural habits of work of a country builder as a builder and not as an architect – a training that even Philip Webb lacked. Thus the latest fashion in architecture could have no effect on his untrained imagination, a thing that no architectural student in a school or articled pupil in a successful office is spared. This was to mean later that he seemed to lack a stylistic basis for his work – which in the end was to have a dire effect on his architecture, and through this, was later to have an equally dire effect on a whole generation of English architects. However, by the late 1880s many of the startling ideas of the 1840s, shorn of their fashionable trappings, had had time to penetrate even to rural Surrey. When he started to build his great Surrey houses, Lutyens was able to make use of what one might call the inner style of the Great Victorians, whilst rejecting the Gothic Revival as such. It was this quality that made his work so immediately appealing to clients – there was nothing doctrinaire about it.

But this form of training has its disadvantages. Lutyens was already hampered by what seemed to him a hopelessly eccentric father,[9] and the sense of not having been properly trained in a proper office, where he could have learned about Architecture with a capital 'A' and the Orders, was never to leave him. This

122

Sir Edwin Lutyens. *Drawing by William Rothenstein*

107   LUTYENS. *Bois des Moutiers, Varengeville*

explains his later theorizing about classical proportions and his frenzied, some might say dishonest,[10] chasing after work throughout his life.

His style, far from being the simple progression to pure classical excellence suggested by Messrs Hussey and Butler,[11] was in fact constantly veering as it came under different influences. Lutyens was, to a suprising degree in such an important architect, much affected by fashion. His first style as a young man, before he met Gertrude Jekyll (1843–1932), was as Nicholas Taylor has shown, the standard Elizabethan–Tudor of the 1890s, which he handled with little or no inspiration, a fact that Lutyens himself acknowledged.[12] Later he essayed a form of Art-Nouveau in the very fine Mackmurdoesque house, Bois des Moutiers at Varengeville in France 107
(1898)[13] and the extraordinary Pleasaunce, Overstrand, (1897–99).[14] In the same year at Overstrand, in another large house, Overstrand Hall,[15] he seemed to be moving to the cranky form of Art and Crafts structural expressionism favoured by E. S. Prior (1852–1932). At other time he designed in a form of streamlined Gothic, not dissimilar to the post–1907 parts of Liverpool Cathedral which Giles Gilbert Scott (1880–1960) had developed by combining the vertical 'Decorated' style of Bodley with the avant-garde Gothic of Leonard Stokes (1858–1925). But some of Lutyens's details in this style, doors made of linen fold panelling running from top to bottom without frames, and chamfers stopped with small domes, occur in some of his earliest buildings, such as Hoe Farm, Hascombe of 1891–92. The prime examples of this style are of course Lindisfarne (1902),[16] Castle Drogo (1910)[17] and

Crooksbury.
Farnham
For Arthur Chapman Esq.

Edwin L. Lutyens Archt
1890

Leonard Martin Delt
1899

108 LUTYENS. *Crooksbury, Farnham*

Campion Hall in Oxford (1934).[18] Later, as Pevsner has shown, he was influenced by the American skyscraper style. Suprisingly enough, in the 1930s, he was also involved in such a consciously fashionable style as 'Vogue Regency' (as Osbert Lancaster has called it). It could indeed be suggested that Lutyens invented this style by combining Art-Deco with careful classical architecture. With mirrors framed in mirrors set against the Delhi Order this style was appropriately seen at its best in Messrs Crane's bath showrooms at 120 Pall Mall, in London (1928).[19]

The style, however, which was to stay with Lutyens most constantly and the one that was to bring him into the mainstream of advanced architectural thought was the style of Philip Webb (1831–1915). The very young Lutyens knew nothing of Webb when he started practice, and he only came under his influence when he had met Gertrude Jekyll in 1889, after he had designed the first part of Crooksbury in a builder's sub-Norman Shaw/Ernest George style.[20] Phené Spiers in his 'Architectural Drawing' illustrates a perspective by Ernest George of Almshouses near Guildford, dated 1879, which look very similar to Lutyens's early perspective of Crooksbury. It was in the Munstead Wood Hut which he designed for Miss Jekyll in 1894 that he began to show the influence of Webb and his attitude to architectural form and materials – in that order. Moreover it is clearly through Webb that Lutyens moved on to Neo-Georgian architecture, and it was from this that he developed to his later more abstract style. By the time that he used it for the War Memorials Webb's puritanical archaism had been left far behind but Luytens's own puritanism was still there (learnt literally at his mother's knee), and it was still informed by Gothic Revival ideals which had now become grafted on to classical architecture.

With this in mind, it is worth giving some thought to the work of Webb's master, George Edmund Street (1824–81).[21] Street, as well as being a designer of great originality, is today often linked with Webb as one of the creators of the Arts and Crafts Movement in the mad rush to trace the 'Origins of the Modern Movement', but he was also deeply involved with another movement and style

108

109

124

which was called by the Victorians the 'Vigorous Style'. It was well enough known to Street's fellow Victorians, but is little discussed today;[22] in its time it created a great deal of controversy. It was this style, related to Webb's Arts and Crafts attitude, that later so much influenced Lutyens. Lord Grimthorpe (1816–1905) in particular detested the style, but his definition is probably the best that we have:

This 'Vigorous' style displays only the vigour of shaving off all projections; making the slopes of buttresses without 'nosings' and twice as steep as they ever were in real gothic, at least in England; window tracery is made as if it were cut out of stone flags; and buildings rise out of the ground without plinths or projecting bases, as if they were mushrooms.[23]

The Vigorous Style was concerned with wall planes and rejected imposed decorations and mouldings, with the result that many of the churches of the 1850s and 60s became matters of pure sculptural form, the shapes, although complex and interlocking, never advancing beyond the front plane of the building, the whole building having a slabby quality with the planes of the walls everywhere dominating, and no decoration being allowed to project forward of the wall surface. Thus the extremities of one façade projected back become the most advanced wall plane of the adjoining elevation. So the whole building has to be thought through from the beginning in three-dimensional terms, as a solid mass, sculpturally stripped to reveal the form and decoration within the mass – in much the way that Michelangelo freed his Moses from the block of marble in which it had been imprisoned.

This style was to have a profound influence on many of the Gothic Revival architects. Brooks always designed in the style[24] and many others such as Butterfield[25] and Bentley often returned to this form of design; indeed, by the end of the century it was accepted into the design vocabulary of most advanced English architects, who in this way learnt to think three-dimensionally, whilst on the Continent the two-dimensional teaching of the Beaux-Arts School was still dominant.[26]

When Lutyens started to work for himself in about 1890, English architecture had perhaps reached its highest peak and the six German volumes of Hermann Muthesius are its greatest monument. The masters of the Gothic church – Street, Butterfield, Pearson, Brooks and Bodley – had done their work, but there were now few young men designing churches. Philip Webb and Norman Shaw were still designing houses and the self-assured younger house architects included Ernest Newton (1856–1922), W. R. Lethaby (1857–1931), C. F. A. Voysey (1857–1941),

110 PHILIP WEBB. *New Place, Welwyn*

Guy Dawber (1861–1938), C. R. Ashbee (1863–1942), M. H. Baillie Scott (1865–1945), Detmar Blow (1867–1939) and many others who were able to design a house both beautiful and practical – all that most clients required. Charles Rennie Mackintosh (1868–1928) won the competition for the Glasgow School of Art at the age of twenty-eight in 1896, and Giles Gilbert Scott that for the Anglican Liverpool Cathedral at the age of twenty-three in 1903. It seemed that everyone was young; the course of English architecture seemed clear for the next century.

On the Continent, however, other things were happening. In England the idea that there ought to be a specific 'modern' style of architecture had been current right through the High Victorian period. One of the most important, though largely unintentional, contributions of Webb and Morris was to wean advanced English design from High Victorian thinking and thus from the idea of a 'modern style'. To the Arts and Crafts designer truth to materials and comfort and conformity to surroundings were much more important than any thought about style. The idea that a building violently out of harmony with its neighbours should be designed, say, to look as if it were built of concrete although it was built of brick would have been quite intolerable to them (though this was something quite accepted by Continental doctrinaire moderns to whom style was more important than the tenets of functionalism). Morris would have been as appalled as Voysey[27] if he had lived to find himself hailed as a precursor of this kind of modern architecture.

At the turn of the century, then, very few people in England believed in the need for a New Architecture as such; current architecture was much too good for them to want to change it. The Arts and Crafts Movement still held the imagination of the young, and because the movement had grown from the Gothic Revival, classical architecture was not much admired. It was into this climate of opinion that the very young Lutyens was brought by the sophisticated Gertrude Jeykll.[28] Philip Webb became his inspiration, and Webb right from the 1870s, like Butterfield before him, was willing to mix Georgian vernacular with Gothic details – a sash window in a Tudor gable.

But Lutyens, perhaps because the simple Georgian classical had lingered on in the builders' yards of rural Surrey, from the beginning used true classical details.

110

Even as early as his first cottage at Crooksbury, built before the house, in 1888, he used a classical scroll to the porch canopy. By the latter half of the 1890s he often used complete classical compositions in his interiors, though not when working for Gertrude Jeykll in her own house. At Fulbrook in 1897 he used an Ionic Order and Roman arches in the staircase hall, with wit but rather clumsily, influenced here perhaps by Norman Shaw's interiors. In the dining room at Orchards in 1898 there used to be a built-in sideboard with small Doric columns on a wooden rusticated plinth, which may have been copied from a rather similar eighteenth-century plinth in the Great Hall of his wife's family home, Knebworth House. At Tigbourne in 1899 a colonnade of oddly coupled Doric columns serves as an entrance porch on an otherwise Early-English-Renaissance front. But it would seem that it was on the garden front at Homewood in 1901 that, for the first time on the exterior of a building, he used classical pilasters to the full height of the façade. This was his firmest step away from Webb who, although he introduced classical mouldings to cornices and fireplaces, would, as a good pupil of Street and the Gothic Revival, never have allowed the hated Orders, and would certainly never have used the non-functionally in the form of pilasters. The pilasters at Homewood are an indication of how fast and how far Lutyens had moved in seven years.

As nearly a child prodigy as architecture is ever likely to see, in those seven years before he married Lady Emily Lytton at the age of 28, Lutyens had built a series of houses that are the grand epitome of the middle-class home, and by the time that he was 33 all the houses on which his reputation really rests were complete: Munstead Wood was built when he was 27; Fulbrook, 28; Orchards, 29; Tigbourne Court 30; Grey Walls, Gullane, 31; Deanery Garden, Marshcourt, Homewood and Folly Farm, 32; and Little Thakeham, 33. These houses, in spite of a noticeable move towards classicism, are still well within the Webb–Morris tradition, a tradition that grew from the Gothic Revival and its violent, not to say hysterical, rejection of classicism in general and the Orders in particular.

Homewood[29] which, significantly, he built for his mother-in-law, the wife of the somewhat hysterical Viceroy of India, Lord Lytton, [30] shows, as we have seen, the first distinct movement away from this tradition, though in some ways it still shows Webb's influence clearly. The similarities to Joldwynds near Dorking (1873) are very great, particularly in the entrance front, where Lutyens's weather-boarded gables (three and two at right angles) echo Webb's six tile-hung gables, as does the odd position of the tall chimney near the bottom of the valley between the two sets of gables. Lutyens's chimneys are very typically Webb – see for example Webb's neighbouring New Place, Welwyn (1878–80).

But the differences should be noticed; in Webb's two houses of the 1870s, there are, surprisingly, sash windows, but Lutyens in 1900 was still using mullions and leaded lights. Lutyens, always more interested in architectural form than details, designed a much more complex series of gables with the end roofs sweeping down much further than the middle valley and with the south-west gables placed just asymmetrically over the ground-floor windows. Thus he created much more tension than Webb had in his Joldwynds façade, which is much blander than one would expect from the architect of No. 1 Palace Green and Clouds.

The tension is further increased at Homewood by the way none of the elevations at first sight seems to bear any relation to any other; it is almost as if each had been designed independently (each is on a different centre-line) and then absent-mindedly rammed together to fit where they would. Each elevation extends backwards, as it were, until it meets its neighbour in a complex clash of hips somewhere near the centre of the house. In a sense this is precisely what is

112

111

110

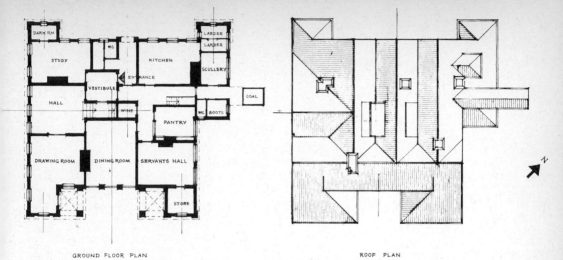

GROUND FLOOR PLAN   ROOF PLAN

111–113 *(Left)* PHILIP WEBB. *Joldwynds, near Dorking;* LUTYENS. *Homewood, Knebworth;* ROBERT VAN T'HOFF. *Huis ter Heide, near Utrecht, a house showing the influence of Lutyens' Homewood*
114 *(Above)* LUTYENS. *Homewood. Plans at ground-floor and roof levels*

happening, only in reverse – for Lutyens sees each façade in three-dimensional terms, and thus sees all its implications projected backwards. This complex interlocking of roof shapes is something that he always enjoyed, the Pleasaunce at Overstrand (1897–99) being perhaps the most extreme example. The whole of Homewood is a virtuoso display by an expert in three-dimensional form, who has learnt all there is to know about handling chimneys, roofs and gables – a technique developed from Nash's villas, through Butterfield and Street parsonages and Norman Shaw's mansions to culminate in the early Lutyens houses. Something more than romanticism is now in the air, however. In this house, both in the elevations and the plans, Lutyens is trying to combine all the expertise of the three-dimensional designing of High Romanticism with the compact shape of the ordinary Georgian house; this is the first time that he ventured on anything quite so complex. It doesn't quite work; it is all too contrived, it should not have been attempted in such a small house; it is far more suitable for the abstract architecture of the War Memorials – the high geometry twenty years ahead.

On entering Homewood we find the same clash between romanticism on the one hand and compactness and symmetry on the other. In Lutyens's earlier houses most of the plans are based on the Tudor scheme, with rooms and wings spreading out from a wide entrance passage. This has the great advantage, when handled by a master, of creating complex vistas and areas of light and dark in the corridors. Philip Webb, on the other hand, usually planned in a more traditional Victorian manner, with the main part of the house compactly round a great central hall, and then allowed the one-storey service wing to stretch out in a tail. Both at Munstead[31] and at Deanery Garden,[32] although Lutyens used a courtyard plan, he planned long wide corridors to run through the whole house, taking light from either side; that at Deanery Garden leads from the front door through the whole house to end magnificently on the terrace. At Homewood, with its compact plan, there are no through vistas. The entrance in the centre of the north front is not on the main centre-line of the house, just as the centre of the west front stands in no relationship to the rest of the plan. Having set himself these problems Lutyens once again puts on a splendid virtuoso display; he devises what must surely be the most convoluted circulation scheme ever forced into such a tight space to resolve what are, after all, the quite simple plan requirements of a small suburban house. But this

114

means that he is able to retain all the complicated spaces and lighting of his more romantic houses and give the impression of a much larger house, though he wastes a great deal of space in the process.

The entrance, which with its rusticated trim looks at first sight like a normal front-door-case, is in fact a void which gives on to an open passage right to the centre of the house, ending at two glazed doors – one to the front and one to the right. It is the right-hand door which is the front door proper and this leads into a square vestibule with four doors, lit very subtly through a pair of octagonal windows which borrow light from the lantern above the staircase – a very typical Victorian trick. This vestibule is crossed diagonally to enter the main hall, a formal and beautiful room with three windows facing south-west. To the left are the double doors to the drawing room. Behind are two grand door-cases, symmetrically placed with an arch between, through which rises the wide staircase (lit by the roof lantern over), climbing nobly through the spine of the house at right angles to the main entrance. Each space along this route is different, and we have, without noticing it, been brought right to the centre of the house and turned 180 degrees in the process; no Hall of Mirrors is designed more subtly!

As we have seen, the gables on the north and west elevations sweep down to no more than seven feet from the ground, but on the southern garden front the low gables disappear and the roof is cut to reveal the Ionic pilasters which one almost feels have been lurking behind the Tudor gables of so many of Lutyens's earlier houses. Even now he seems not quite sure of the propriety, good Arts and Crafts man that he still is, of using pilasters conventionally; so, as if with a note of apology, he adds half-way up each pilaster a Jacobean lozenge.

Within five years of the still very traditional Homewood, Lutyens declared himself unequivocally in the Mannerist Baroque of Heathcote, but this turned out to be as much a stylistic dead end for Lutyens as did the Art Nouveau of Varengeville, and he soon returned to Philip Webb, the Webb of Standen (1891)[33] and Smeaton (1877)[34] which were designed in a completely indigenous red brick classicism with tall chimneys, hipped roofs and sash windows. It was this style of Webb and not the Arts and Crafts fun and games of Lutyens's earlier architecture which through Lutyens was to have such an influence on the younger generation of school-trained architects.

This style, when used on houses of reasonable size, could produce a building that anyone who was, or wished to be, a gentleman would be happy to live in. It soon became known – as much after the reigning monarch as after his Hanoverian predecessors – as Neo-Georgian. From its beginning it was quickly accepted as the perfect English compromise between the extremes of Gothic Revival Arts and Crafts on the one hand, and academic classicism on the other. It seems particularly to have appealed to the first generation of architects who were trained in the Orders at the new schools of architecture, but had been taught to see by reading Ruskin and his followers. The style lasted for approximately fifty years, and can be seen as one of the more civilized contributions to an architectural debate which at that time was bedevilled by much doctrinaire talk and little good design. Expanded over the great flanks of twentieth-century office buildings or blocks of flats, Neo-Georgianism, relying so much on small variations of proportion, lost its inspiration, and inevitably gave way to the onslaught of the equally boring, but considerably cheaper 'Modern' style of the early 1950s.

In point of fact Lutyens used the full-blown Neo-Georgian style on comparatively few of his buildings. Butler's list shows that only about one third of the major buildings are in this style, but none the less he can be blamed in many ways for the misuse of the style. During the 1920s and 30s he was consultant architect to the Westminster estate, and in a mad attempt to make enough money to keep his wife and family in the manner to which he believed that they should have been accustomed, he spread his Neo-Georgian façades – often masking other architects' frames – all over the rebuilt acres of Mayfair. Park Lane is not a happy monument to a very great architect. Some of his banks of this period, in a kind of Neo-Edwardian-Baroque without the curves, are often surprisingly good, although completely anti-functional, with such things as *piano nobile* windows divided horizontally to fit in two floors of offices.

It is important to differentiate between Neo-Georgian, essentially an architecture growing from the Arts and Crafts Movement – even the Hall of the Art Workers Guild (1914) by F. W. Troup (1859–1941) is Neo-Georgian – and Neo-Classicism, a foreign style which only came to this country when the schools of architecture began to take over from the architects' offices as the main training grounds for architects (just as it was the schools who were later to force Modern architecture on to their students).

Whilst Neo-Classical and Edwardian Baroque were completely separate styles, Neo-Georgian and Neo-Tudor had by the 1920s merged, a fact that would have delighted William Morris.[35] The real divide was between the Neo-Classicist Modernists on the one side and the Neo-Georgian Arts and Crafts designers on the other, and in this matter, *pace* Hussey and Butler, Lutyens and most English architects even after 1920 still stood firmly with the Arts and Crafts Movement.

Neo-Georgian architecture is not easy to write about – there are no obvious masterpieces. The best buildings in the style are good for the very reason that they are not noticeable, that they politely blend with their neighbours. It is an architecture most suited to medium-sized houses, banks and pubs, and it was those practices which specialized in this type of work, never those to be much noticed, which designed most in this style. This essay does not pretend to be a history of Neo-Georgian architecture, but mention must be made of Crabbet Park of 1873, designed in a completely Neo-Georgian style it is said by its owner, Wilfrid Scawen Blunt, or possibly his wife Lady Anne Blunt[36] (Blunt was a cousin of Percy Wyndham, the builder of Clouds). Crabbet however seems to be more a case of very sophisticated survival than the herald of a new style, though both Lutyens and Detmar Blow married wives who were distantly related to Blunt, and both may well have known the house.

Ernest Newton (1856–1922)[37] twelve years older than Lutyens, was an early practitioner in the style. He joined Norman Shaw in 1873, working on Flete, and started practice on his own in 1879. In Shaw's office at this time were many of the younger leaders of the Arts and Crafts Movement, such as E. S. Prior (1852–1932), Mervyn Macartney (1852–1931) and E. J. May (1853–1941), and they together formed the St George's Art Society (named after Hawksmoor's St George's, Bloomsbury!), which later became the Art Workers Guild. Newton's practice started slowly, and only in 1889, with Buller's Wood, Chislehurst, did he really begin to be important. However, with its heavily dentilled cornice over leaded windows, this house already shows strong Neo-Georgian tendencies, though obviously, like much work by Macartney and May, derived from their master's 170 Queens Gate, built in 1888.

In the 1890s, whilst Lutyens was designing with wild imaginative romance, Newton was building a series of wonderfully restrained houses, well, and more or less symmetrically, planned, using sash windows, tall chimneys, curved bays with decorative lead work and excellent workmanship carried through to completion by his great assistant W. R. Lethaby (1857–1931). Redcourt, Haslemere (1894), is a typical example of this style. Ian Nairn in *The Buildings of England: Surrey* considers

115   ERNEST NEWTON. *Redcourt, Haslemere*

the house[38] to be an ominous precursor of Lutyens, particularly as it was built four years before the classical front to Crooksbury. There is however nothing ominous about it; it is merely the natural progression from romanticism to a more restrained style, by a master of the Arts and Crafts Movement.

In 1898 Newton designed a row of shops in the High Street of Bromley including both an inn and a bank,[39] and these buildings were to have a profound effect on the future. The bank, recently scandalously mutilated, is very simple, with two lead-faced bow windows rising to curved-headed dormer windows; below are two doors between windows with stone mullions. There is nothing specifically classical or Georgian here – the windows are in fact leaded – but it has in its calculated reticence and balance all the qualities that were coming to be admired in Georgian street architecture, and showed clearly how this could be achieved again. The inn next door, for which Newton supplied only the exterior elevations, is more obviously Neo-Georgian and more assertive, with its heavily dentilled cornice, sash windows and alternating bays. The pargetted strapwork panels on the bays are not on Newton's original drawing and may have been added later by the owner. However, Newton throughout his career was as willing to design in the Tudor or Elizabethan style as the Georgian. The Memorial Hall of Uppingham School in 1921,[40] his last work, is firmly Neo-Elizabethan in the manner of Kirby. There is in his career no sense of progression from one style to another; thus he is quintessentially the architect's, rather than the architectural historian's, architect. Every building seems to have been designed with a specific client in mind; there is no forcing to achieve effect either in the plan or the elevation, something that can never be said of Lutyens.

Of the other architects of Lutyens's generation, it was Arts and Crafts architects like C. H. B. Quennell (1872–1935) and Guy Dawber (1861–1938) who turned to Neo-Georgian, but once again they treated it as a style that was interchangeable with Tudor. Hampstead Garden Suburb, with Lutyens's excellent Neo-Georgian terraces (1908–10), is as fine an example of the style as any. Even Parker and Unwin forsook Arts and Crafts free-Tudor for Neo-Georgian in Hampstead.

At this time the London County Council's Architect's Department, much influenced as it was by Lethaby,[41] also took up the style and in many housing estates and fire stations displayed an excellent architectural sense. Typical of the earlier Neo-Georgian estates are the Old Oak Estate, in Hammersmith (1912), showing strong Lutyens influence, and the Webber Row Estate (1906), with its fine hand-made iron work. The LCC continued to design in a Neo-Georgian style until the 1950s. Some estates are very good, but slowly the detailing and forms become more and more standardized and the Arts and Crafts influence dies away, leaving little else of interest.

During the 1920s and 30s, reflecting the move to prohibition which had been general on both sides of the Atlantic, pubs were being forced by the magistrates to undergo considerable changes.[42] It was to the Neo-Georgian style that the brewers turned, influenced very probably by the romantic fantasies of Cecil Aldin (1870–1935). In an important series of coloured lithographs of the 1890s, Aldin drew eighteenth-century taverns populated by country squires and rosy-cheeked wenches, which made a considerable contrast to the supposed licentiousness in both morals and design of the Victorian Gin Palace. The influence of the children's book illustrators on the various designers of the early twentieth century is a matter that is deserving of serious study. Certainly Lutyens admitted to having been influenced by the work of Randolph Caldicott, and this is obvious in some of his early farmhouse designs. Alas his only essay in this pub style was the very late and disastrously out-of-scale whimsy of the Drum Inn at Cockington, Devon (1934).[43] The cynicism displayed in this thatched piece shows how bored Lutyens had become by this time with anything but the most personal displays of abstract form.

Fortunately for him and for his reputation, it was the commission for such War Memorials as the most subtle Cenotaph[44] and the Thiepval Memorial Arch which saved his reputation as a serious architect. But with these designs he turned his back completely on Webb-inspired Arts and Crafts Neo-Georgian and returned to an even earlier influence, that of High Victorian Gothic. This can be particularly seen in the Thiepval Memorial Arch (1924).[45] The purpose of this, the largest War   116
Memorial, was to record the names of the 73,357 missing of the Somme battles of July 1915 and March 1918; the main brief was the rather macabre one of finding enough flat surfaces to carve all the 73,357 names. It was because of this that   119
Lutyens hit on his idea of a fully three-dimensional triumphal arch. The triumphal arch had, of course, been devised by the Romans as basically two-dimensional, the beginning and end of a tunnel pressed together, the sides signifying very little. A two-dimensional arch that can be viewed from all sides is always absurd and for Lutyens with his three-dimensional imagination such a design could never be satisfactory. In New Delhi[46] he tried to create a three-dimensional form by surmounting his arch with a flat saucer dome, a solution both absurd and unsuccessful. At Thiepval, however, he went for something more complex.

Taking the standard tripartite Roman arch made up of a large opening and two related lower openings he arranged to interlock a similar but smaller arch at right angles to it. He did this in such a way that the entablature above the keystone of the central arch of the smaller set of arches is at the spring of the larger arch at right angles to it, but this smaller central arch relates back again to the side arches on the main front, and not to the related lower arches on the same front. Each arch relates to an arch on the plane at right angles to it. Thus the proportions of the arches are related never directly but by reference to a second set piercing them at right angles. Once again as at Homewood the elevations are projected backwards into each other to create an elaborate architectural form, but here with much more subtlety and mathematical elegance. The attic over is dispensed with, and the whole area over the arches has been cut back to reveal a sculptured tower; as each plane of the wall is removed it seems to expose more elaborate forms and even carving beneath.[47] Most buildings from outside seem to impinge on space and from the inside to enclose space, but at Thiepval, because of the relationship of the arches in

116 LUTYENS. *Memorial to the missing on the Somme, Thiepval*

three dimensions, space seems to flow through and around the building with a special rhythm which is given further *rubato* by the relationship of the wall planes, sometimes setting back on one elevation, sometimes on the other, but rarely on both elevations at the same time – a trick incidentally also used by Lutyens to great effect on the Cenotaph.

The result is that the mind has difficulty in deciding exactly what type of building Thiepval really is. The triumphal arch becomes a memorial cenotaph in one view, in another it is a solid memorial tower, its base pierced by arches in all directions. In fact it is all these forms, all interlocked in one building. For the first time in two thousand years an architect has found something new to do with a triumphal arch, and he was in a position to do this because he was brought up within the tradition of the Gothic Revival with a Gothic Revival sense of form. For instance in the spire of G. E. Street's St Mary at Wheatley (1856) we find, if we ignore the style of the two buildings, considerable similarities with Thiepval, though Street's is of course a much less complex design, but the treatment of the wall planes is very similar. At the bottom of the spire the plane of the east wall of the spire runs up straight, whereas that on the south wall drops back; note the flat areas of masonry and the way that the elevations are projected back into each other. The openings are punched straight through the wall without mouldings, and any

117

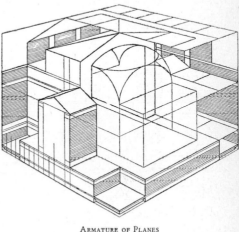

ARMATURE OF PLANES

117   G. E. STREET. *Spire of St Mary, Wheatley*
118   *Diagram to illustrate the 'Armature of Planes', drawn by Robert Lutyens*

decoration is carved out from inside the form. Such similarities with Lutyens's work, which can be found also in many other Victorian buildings of the period, might perhaps be seen as coincidental were it not for the fact that whilst he was designing the Thiepval arch, Lutyens was also working on something that he called the 'Armature of Planes'. This was an attempt to arrive at a three-dimensional proportioning system. Robert Lutyens describes his father's style thus:

A building is made up of solids and voids, all of which have definite shapes and are   118
geometrically related . . . To state this relationship it is first of all necessary to visualise space . . . as divided along three series of planes, mutually at right angles, into a number of cubical compartments or cells. One series of the planes is horizontal . . . each plane extending over the whole area. The two other series of planes are vertical, at right angles to one another, and should also be visualised as extending to the limits of the future building.
   This visualisation of a space divided in all directions becomes an 'armature of planes', or foundation of three-dimensional relationships. It should be thought of not as a grid or frame of three intersecting sets of lines or arrises, but as almost invisible 'lines of cleavage', the whole being like a glass cube made up of smaller glass cubes.[48]

The 'Armature of Planes' was an idea that could not have been conceived on the drawing board; it is in fact a system that thinks in terms of form rather than two-dimensional shapes. It is entirely concerned with wall planes in three dimensions, the three-dimensional consequences of projecting façades backwards, and thus brings us, and Lutyens, back almost a century to the architecture of the 1850s, the architecture of Philip Webb's master, G. E. Street. It was therefore inevitable that the people who rejected Victorian architecture should also reject Lutyens; it was not his classicism that they hated but his Victorianism. Although they in theory rejected classical architecture, most of the early practitioners in the style were classicists. As long as the orders as such were rejected the rest of the design could remain entirely classical in conception and detail – indeed the Georgian house became the *beau idéal*. Such classicists as Otto Wagner and Charles Holden were hailed as early masters of the Modern Movement, but the true followers of Williams Morris, and the Arts and Crafts Movement, were made objects of derision. This, alas, is something that still continues to this day. It is only when it becomes generally accepted that the principles of William Morris were not those of the Modern Movement that English architecture will be able to hold up its head again.

When Lutyens designed brilliantly without using the Orders, as at Thiepval, the Moderns still hated him. It was of course inevitable that they should do this but a pity; for here was a man who combined all that was best in a hundred years of magnificent architecture. Pugin began work in the 1830s; Lutyens's career came to an end in 1939. Between those years lies the greatest period of English architecture.

119 LUTYENS. *Detail of the Thiepval Arch, showing the two smallest sizes of arch, and panels with the names of the missing*

Acknowledgments and Notes on the text

I William Burn

This chapter was first written in 1969 and completely rewritten in 1970, minor amendments being made over the following five years as further information came to hand. At that time it was the first serious study of Burn's career since that by T. Harold Hughes published in 1925, and for the convenience of other scholars a typescript of the original 1969 version was lodged in the National Monuments Record of Scotland library pending publication, which has however taken six years to come to fruition. In the interval Dr James Macaulay has published 'William Burn and the Country House' as Chapter XVII of his *Gothic Revival 1745–1845* (Edinburgh 1975). The conclusions he has reached and the comparisons he has made are generally similar to those expressed here, although lay-out and treatment are different, fewer houses being discussed in greater detail with some interesting quotations which illustrate Burn's dealings with his clients. Although in some degree overtaken by the Macaulay volume, my original account of his career together with a list of his principal buildings still seemed worth publishing as a more complete picture of his work and development. The reader may take it that at the two main points where the two books differ on matters of fact, viz the location of Brownlow Hall at Lurgan and the authorship of the porte-cochère at Auchterarder, the information given here is correct. Belmont, a Playfair house referred to by Dr Macaulay, is not included in my chapter as it is in fact the Italianate house at Corstorphine, Edinburgh and not the Perthshire castle, which was built before 1793 and reconstructed with its present Falkland profile by James Thomson in 1885.

At the time the chapter was written little work had been done on Burn and I required a great deal of help. To Dr J. Mordaunt Crook I owe a particular debt for information on the all-important Jacobean houses by Smirke, and to Dr A. J. Rowan for help with Burn's Irish houses, and the early Jacobean revival work of Rickman and Lugar. Sir Nikolaus Pevsner, Mr Colin McWilliam and Mr Nicholas Taylor all read the script and helped greatly with information and advice. To Miss C. H. Cruft of the Scottish National Monuments Record, to Mr John Harris of the RIBA library and to the staff of the National Monuments Record in London, I owe an immense debt for help with photographs and Burn's original drawings. Mr Howard Colvin kindly pooled his knowledge of Burn with mine and saved me from serious error. The Earl of Haddingon, Lord Lovat, Mrs Jill Allibone, Mr A. S. Bell, Mr H. K. Cox, Mrs Enid Gauldie, Dr A. H. Gomme, Mr G. L. M. Goodfellow, Mr Felix Hull, the late A. G. Lochhead and Miss A. M. Pilkington have all helped with more specific queries; without their help the essay would have been much less accurate than it is. Mr John Dunbar of the Royal Commission on Ancient and Historical Monuments in Scotland kindly allowed me to see their then unpublished research on Gallanach. Mr David Crichton of Dundee Public Library and Mr William Davidson of Perth Museum have both helped greatly with old photographs of lost houses; and to the many owners or custodians who have, at one time or another, shown me over their houses, my most grateful thanks.

The reader should also be referred to John Cornforth's articles on Bowhill (*Country Life*, 5/26 June 1975) which give a most excellent account of how Burn secured and retained the patronage of his great client the 5th Duke of Buccleuch despite the lifelong hostility of his duchess.

1 See *Transactions of the RIBA*, 1866/67, and Dr J. Mordaunt Crook in *Country Life*, 13 April 1967.

2 See list of works, mainly extracted from following sources: T. L. Donaldson's Memoir, *Transactions of the RIBA*, 1870; plans at RIBA, or dispersed to County Record Offices, private owners and Scottish National Monuments Record; Schinkel Diaries (Carl Friederich Schinkel, *Aus Schinkels Nachlass*, Berlin 1862–63); Saltoun muniments, National Library; Dundas muniments; Balnamoon muniments; Charleton muniments; Gallanach muniments; Seggieden muniments (Killiecrankie); Arthurstone muniments; Lamport muniments; Carfrae of Bourhouse muniments, Forbes-Sempill muniments and Heritors' records, Scottish Record Office; and Small's *Castles and Mansions of the Lothians*, Edinburgh, 1883. The only biography of Burn other than Donaldson's is that by T. H. Hughes in the *Royal Incorporation of Architects in Scotland Quarterly*, 1925, but useful notices of individual houses will be found in Sir Nikolaus Pevsner's *Buildings of England* series.

3 Scottish Record Office G D 35/196, 1837.

4 National Library, Saltoun Muniments.

5 A. J. Rowan in *Country Life*, 19/26 April 1973. Part of the old house was retained in the service court. It is of interest that Gillespie Graham who had hitherto dominated the country house field had been consulted earlier. 'Mr Gillespie there is nothing he would hesitate about,' observed Burn to Cockerell in 1824 (National Monument

correspondence, National Library), but he nevertheless would have left more of the old house.

6 These houses, and the Elizabethan and Jacobean revival generally are well dealt with in Sir Nikolaus Pevsner's 'Good King James's Gothic' (revised in *Studies in Art, Architecture and Design* I, London, 1968, pp. 18–37) and Mark Girouard's 'Elizabethan Retrospects' in *Concerning Architecture* (ed. Sir John Summerson) London, 1968, which should be read as general background to Burn's Jacobean revival. Repton's design for Great Tew is illustrated by Dorothy Stroud in *Humphry Repton,* London, 1962, p. 116. A few isolated mid-eighteenth-century instances of Jacobean gables can be found; e.g. Ecton, Northants (1756) and King John's Lodge, Odiham, Hants.

7 See Mark Girouard in *Country Life,* 17 and 24 February 1966.

8 He returned to Neo-Tudor in later years however, e.g. at Taplow, Bucks (1855).

9 I am much indebted to Dr J. Mordaunt Crook for these details. It is to be hoped he will soon publish a study of these obscure houses by Smirke as they were an important influence on the revival of Jacobean.

10 Illustrated in Sir John Stirling Maxwell *Shrines and Homes of Scotland,* London 1937, pl. 103. The building accounts (1828–32) are in the Scottish Record Office. Pugin designed the unexecuted interiors (see Phoebe Stanton, *Pugin,* London, 1972, p. 195). It is of interest that the drawing room was to be 'Louis XIV'.

11 Burn seems not to have actually seen Abbotsford until 1831. The event is recorded in Scott's journal, 5 May 1831: 'Mr Burn the architect came in, struck by the appearance of my house from the road. He approved my architecture greatly.' It seems to have been through Scott's influence that Burn took the Drumlanrig commission from Atkinson (Scott correspondence, National Library).

12 Figures based on Ochtertyre. True prices are difficult to obtain because of the use of estate labour and material, but a house such as Dupplin must have cost about £40,000. Falkland is said to have eventually cost £30,000, although the original estimate was for £18,000. The contract for Stoke Rochford was £60,000.

13 Original plans for all these Playfair buildings preserved in Edinburgh University Library.

14 National Library, Rutherford correspondence, per A. S. Bell.

15 Notes on 1855 pre-demolition survey plans at Arthurstone. The wing was re-erected in edited form as Cardean House, 1855–56, now also demolished. Whether built for James Munro MacNabb or for Patrick Murray as tenant is unclear. Murray bought the property in 1838. Burn designed a new house at Meigle for Murray in 1834 but only an addition was executed. (Sketch plans at RIBA.)

16 See Christopher Hussey, *English Country Houses, Late Georgian,* London, 1958, and Sir Nikolaus Pevsner and John Harris, *Buildings of England: Lincolnshire,* London, 1964, which also gives further particulars of Belvoir, Stoke Rochford, Rauceby and Revesby to which the writer is indebted. George Meikle Kemp (1795–1844), of Scott Monument fame, was in the office from the early 1830s, and doubtless assisted in the spectacular detailing of these houses. Contemporaries regarded Burn as a 'fast friend' to that unfortunate artist, but for Kemp's own view see Thomas Bonnar, *Biographical Sketch of George Meikle Kemp,* Edinburgh, 1892.

17 Why dressing and sitting rooms for Mr Ramsay were not provided is not known, but it is interesting to note that Burn provided two servants' rooms in the appropriate position so that the omission could easily be remedied later.

18 The preliminary plans for Stoke Rochford (1839) are illustrated by T. H. Hughes in the *Royal Incorporation of Architects in Scotland Quarterly,* No. 16, 1925.

19 For Prestwold see *Country Life,* 16/23 April 1959, and Mark Girouard, *The Victorian Country House,* London, 1971, pp. 71–72; for Raby see *Country Life,* 22 January 1970.

20 *Builder,* 27 May 1876.

21 In 1839–41 Burn had five churches, the immense Morningside Asylum, and the North British Assurance Building at Edinburgh on hand in addition to his country house commitments. After he moved to London he refused virtually all public commissions except for Glasgow Post Office (1855, demolished).

22 National Library, Blackwood correspondence.

23 With Invermark (Glenesk) these are the correct versions of Henry-Russell Hitchcock's 'Gaelic litany of place names' (quoted as misspelt by the *Builder*) in *Early Victorian Architecture in Britain,* London, 1954. The *DNB* is also somewhat inaccurate on Bryce; the dates of election to the Royal Scottish Academy should be 1851 and 1856.

24 Illustrated in Henry-Russell Hitchcock, *op. cit.,* VIII 31, with main front of 1849 scheme, VIII 30.

25 Illustrated in Henry-Russell Hitchcock, *op. cit.,* VIII 29, with plan as executed. Robert Kerr published this plan (with detail variations) as 'Modern Scotch Example' in *The Gentleman's House,* London, in 1864. Burn memorialized the Council of the RIBA on the subject in the following year as Kerr did not have consent to study his plans; Burn had had a similar experience in 1823 when the Nicholsons pirated his Carstairs design in their *New Practical Builder,* London, 1823–25. The patronizing impudence of Kerr's book must have irritated Burn even more, for although he found himself described as 'that great master of our subject' he also found that the merits of his school made 'but modest pretensions to be of artistic order', and criticism of the lack of a vestibule cloakroom

and of his internal courts and corridors, the implication being that Kerr's plans would be both artistic and faultless. It may well have influenced John Walter into switching from Burn to Kerr for Bearwood, where all the supposed deficiencies of Burn's plans were remedied. It does not have the much admired private wing, however, but a first-floor suite with private boudoir stair to the principal rooms. Walter found Kerr did not have Burn's personal qualities also, however: see Mark Girouard in *Country Life*, 17 and 24 October 1968.

II Philip and Philip Charles Hardwick

Even for such a brief article, it has been necessary to trouble a number of people with requests for information or for permission to see their houses. I am most grateful to Earl Beauchamp for showing me Madresfield Court, to Earl Spencer for allowing me to use the Althorp records of the Hardwicks' work at Althorp and Spencer House, and to the Duke of Wellington for lending me some Hardwick correspondence. I am indebted to the archivists and librarians and the governing bodies of the following institutions for whom the Hardwicks worked: the Goldsmiths' Company, the Honourable Society of Lincoln's Inn, St Bartholomew's Hospital, the Bethlehem Royal Hospital, Charterhouse School. Mr & Mrs Charles Chichester took great trouble to show me Hall, Mr Anthony Quick was kind enough to show me round Rendcomb College, of which he is headmaster, and Mr R. H. V. Cooke of Cleaver-Hume Ltd was most helpful over Aldermaston Court, as was the Secretary of the City of London Club in letting me see the Club premises.

Finally, I must thank Mr Mark Rittner and Mr Arthur Lyons, both Hardwick descendants, who were extremely kind and helpful and provided me with information and also allowed me to make use of family records.

1 Professor H.-R. Hitchcock, *Early Victorian Architecture in Britain*, London, 1954.
2 H. M. Colvin, *A Biographical Dictionary of English Architects (1660–1840)*, London, 1954. Information from descendants of the Hardwick family. There are sketchbooks at the RIBA and in the possession of descendants.
3 See archives of Goldsmiths' Company, St Bartholomew's Hospital, Royal Bethlehem Hospital. There are plans and elevations among Bethlehem records.
4 Though Telford prepared the plan of 1824, both he and Hardwick signed that of 1827, showing the intended docks and warehouses (list at Guildhall Record Office). Unfortunately, both these plans seem to have disappeared from the archives of the Port of London Authority.
5 See his letter to his father from Paris, 5 September 1815: 'I soon found that my attention should be entirely directed to the Works in

Iron as they are many many years before us in this branch of building.'
6 Three of his warehouses survive in an altered or partially demolished form, now warehouses A, B and C.
7 Goldsmiths' Company, *Court Minutes*, Vol. 32, fo. 413. He resigned on 29 January 1868.
8 Of *brocatelle* or *verde antica*.
9 See note for carver among drawings, instructing him to copy Mars Ultor.
10 *Civil Engineer and Architect's Journal*, 1837, p. 221.
11 I am indebted to the Secretary for permission to see over the Club.
12 'Resolved that the new Building over the Principal Entrance be appropriated to the residence for the house surgeons, and the same to be completed forthwith with stoves etc . . .' See *Journals*, 1826–41, 8 July 1834, fo. 280. 'The principal entrance from Smithfield . . . is by a handsome gateway lately erected.' See report of Charity Commissioners, Vol. 32, Pt 6, 1840, p. 63.
13 His initials are on the gable end of Lincoln's Inn, and his name was also on Euston Station. His son's name is on a plaque at Hall, near Barnstaple.
14 I am indebted to the late Duke of Wellington, and his archivist, Mr Francis Needham, for this information. P. C. Hardwick built a riding school for the second Duke in Knightsbridge in 1856–61.
15 Philip Hardwick's drawings for clients and his polished perspectives are presented in pen or pencil and sepia wash.
16 Contract drawings among Goldsmiths' Company Records.
17 See his sketchbooks at the RIBA.
18 Memorial from Builders, 7 March 1833; Goldsmiths' Company Records, *Committee Minutes*, 1833–37: The contract sum was £3,470 (tenders received 1 July 1830). Hardwick felt the builder had a case in equity if not in law.
19 Colvin's *Dictionary*. The present owner tells me that no correspondence or plans of the building are available. According to N. Pevsner, *Buildings of England: Cambridgeshire*, London, 1970, p. 229, it was further enlarged in 1864.
20 *The Victoria County History of Worcestershire*, Vol. III, p. 234–36. The house has now been divided into flats so the extent of Philip Hardwick's work is difficult to judge.
21 See sketchbooks at RIBA.
22 John White (d. 1850), District Surveyor for St Marylebone, who worked with his father on the Duke of Portland's Marylebone Estate. *Lincoln's Inn Records: Printed Black Book*, Vol. IV, 6 March 1839, p. 200 *et seq*.
23 *MSS. Black Book*, Vol XXIII, pp. 278–80.
24 Hardwick was instructed to prepare sketches and plans on 24 April 1839. *MSS. Black Book*, Vol. XXIII, p. 281.
25 *MSS. Black Book*, Vol. XXIV, pp. 22–23. Stone Building is now thought to be designed

by Brettingham and Paine, and merely supervised by Taylor. *Black Book*, Vol. IV, p. 5.

26 MSS. *Black Book*, Vol. XXIV. p. 164.

27 MSS. *Black Book*, Vol. XXIV, pp. 164–69. Report presented at a Special Council, 16 July 1842.

28 E.g. *Builder*, 14 January 1871, p. 24.

29 See bound volumes of drawings and plans at Lincoln's Inn.

30 J. L. Pearson wrote seventy years later, when both Hardwicks were dead, to claim much of the credit for the building. *RIBA Journal*, 5 May 1892. *Proceedings of the RIBA*, 1892, New Series 8, pp. 191–92. 'I was to assist in preparation of the drawings for this building for the surveyors ... and a hard time I had of it ... All the working drawings were either made by me or they passed through my hands, and I superintended almost daily the building until it was all covered in,'

31 *Builder*, 1 November 1845, p. 522.

32 He kept on his appointment at St Bartholomew's until 1856, and with the Goldsmiths' Company till 1868; he was attending meetings of the Merchant Taylors' Company in 1854 (Merchant Taylors Est. Com. Mins. 1845–55, fo. 253).

33 Professor H.-R Hitchcock *op. cit.*, Vol. I, p. 211.

34 Drawing exhibited at the RA by Philip Hardwick in 1844, probably that at the RIBA in the Drawings Collection (U 14/8).

35 The inscription in the Great Hall reads:
'Philippus C. Hardwick
Londoniensis Architecton'
'R. C. Gould
Operum director et delineator',
but these should be read in conjunction with another inscription in the hall:
'In ligno, pigmento, vitro, metallo et saxo ornamenta et omnia pertinentia ipse fundator eligit et variis usibus accommodari jussit 1847–8–9.'

36 The Euston Arch was, of course, swept away in 1961–62, but the Birmingham Arch lingers on, considerably altered, as the Curzon Street goods station. For a contemporary illustration see *Companion to the Almanack*, 1839, p. 237.

37 *The Civil Engineer and Architect's Journal*, 1837, Ralph Redivivus No. 8, The Railway Entrance, Euston Square, p. 276.

38 *London and Birmingham Hotel Minute Book*, British Transport Historical Records, 25 May 1838 and *passim*.

39 *London and Birmingham* Board minutes No. 1921, 13 May 1842.

40 *London and Birmingham* Board Minutes No. 3204, 2 April 1846. See contract drawings signed by Philip Hardwick and William Cubitt, 25 August 1846, BTHR/LNW/276.

41 There are some two or three hundred drawings in four folders, one of which contains the signed contract drawings of August 1846, mostly altered subsequently, BTHR/LNW/274–7.

42 The Great Hall and Shareholders' Meeting Room were elaborately restored in 1952, but the entire complex was demolished ten years later, including all Thomas's figures. A drawing of the Great Hall was exhibited by P. C. Hardwick at the RA in 1849, probably the drawing at the RIBA (U 14/16).

43 H.-R. Hitchcock, *op. cit.*, Vol. I, p. 212.

44 Uxbridge House, Burlington Gardens, now the Royal Bank of Scotland; see *Survey of London*, Vol. XXXII, Pt II, p. 465. Hull Branch Bank, exhibited at the RA, 1856.

45 *Builder*, 15 October 1864, pp. 758–59.

46 *Builder*, 26 August 1865, p. 609.

47 He was never official surveyor to the Goldsmiths' Company, but he was made a freeman in 1844, and a liveryman in 1848, which indicates an important relationship with the Company.

48 See the staircase illustrated in Joseph Nash, *Mansions of England in the Olden Time*, London, 1839–49, Vol. III.

49 H.-R. Hitchcock, *op. cit.*, Vol I, pp. 234–35.

50 It is attributed to Philip Hardwick in N. Pevsner, *Buildings of England: Hertfordshire*, London, 1963, p. 96, but J. S. Nicholl in the obituary notice of P. C. Hardwick claims it for him. *RIBA Proceedings*, 1892. Drawing at RIBA (W. 14/5).

51 Drawings exhibited at Royal Academy, 1856, probably those now at RIBA (U 14/4 [1–3]).

52 Exhibited RA, 1854. Drawing now at RIBA (U 14/6).

53 *Builder*, 10 June 1865, pp. 412–13.

54 The third Earl Spencer (1782–1845) d. S.P., succeeded by his brother, the fourth Earl (1798–1857). I am indebted to the late Earl for permission to use the Spencer records at Althorp and for help in interpreting them.

55 See correspondence at Althorp: *Spencer House Letters and Bills, 1766–1847, 1848–78*.

56 *Country Life*, 26 May 1960, p. 1188.

57 Correspondence and drawings at Althorp House. Also photographs in 1892 volume.

58 Drawings of Little Brington exhibited at the RA, 1850, now at RIBA (U 14/12). Lodge dated 1852.

59 Hardwick to Lord Spencer, 11 January 1855, 22 January 1855, 9 October 1855. The drawings are at Althorp. Hardwick also designed a curate's house which was not built.

60 Carried out by Mr Hardwick and Mr Morris, according to a contemporary account in the *Builder*, 17 January 1852, p. 39. H.-R. Hitchcock, *Early Victorian Architecture*, Vol. I, p. 330. From the date and the fact that the roof construction was said to resemble that of Euston Great Hall, it could have been P. C. Hardwick's work.

61 Littlecote Hall is included in the list of works supplied by J. S. Nicholl in 1892. It is not clear what exactly he did to the chapel, possibly work to the roof, and probably the pulpit and the

panelling under. He may have done other work to the house, such as the Long Gallery plaster ceiling, reputedly restored in early Victorian times, or the panelling in the Long Gallery.

62 Hardwick restored only the tower as money was short, though he did drawings for the whole building. There are alternative treatments at the RIBA (U 14/25 [1–2]).

63 *Country Life*, 15, 22 and 29 May 1969, pp. 1230–34, 1302–6, 1366–69. I am indebted to John Cornforth for additional information.

64 See Caroline, Countess of Dunraven, *Memorials of Adare Manor*.

65 There is a drawing for this tower at the RIBA, rather curiously labelled 'design for addition of a tower to a 16th century mansion' (U 14/9).

66 *Country Life*, 29 May 1969, p. 1367.

67 See letters and plans at Durham County Record Offices: D/LO/C 195, D/LO P 290:291:292.

68 See drawing at RIBA (U 14/11).

69 A drawing was exhibited at the RA in 1861.

70 *The Victoria County History of Worcestershire*, IV, p. 134. This roof was removed in the 1880s and the internal courtyard remodelled. According to Lord Beauchamp, this work was not carried out by Hardwick.

71 It is quite clear from the sixth Earl's own account, read to the Worcestershire Diocesan Archaeological Society, meeting at Madresfield in 1881, that reconstruction was substituted for repair'. *Assoc. Archit. Soc. Rep.*, XVI, pp. 104–10.

72 A drawing was exhibited at the RA by P. C. Hardwick in 1852, probably that now at the RIBA (U 14/15). The building was demolished in 1933.

73 Exhibited Royal Academy 1852, 'an appropriate design, admirably well set forth'. *Builder*, May 1852, p. 289.

74 Exhibited RA, 1854. Probably RIBA (U 14/13).

75 *Builder*, 8 May 1869, p. 357. There are a number of other references in the *Builder*: 6 July 1870, pp. 566–67, 14 December 1872, p. 987.

76 Nairn in N. Pevsner and I. Nairn, *Buildings of England: Surrey*, London, 1962, p. 121.

III Sydney Smirke

1 Patronage, pupillage and the fragmentation of 'the architectural professions' are all discussed in J. Mordaunt Crook, 'The Pre-Victorian Architect, 1800–37', *Architectural History*, XII, 1969. For a vehement contemporary critique, see J. T. Emmett, *Six Essays*, 1891, ed. J. Mordaunt Crook, London, 1972.

2 A useful biographical note, with a general list of works – invaluable but incomplete – is contained in Wyatt Papworth, *Dictionary of Architecture*, Architectural Publications Society, 1852–92. For obituaries see *Building News*,

XXXIII, 1877, p. 583; *Architect*, XVIII, 1877, p. 327; *British Architect*, VIII, 1877, p. 288–89; *The Times*, 12 December 1877, p. 11; *Builder*, XXXV, 1877, p. 1256; *Illustrated London News*, LXXXI, 1877, p. 605.

3 'Diary of Joseph Farington' (BM typescript), p. 2457, 6 December 1803. 'His designs will sell any book, be it ever so bad' (Southey to Sir George Beaumont, 11 December 1807, *Memorials of Coleorton*, ed. W. Knight, II, 1887, pp. 27–28). He was 'a man of strong likings and dislikings' (*Gentleman's Magazine*, 1845, XXIII, p. 319).

4 *Archaeological Journal*, XXXII, 1875, p. 326

5 *Gentleman's Magazine*, 1803, Pt I, p. 204; 1815, Pt I, p. 477.

6 Farington, *op. cit.*, pp. 1269, 2489, 2658, 2872, 3410, 3605.

7 Farington, *op. cit.*, p. 6944, 17 June 1815, and p. 6680, 3 June 1816; Sir Herbert Baker, *Architecture and Personalities*, 1944, p. 12.

8 J. Mordaunt Crook, 'Architect of the Rectangular: a Reassessment of Sir Robert Smirke', *Country Life*, CXLI, 1967, pp. 846–48; 'Sir Robert Smirke: a Centenary Florilegium', *Architectural Review*, CXLIII, 1967, pp. 208–10; 'Sir Robert Smirke: a Regency Architect in London', *Journal of the London Society*, March 1968, pp. 2–11.

9 Farington, *op. cit.*, p.3775, 9 July 1807, and p. 4440, 12 August 1809.

10 Sydney Smirke's travel sketches and correspondence, RIBA; J. Mordaunt Crook and M. H. Port, *The History of the King's Works, VI, 1782–1851*, London, 1973, pp. 676–77.

11 *Gentleman's Magazine*, 1841, Pt I, p. 91. A son, Sydney Smirke Jr (1838–1912), 'practised for many years in America', according to Arthur Cates (*Transactions of the RIBA*, 1883–84, p. 175).

12 J. Mordaunt Crook, 'Sir Robert Peel: Patron of the Arts', *History Today*, XVI, 1966, pp. 3–11.

13 *Builder*, IX, 1851, p. 547.

14 Illustrated in D. Sutherland, *The Yellow Earl*, 1965, p. 112. For Wellington Pit, Whitehaven, see *Country Life*, CLVIII, 1975, p. 1088.

15 N. Pevsner, *Buildings of England: Leicestershire and Rutland*, London, 1960, p. 317.

16 *Gentleman's Magazine*, 1851, Pt II, pp. 190, 388, 644.

17 *Gentleman's Magazine*, 1842, Pt I, p. 647.

18 G. F. Prosser, *Select Illustrations of Hampshire*, London, 1833.

19 Public Record Office, H. O. 20/4; Parliamentary Papers, 1837–38, XXX (141), p. 213; White's Directory, 1859, p. 602; *Civil Engineer and Architect's Journal*, I, 1837, p. 14; Heather Tomlinson, 'Victorian Prisons: Administration and Architecture, 1835–77' (PhD, London, 1975). Appendix 8.

20 W. Sandby, *History of the RA*, II, London, 1862, p. 318.

21 Will, dated 12 January 1872, at Somerset House.

22   N. Pevsner, 'Early Working Class Housing' in *Studies in Art, Architecture and design*, II, London, 1968, pp. 18–37. See also Sydney Smirke's 'Water Service to the Poor', *Builder*, XVI, 1858, p. 141; 'On Water Supply to Towns', *Transactions of the RIBA*, VIII, 1858, pp. 107–8.

23   They were planned on a smaller scale as early as 1807; see plans and correspondence in Hereford Chapter Records, 3564, 3581; W. W. Capes, *The Hospital of St Katherine at Ledbury*, n.d. Cockerell admired their 'iron gutters [used] as cornice under [the] eaves, carried by small corbels.' See 'Diary of C. R. Cockerell', 18 July 1822.

24   Murray's *Guide*, quoted in *Country Life*, CXXXIX, 1966, p. 728.

25   Goodhart-Rendel card index, RIBA; N. Pevsner and E. Radcliffe, *Buildings of England: Essex*, London, 1965, pp. 383–84.

26   *Ecclesiologist*, I, 1843 ed., p. 210.

27   E.g. 'The origin of the pointed arch', *Archaeologia* XXI, 1826, pp. 521–33; 'A sepulchral monument in the Campo Santo at Pisa', XXIII, 1830, pp. 1–6; 'The mausoleum of Theodoric at Ravenna', *ibid.*, pp. 323–36; 'The palace at Whitehall', XXV, 1833, pp. 113–18; 'The church of St John, Syracuse', *ibid.*, pp. 275–78; 'The palace at Ravenna, reputed to be that of the Gothic King Theodoric', *ibid.*, pp. 579–83; 'The archiepiscopal throne in the conventual church at Assisi', XXVI, 1836, pp. 472–74.

28   Goodhart-Rendel index; *Civil Engineer and Architect's Journal*, IX, 1846, p. 81; P. G. Thompson, *Parish Church of Loughton, Essex*, 1946; N. Pevsner and E. Radcliffe, *Buildings of England: Essex*, London, 1965, pp. 287–88.

29   *Ecclesiologist*, XI, 1850, pp. 198–99. The aisle and clerestory were rebuilt by A. R. Barker, 1880–84.

30   N. Pevsner and I. Nairn, *Buildings of England: Sussex*, London, 1965, p. 573. Sydney Smirke also made alterations to Turner's house – Brickwall, Northiam – later rebuilt by Devey. See *Country Life*, VIII, 1900, pp. 400–407.

31   D. R. Thomas, *History of the Diocese of St Asaph*, London, 1874.

32   N. Pevsner, *Buildings of England: Leicestershire and Rutland*, London, 1960, p. 147. Remodelled by Flint and Wicks in 1855; and by Teulon in 1871.

33   Goodhart-Rendel index; N. Pevsner and D. Lloyd, *Buildings of England: Hampshire*, London, 1967, pp. 79–80. The church cost between £25,000 and £30,000 (White's *Directory*; Kelly's *Directory*) and was altered in 1872–87 by William White.

34   *Yorkshire Gazette*, 1829–31, *passim*; *Gentleman's Magazine*, 1830, Pt I. p. 631; 1830, Pt II, pp. 26, 405; 1831, Pt I, pp. 33, 98, 127, 252; 1832, Pt I, p. 458; and 1833, Pt I, p. 298; *Builder*, III, 1845, p. 158; *Athenaeum*, 1830, p. 298, and 1831, p. 75; *British Almanac and Companion*, 1833, p. 213.

35   *Ecclesiologist*, I, 1843 ed., p. 200; and IV, 1845, pp. 138–39. 190; *Builder*, I, 1843, p. 340; II, 1844, pp. 83, 317; and III, 1845, pp. 158, 202, 295, 306, 394; *Athenaeum*, 1840, pp. 175, 462; and 1844, p. 271; *Gentleman's Magazine*, 1840, Pt I, pp. 643–44; *Civil Engineer and Architect's Journal*, VII, 1844, p. 10; *Illustrated London News*, VI, 1845, pp. 97, 572; *Surveyor, Engineer and Architect*, III, 1842, pp. 155–57; *Illustrated Builder's Journal*, 1865, p. 92; G. W. O. Addleshaw, 'Architects, Sculptors, Painters, Craftsmen, 1660–1960, whose work is to be seen in York Minster', *Architectural History*, X, 1967, pp. 90–119; N. Pevsner, *Buildings of England: Yorkshire, East Riding*, London, 1972, p. 83.

36   J. Mordaunt Crook, 'The Restoration of the Temple Church: Ecclesiology and Recrimination', *Architectural History*, VIII, 1965, pp. 39–51; Sydney Smirke, 'An Account of the Temple Church' in J. Weale (ed.), *Quarterly Papers on Architecture*, ii (1844).

37   *Builder*, XXIV, 1866, pp. 117–19; accounts and correspondence in P.R.O. D.1. 41/79. See also *Building News*, xi, 1864, p. 539 and xxxiv, 1878, p. 76.

38   *Ecclesiologist*, XVIII, 1857, p. 178; *Civil Engineer and Architect's Journal*, XXIII, 1859, pp. 29–30; and XXIV, 1860, p. 4; *Building News*, VI, 1860, p. 684, and XI, 1864, p. 602; *Builder*, XVII, 1859, pp. 414, 796, XVIII, 1860, pp. 44, 584; XX, 1862, p. 168; and XXII, 1864, p. 865; A. Graves, *RA Exhibitors*, VII, 1906, p. 164.

39   N. Pevsner and I. Nairn, *Buildings of England: Surrey*, London, 1962, pp. 444–45. Also the nearby Convalescent Hospital.

40   N. Pevsner and I. Nairn, *Buildings of England: Sussex*, London, 1965, p. 615.

41   Inner Temple records: Bench Table Orders, *passim*; plans and correspondence in the Surveyor's office; *Civil Engineer and Architect's Journal*, 1848, p. 230; W. J. Loftie, *Inns of Court and Chancery*, 1895, p. 123. Sydney Smirke also designed Dr Johnson's Buildings (1857–58).

42   Inner Temple Records, *op. cit.*, illustrated in E. A. P. Hart, *Inner Temple Hall*, 1952. Sir Robert Smirke had rebuilt the original hall in 1816–17, 1827, 1837; Sydney Smirke's reconstruction of 1867–70 was gutted in 1940–41 and completely rebuilt after World War II by Sir H. Worthington and Sir E. Maufe.

43   *Archaeologia*, XXVI, 1836, pp. 406, 415–16; XXVII, 1837, pp. 135–37, p. 139, and L 1860, p. 6; *Gentleman's Magazine*, 1834, Pt II, p. 309; and 1838, Pt I. p. 55; *Literary Gazette*, 1834, p. 660; *Architectural Magazine*, III, 1836, p. 40; *British Almanac and Companion*, 1836, p. 227; J. L. Pearson, *Report on Westminster Hall*, 1884.

44   C. Hussey, 'Lambton Castle, Durham', *Country Life*, CXXXIX, 1966, pp. 664–67, 726–29. See also *Building News*, xi, 1864, p. 433 and xii, 1865, pp. 25–26, 50.

45   *Survey of London*, XXXI–II, 1963, pp. 268–83; *Gentleman's Magazine*, 1834, Pt II, p. 87,

and 1835, Pt I, p. 44.

46 *Builder*, I, 1843, p. 347; *Civil Engineer and Architect's Journal*, VII, 1844, p. 305; *Athenaeum*, 1844, p. 714; *Illustrated London News*, V, 1844, p. 60; R. Colby, 'Shopping off the City Streets', *Country Life*, CXXXVI, 1964, pp. 1346–51. In redeveloping this portion of the Marquess of Exeter's property, Sydney Smirke also designed two buildings in Wellington Street: the *Morning Post* office and Bielefeld's papier mâché works.

47 T. W. Horsfield, *Sussex*, II, Lewes, 1835, p. 212; E. J. Salmon and A. Pilmore, *The Two Shorehams*, Shoreham, 1902, p. 12; W. Ison, *Georgian Buildings of Bristol*, London, 1952, p. 44; H. B. Allsopp, *Historic Architecture of Newcastle upon Tyne*, Newcastle, 1967, p. 50.

48 *Gentleman's Magazine*, 1845, Pt. I, p. 82; drawings for library bookcases, RIBA J11/57, 1849.

49 *Athenaeum*, 1850, p. 1072; *Builder*, VIII, 1850, p. 534; J. Mordaunt Crook, *Victorian Architecture: a Visual Anthology*, London, 1971, p. 31.

50 *Civil Engineer and Architect's Journal*, 1838, pp. 99, 297; and VII, 1844, p. 411; *Illustrated London News*, II, 1843, pp. 207–8, and VI, 1845, p. 100; *Athenaeum*, 1845, pp. 1084, 1130; *Country Life*, LIX, 1926, pp. 361, 371–74; E. and W. Young, *Old London Churches*, London, 1956, p. 269. The dome was partly burnt and rebuilt in 1968–69.

51 *Country Life*, VIII, 1900, pp. 656–64.

52 H. Avray Tipping, 'Oakley Park, Suffolk', *Country Life*, XXIII, 1908, pp. 18–26.

53 *Survey of London*, XXIX–XXX, 1960, p. 422; *Civil Engineer and Architect's Journal*, I, 1837, pp. 15, 59; *British Almanac and Companion*, 1837, p. 245; and 1838, p. 235. N. Taylor, *Monuments of Commerce*, RIBA, London, 1968, p. 31. The interior of the club was restored in 1972–73.

54 *Civil Engineer and Architect's Journal*, I, 1838, p. 67; and III, 1840, p. 222; *Surveyor, Engineer and Architect*, I, 1840, p. 160. J. Mordaunt Crook, *The Reform Club*, London, 1973.

55 *Survey of London*, XXIX–XXX, 1960, pp. 478–84; *Builder*, II, 1844, p. 498; and II, 1845, p. 229; *Athenaeum*, 1844, p. 114; and 1845, p. 96; *Civil Engineer and Architect's Journal*, VI, 1843, pp. 331–32; and VII, 1844, pp. 43, 66, 270; *Illustrated London News*, IV, 1844, p. 85; VI, 1845, p. 121; and VII, 1845, p. 55; *British Almanac and Companion*, 1845, pp. 242–44; *Building News*, VI, 1860, p. 553; *Country Life*, CIV, 1948, p. 333. The interior was reconstructed as offices in 1964.

56 *Survey of London*, XXIX–XXX, 1960, pp. 354–59; *Builder*, II, 1844, p. 233; III, 1845, p. 269; V, 1847, p. 218; XI, 1853, p. 685; and XIII, 1855, pp. 282, 331; *Civil Engineer and Architect's Journal*, III, 1840, p. 336; VI, 1843, p. 36; VII, 1845, p. 279; and X, 1847, pp. 127, 174, 297; *Building News*, VII, 1861, p. 95; BM Add. MS 40609, ff. 30–31.

57 'Diary of C. R. Cockerell', 25 February 1824.

58 *The Whitehaven News*, 1 January 1970.

59 This design is now in the Metropolitan Museum of Art. It is illustrated in J. Harris, *Catalogue of British Drawings for Architecture, Decoration, Sculpture and Landscape Gardening, 1550–1900, in American Collections*, New Jersey, 1971, pp. 224–25, Pl. 169.

60 N. Pevsner, *Buildings of England: London*, I, London, 1962, pp. 568–69.

61 *Survey of London*, XXXII, 1963, pp. 390–429; R. Phené Spiers, 'Burlington House', *Architectural Review*, XVI, 1904, pp. 147–57, 202–9; H. B. Wheatley, 'The Royal Society', *Country Life*, XXXII, 1912, pp. 84–88; C. Hussey, 'Burlington House', *ibid.*, LV, 1924, pp. 694–72; S. C. Hutchison, *The Houses of the RA*, 1956, pp. 19–30; and *History of the RA*, 1968, pp. 122 *et seq*.

62 *Builder*, XIV, 1856, pp. 113–14, 125–26.

63 *Builder*, XVII, 1859, pp. 456–57, 297; *Building News*, V, 1859, p. 830; and VII, 1861, p. 241; A. Graves, *RA Exhibitors*, VII, 1906, p. 164; 1862 Exhibition, catalogue prospectus and guide (BM press marks 7957 bb.20, 7055 d.44 and 7957 c.19); G. F. Chadwick, *The Park and the Town*, New York, 1966, pp. 149–50; W. Ames, *Prince Albert and Victorian Taste*, London, 1967, pp. 128–30. See also *The Architectural Review*, CXXXII, 1962, pp. 15–21; and *Survey of London*, XXXVIII, 1975, pp. 125–29.

64 *Building News*, IV, 1858, p. 315; *Builder*, XV, 1857, pp. 116–18, 127–29, 148–50, 171–73; XVI, 1858, pp. 101–2, 120–22, 139–41, 151–52; XVII, 1859, pp. 107–9, 133–34, 168–70, 191–92; XVIII, 1860, pp. 65–68; XIX, 1861, pp. 65–69; XX, 1862, pp. 40–41, 57–59, 73–74, 90–92, 109–11, 128–30, 143–45, 234–35, 262–63; XXI, 1863, pp. 126–29; XXII, 1864, pp. 38–40, 54–56; and XXIII, 1865, pp. 38–40, 60–62. See also three articles by Sydney Smirke: 'Architectural Colouring', in *Universal Decorator*, ed. F. B. Thompson, Pt XI, 1859, pp. 93–4; 'Mouldings as Ornaments in Architecture', *ibid*, XVI, 1859, pp. 51–52; 'Natural Forms in Architectural Embellishment', *ibid.* XVIII, 1859, p. 57. J. B. Waring, later something of an expert in this field, was briefly a pupil in 1846 (J. B. Waring, *A Record of My Artistic Life*, 1873, p. 60).

65 *Journal of Design*, VI, 1851, p. 96.

66 For a discussion of this crisis of confidence, see Sir John Summerson, *Victorian Architecture: four studies in evaluation*, New York, 1970; R. Kerr, *The Gentleman's House*, London, 1871, ed. J. Mordaunt Crook, 1972; J. T. Emmett, *Six Essays*, 1891, ed. J. Mordaunt Crook, 1972.

67 For full details of the museum's architectural history, see J. Mordaunt Crook, *The British Museum*, 1972; J. Mordaunt Crook and M. H. Port, *The History of the King's Works, VI, 1782–1851* (1973), pp. 403–21.

68 Sydney Smirke was a leader of the 'classical' lobby at the RIBA. In 1865 he helped to secure the Gold Medal for Penethorne by making a

'heated speech' against Butterfield (P. Thompson, *William Butterfield*, 1971, p. 68, n. 25).

IV   J. L. Pearson

I should like to thank Mr Paul Joyce for making available his card index of the works of J. L. Pearson, one of several indexes he has compiled on the works of major Victorian architects. The Pearson index is extraordinarily thorough, and covers every known work, giving dates of design, construction and completion and extensive references to periodicals and other publications. Without the availability of this card index, the chapter would have been less comprehensive, and possibly less accurate. Furthermore Mr Joyce's own enthusiasm for the works of Pearson, particularly those of his early to middle career, was an enormous stimulant to the writer in his understanding and enjoyment of the buildings.

Also invaluable were the splendid series of photographs, taken by Mr Gordon Barnes, in the National Monuments Record, covering most of the major churches, inside and out. These helped to remind me of churches long after visiting them, or, in some instances, conveyed the character of the churches I had not been able to visit.

General references to Pearson's works are the obituaries in the *Builder*, 18 December 1897; *Building News*, 17 December 1897; *Illustrated London News*, 18 December 1897; and *Journal of the RIBA*, 8 November 1898. Also articles in the *Architectural Review* of November 1896 (the first article in the first issue of the AR) and May 1897; and, of course, Rev. Basil Clarke's *Church Builders of the Nineteenth Century*, London, 1938, reprinted Newton Abbot, 1969.

1   Ignatius Bonomi is an architect whose work deserves study. Often it was of high quality, e.g. in the Roman Catholic church at Brough in the North Riding, exquisitely Gothic, and in the later, convincingly Norman, church at Oxenhope in the West Riding. He designed the first railway bridge (still existing) over the River Skerne at Darlington in 1825. See Colvin, *Dictionary of British Architects*; N. Pevsner, *Buildings of England: Durham*, London, 1953; *Northumberland*, 1957; *Cumberland*, 1967; *North Riding*, 1966; *West Riding*, 1959; *York and the East Riding*, 1972; and article by A. F. Sealey and D. Walters in the *Architectural Review*, May 1964.

2   W. G. Pickering designed a number of churches in County Durham, often Neo-Romanesque, which have some quality.

3   The Salvin family, of long ancestry, lived at Croxdale Hall, just south of Durham.

4   See Hermione Hobhouse's essay on Philip Hardwick, p. 38.

5   Elloughton was, in fact, a rebuilding of a medieval church of which parts survive (e.g. the tower). It was fire-damaged in 1964 and subsequently restored, but the exterior is mostly as Pearson left it.

6   Weybridge Church replaced a small picturesque building in the Home Counties vernacular with a wooden belfry. It was added to several times by Pearson – chancel aisles 1856, outer south aisle 1864, chancel extended 1889 and redecorated 1894 (P. Joyce). The mature work in the chancel contrasts interestingly with the earlier work.

7   The construction of the vaulting at Stow was under way in 1851. See the *Ecclesiologist*, 1851, and the *Builder*, 9 August 1851. The restoration was probably completed in 1856.

8   Another notable early restoration, or partial rebuilding, was at Garton-on-the-Wolds, in the East Riding, in 1856–57 – for the redoubtable Sir Tatton Sykes of Sledmere, agricultural improver and prolific rebuilder of churches (for which he usually employed G. E. Street).

9   There is a photograph in the National Monuments Record showing Dalton Holme church under construction, with the medieval church (shortly afterwards demolished) in the background.

10   For St Peter's, Vauxhall, see the *Builder*, 2 September 1865, and *Building News*, 18 August 1865, 13 October 1865 and 27 October 1865. The church was designed in 1860 and begun in 1862 (P. Joyce).

11   Adjoining St Peter's is a remarkable group of secular buildings associated with the church making a tough, romantic composition with gables, turrets and irregular massing. The adjoining Vicarage was contrived out of a Georgian house, oddly but effectively, by Pearson in 1862, and the present St Peter's House to the north of the church may date from 1863. St Peter's was intended to have a tower and spire, in the angle between nave and north transept, but none of this was ever built.

12   Other notable houses by Pearson are Roundwick, near Kirdford in Sussex (1868), and Treberfedd in Breconshire, designed by Pearson in 1848, standing by the church of Llangasty-tal-y-llyn (which he rebuilt at the same time) on the shores of Llangorse Lake. See David Verey, *Shell Guide to Mid Wales*, London, 1960.

13   For St Augustine's, Kilburn, see *Building News*, 27 September 1872. It was designed in 1870 (P. Joyce).

14   The rood screen was constructed in 1890 (illustrated in *Building News*, 2 January 1891).

15   Another powerful, though simple, early work of Pearson is Titsey Church, Surrey (1859–61).

16   N. Pevsner, *Buildings of England: South Lancashire*, London, 1969.

17   St John's, Norwood was designed in 1875, but not started till 1880 (P. Joyce). The very fine spire was never built.

18   St Michael's, Croydon, was designed in 1876 but not started till later. The very fine spire would have been an invaluable landmark in

present-day Croydon with its cluster of crude commercial towers. A recent offer to pay for its construction according to the original design was, astonishingly, turned down.

19 The nave of St Stephen's, Bournemouth, was built in 1881–85, the chancel in 1896–98, and the tower (under F. L. Pearson) in 1907–8 (P. Joyce). An illustration in the *Building News* of 22 February 1884 shows the spire as intended.

20 The intended complete external design for All Saints', Hove, is illustrated in the *Architectural Review*, 1896. It was to have had a massive south-west tower with a West Country-type pinnacled parapet, and no spire.

21 As at All Saints', Hove; at Chute Forest (see p. 76; and also at St John's, Redhill, Surrey, an earlier nineteenth-century church reconstructed by Pearson in 1889, with a very fine spire added in 1895.

22 Much the same effect, on a smaller scale, as at Wentworth, Yorkshire. See p. 75.

23 For the Hythe restoration see *Building News*, 6 March 1891. The nave had previously been restored by Street.

24 For the restoration at the Lord Mayor's Chapel (St Mark's) at Bristol, see the *Builder*, 26 January 1889.

25 His work at Lincoln was extensive but very conservative; he saved the south-west tower from complete collapse in 1880, having to rebuild part of it, as much as possible with the old materials; he restored the vaulting of the north transept, the chapter house and the cloister.

26 At Norwich he designed the Bishop's Throne in 1894.

27 At Rochester he restored the west front and the choir screen. See the *Architectural Review*, May 1897.

28 At Chichester he designed a new north-west tower to match, though not to copy, the existing south-west one. The original north-west tower had collapsed in the seventeenth century (the *Builder*, 13 November 1897). This work (1897–1901) was carried on after his death by his son.

29 Pearson took over from Street as architect to Bristol Cathedral after Street's death. He completed Street's west towers, and then restored, and refitted, the medieval parts of the cathedral. The screen and reredos and restoration of the medieval sedilia were designed in 1895; the reredos was erected in 1898. See the *Builder*, 18 June 1892, 4 February 1893, 24 June 1893, 24 March 1894, 14 July 1894, 10 November 1894, 5 January 1895, 2 March 1895, 26 February 1898 (illustration of reredos, which is one of the best of the many that Pearson designed).

30 For the restoration of the north transept of Westminster Abbey, see *Building News*, 5 June 1891. Pearson also designed a Monumental Chapel (for the reception of many of the monuments in the Abbey) in a flamboyant Perpendicular style to match Henry VII's chapel. See the *Builder*, 23 February 1889 and 27 December 1890, for illustrations. There are drawings in the RIBA collection.

31 For the rebuilding of the central tower and restoration of the choir at Peterborough, see the *Builder*, 13 January 1883, 20 January 1883, 22 September 1883, 10 November 1883, 17 May 1884 (a long article), 10 January 1885 (editorial), 17 January 1885, 24 January 1885, 25 April 1885 (editorial), 18 October 1890, 11 June 1892 (editorial), 10 March 1894 (screen). There is a drawing of the projected spire in the RIBA collection

32 For the controversy over the restoration of Peterborough west front, see the *Builder*, 1 June 1895, 4 January 1896, 12 September 1896, 31 October 1896, 5 December 1896, 19 December 1896, 26 December 1896, 2 January 1897, 9 January 1897, 16 January 1897, 23 January 1897, 13 February 1897; and *Building News*, 26 February 1897 and 9 March 1900.

33 See the *Builder*, 16 January 1897.

34 For the restoration of Westminster Hall and the controversy over it, see the *Builder*, 26 July 1884, 29 November 1884, 11 April 1885, 9 May 1885 and 4 July 1885; also *Building News*, 18 July 1884, 19 September 1884, 5 December 1884 and 12 December 1884. See also correspondence in *The Times*, 1884–85.

35 N. Pevsner, *Buildings of England: London I*, London, 1962, revised 1973.

36 Alfred Waterhouse, Ewan Christian, James Brooks, Sir Arthur Blomfield, J. Oldrid Scott and William White all supported Pearson. One of his opponents was J. J. Stevenson.

37 Pearson's proposed upper storeys to the Westminster Hall towers are illustrated in the *Building News* of 19 September 1884. There are drawings in the RIBA collection.

V G. F. Bodley

1 Sir Ninian Comper, unpublished manuscript kindly lent by Mr Anthony Symondson.

2 B. F. L. Clarke, *Church Builders of the Nineteenth Century*, London, 1938.

3 F. M. Simpson, 'George Frederick Bodley' in *RIBA Journal*, 11 January 1908.

4 C. L. Eastlake, *A History of the Gothic Revival*, London, 1872, p. 289. Reprint ed. J. Mordaunt Crook, Leicester, 1970.

5 G. F. Bodley, unpublished correspondence preserved at France Lynch Church, Gloucestershire.

6 David Verey, Presidential Address, Bristol and Gloucestershire Archaeological Society, Vol. 92.

7 The glass made by Morris and Co. for Bodley throughout his career can now be easily referred to in A. C. Sewter, *The Stained Glass of Morris and his Circle*, New Haven and London, 1974.

8 Paul Crossley, article in *Trinity Review*, Summer 1968.

9 Paul Thompson, *The Work of William Morris*, London, 1967, p. 69.

10 E. Warren, 'The Life and Work of George Frederick Bodley' in *RIBA Journal*, 19 February 1910, p. 308.

11 Peter F. Anson, *Fashions in Church Furnishings*, London, 1960.

12 J. Brandon-Jones, letters from Bodley to Webb, published in *The Journal of the Society of Architectural Historians of Great Britain*, Vol. 8, 1965, p. 64.

13 E. Warren, *op. cit.* p. 316.

14 *Leeds Arts Calendar*, No. 62, 1968.

15 E. Warren, *op. cit.* p.329.

16 Exhibition Catalogue, *Victorian Church Art*, Victoria and Albert Museum, 1971, p. 112.

17 G. W. O. Addleshaw, *The Journal of the Society of Architectural Historians of Great Britain*, Vol. 10, 1967, p. 94.

18 William Morgan, Department of Fine Arts, University of Louisville, Kentucky, 1976.

VI Alfred Waterhouse

1 Small pocket notebook preserved by Mrs Michael Waterhouse.

2 Holy Trinity, Platt Lane, 1844. Rusholme is now an inner suburb of Manchester.

3 Journal of Mary Waterhouse. Undated. Printed privately after her death.

4 Removed from original covers and pasted into a new book, in the process losing half the entries. In the possession of Mrs Michael Waterhouse.

5 Preserved by David Waterhouse.

6 Now Lakes District Council Offices.

7 Demolished. It stood in Chester Street, Chorlton – on Medlock.

8 Recorded in pocket notebook numbered 1, and preserved by Michael Waterhouse. Pages are not numbered.

9 *Ibid.*

10 *Ibid.*

11 *Ibid.*

12 *Ibid.*

13 *Builder*, 15 January 1859, pp. 42–43.

14 Waterhouse visited the site 10 November 1855, having been approached by Bushnell the previous week. It is to be assumed that plans were ready by the spring of 1856 since the *Builder* article describes the house completed and occupied.

15 Twenty-five feet square, the largest room in the house.

16 Now Midland Bank, Darley Street, Bradford.

17 Barcombe Cottage, Fallowfield, demolished in 1966.

18 Before beginning work Waterhouse visited the Town Halls of Bruges, Ypres, Ghent, Oudenaarde, Brussels, Louvain, Malines, Antwerp and Courtrai.

19 *Building News*, 15 April 1859, p. 365.

20 *Building News*, 15 April 1859, p. 366.

21 French capitals for St Nicholas from the Ste Chapelle. Sir Gilbert Scott, *Personal and Professional Recollections*, London, 1879, p. 202

22 *Ibid.* p. 159.

23 *Ibid.*

24 The *Building News* in 1857 endorsed it most emphatically and drew the parallel with music where original compositions of great merit were based on remembered folk tunes.

25 Visited in 1867.

26 Visited in 1861.

27 Visited in 1872.

28 Visited in 1861.

29 Visited in 1871.

30 H. S. Goodhart-Rendel, *English Architecture Since The Regency* London, 1953.

31 There were clearly two separate contests but it was the intention of the General Purpose Committee that the competition be considered a two-stage one; the first phase being open to attract as many ideas as possible, and the second to allow more mature judgment on the part of the twelve best candidates.

32 The committee was authorized to invite as many as twelve of the ten designs selected, two were double entries.

33 As published in the *Manchester Guardian*, 11 March 1868.

34 The stone bridges connecting the central hall with the first-floor corridor were suggested by Donaldson and Street's report.

35 Le Corbusier, *Towards a New Architecture*, 1923.

36 E. H. Pitcairn, *Unwritten Laws and Ideals of Active Careers*, London, 1885, p. 343.

37 *Building News*, 1 February 1889, p. 23.

38 *RIBA Journal*, Vol. I, 1894, p. 23.

39 *Ibid.*

40 Beginning with the Binyon and Fryer Warehouse, he employed a rolled-iron system of girders in every large office and commercial block.

41 Address to the Birmingham School of Art as reported in the *Building News*, 2 March 1883.

42 Ralph Dutton, *The Victorian Home*, London, 1954, p. 126.

43 As reported in the *Architect*, 8 June 1878, p. 343.

44 C. H. Reilly, *Scaffolding in the Sky*, London, 1938.

45 *The British Architect*, 30 October 1896.

46 For the purposes of probate, the estate was sworn at £163,575 0s. 0d. compared with the approximate £130,000 left by G. G. Scott.

47 *The British Architect*, 1 September 1905, p. 147. As reprinted from *The Times*.

VII Edwin Lutyens

1 Unlike the careers of most of the other architects in this book, that of Lutyens is fully documented in *The Lutyens Memorial, The Life*, by Christopher Hussey, and *The Architecture* by

A. S. G. Butler, 3 vols., London, 1950, and the more accurate Lawrence Weaver, *Houses and Gardens by E. L. Lutyens*, London, 1913. Nicholas Taylor's as yet unpublished book should also be a valuable source.

2   Robert Furneaux Jordan, *Victorian Architecture*, Harmondsworth, 1966, p. 235.

3   Michael Edwards, *Raj, British India 1772–1947*, London, 1967, p. 205.

4   Nikolaus Pevsner, *Buildings of England: Middlesex*, London, 1951, p. 62.

5   Robert Furneaux Jordan, *Reminiscences of Sir Edwin Lutyens, AA Journal*, Vol. LXXIV, No. 830, March 1959, p. 231.

6   But old and bad habits die hard, as recently as 1975 in the BBC book 'Spirit of the Age' Patrick Nuttgens talks of Lutyens's 'change of mood and of scale from those early houses to the pompous banalities of the public buildings'. To prove his point he illustrates Baker's Government Buildings in New Delhi, claiming them to be by Lutyens and saying that they are 'outrageous in scale', which they are not!

7   Paul Thompson, in P. Kidson, P. Murray and P. Thompson, *A History of English Architecture*, Harmondsworth, 1965, p. 308.

8   Herbert Baker, *Architecture and Personalities*, London, 1944, p. 15.

9   Lutyens's early years and his somewhat cloying relationship with his mother, and the other older women who dominated his life, are described between pp. 3 and 14 of *The Life*.

10   The history of Lutyens's and Detmar Blow's peculations at the expense of the Duke of Westminster has yet to be written.

11   See for instance *The Life*, Chap. VIII, pp. 185–234.

12   See for instance *The Life*, p. 326

13   Illustrated, *The Life*, p. 15.

14   The Pleasaunce, Overstrand and Overstrand Hall are fully described in Weaver, *Houses and Gardens*, Chap. III, pp. 48–52.

15   See note 13 above.

16   Illustrated, A. S. G. Butler, *op. cit.*, Vol. I, pls. 134–40.

17   Illustrated, *ibid.*, Vol. I, pls. 141–74.

18   Illustrated, *ibid.*, Vol. II, pls. 263–77.

19   Illustrated, *ibid.*, Vol. III, pls. 77–81.

20   Nicholas Taylor has noted that Butler is almost certainly wrong to suggest on p. 26 of *The Life* that Webb was an influence before Lutyens met Miss Jekyll; see note 28 below.

21   I am most grateful to Paul Joyce for letting me see his notes on G. E. Street and for his advice and guidance in this and many other areas.

22   Though H. S. Goodhart-Rendel in *English Architecture Since the Regency – an Interpretation*, London, 1953, pp. 139–42, discusses the style at some length. Stefan Muthesius in *The High Victorian Movement in Architecture 1850–1870*, London, 1972, considers the style briefly.

23   Sir Edmund Birkett, *A Book of Building*, London, 1876, p. 97.

24   See for instance St Columba's Church, Kingsland Road, London, E.2. (1867–71).

25   The influence is particularly evident in Butterfield's work in *Instrumenta Ecclesiastica*, 1st Series, 1847, pls. 65 and 66 (design for a 'Stone Lich Gate').

26   Though not in the work of H. P. Berlage (1856–1934), who in the Amsterdam Exchange of 1898–1902 created one of the finest, if one of the latest, examples of the 'Vigorous Style'. The development of this style, and its relationship back to Lutyens's work, by such masters as W. M. Dudok (1884–1974), has yet to be studied. See note 29 below.

27   Though Noel Rooke told John Brandon Jones that C. F. A. Voysey's startling white house on South Parade, Bedford Park, was much disliked by the Bedford Park residents when it was built, not because it was too 'modern' but because it was too 'old fashioned' since its walls were stuccoed and it used leaded lights instead of the simple 'modern' sashes of the rest of the suburb.

28   See *The Life*, Chap. II, Part 3, pp. 22–35, titled significantly 'Gertrude Jekyll and Philip Webb'.

29   Homewood was one of the Lutyens houses to have a considerable influence abroad. A full-page plate appears in '*Deutsche Kunst und Dekoration*', Vol. XXIX, 1911, p. 53. Of particular interest in this context are the two houses by Robert Van t'Hoff (1887–?) at Huis Ter Heide near Utrecht. One, 'Bosch en Duin', was built in 1911–12, and is very clearly influenced by Homewood; its neighbour, more famous, was built in 1915–16, and is strongly influenced by Frank Lloyd Wright's Oak Park Houses.

30   See for instance Robert Blake, *Disraeli*, London, 1966, pp. 657–58.

31   Plans reproduced in Weaver, *House and Gardens*, fig. 36, p. 18.

32   Plans reproduced, A. S. G. Butler, *op. cit.*, Vol. I, pl. V.

33   Illustrated, W. R. Lethaby, *Philip Webb and His Work*, Oxford, 1935, p. 84.

34   Illustrated, Peter Ferriday, *Victorian Architecture*, London, 1963, pl. LXXXIX.

35   A book which clearly shows this is P. A. Barron, *The House Desirable*, London, 1929. Although dedicated to Neo-Tudor architecture, Barron is quite willing to show Neo-Georgian examples, including work by Lutyens.

36   See Shane Leslie, *Men Were Different*, London, 1937, p. 230.

37   Newton's career is reasonably well documented with: Ernest Newton, *A Book of Country Houses*, London, 1903; William G. Newton, *The Works of Ernest Newton RA*, London, 1925.

38   N. Pevsner and I. Nairn, *Buildings of England: Surrey*, London, 1962, p. 263.

39   Illustrated, Newton, *The Works of Ernest Newton*, pp. 42–45.

40   Illustrated, *ibid.*, pp. 202–7.

41   See for further information and many illustrations, David Gregory Jones, *AA Journal*, Vol. LXX, November 1954, p. 95.

42   The book that most clearly illustrates the movement is Basil Oliver, *The Renaissance of the English Public House*, London, 1947 (well illustrated with photographs and plans). Robert Thorne's article in the *Architectural Review*, Feb. 1976, on the 'reformed drinking house' and his description of the post-1914 pubs in Alan Crawford and Robert Thorne, *Birmingham Pubs 1890–1939* University of Birmingham, 1975, are pioneering studies in a relatively untouched field.

43   Illustrated, A. S. G. Butler, *op. cit.*, Vol. I, figs. CVIII–CX, pls. 269–71.

44   Illustrated, *ibid.*, Vol. III, figs. LXIV–LXVI and Frontispiece.

45   Illustrated, *ibid.*, Vol. III, figs. LXXIV–LXXVI, pls. 104–8.

46   Illustrated, *ibid.*, Vol. III, pl. 98.

47   That Street approached architectural form in this way can be seen in many of his buildings, such as the spire of St John the Evangelist, Howsham, Yorkshire (1859–60), but more particularly in the north wall of the exactly contemporary St John the Evangelist, Ardamine, County Wicklow, where the wall is cut back in only a few places to reveal what seems to be a complete arcade of columns and brick arches embedded in the stonework.

48   Robert Lutyens, *Sir Edwin Lutyens, An Appreciation in Perspective*, London, 1942, pp. 57–65.

Check-lists of chief works

I   William Burn

Burn is said by Donaldson to have had a hand in about seven hundred buildings. About three hundred of these have been identified. The balance of four hundred probably consisted of minor estate buildings or unexecuted proposals. Buildings which appear without qualification are new buildings, or virtually so: R in square brackets indicates a complete reconstruction; A a substantial addition or alteration; C a conversion; Rn a restoration in which the original design was in large part respected; IR internal remodelling; IW interior work. Buildings marked ★ are known to the writer either to have been destroyed or to have lost any work by Burn; buildings marked★★ have also been credited to Bryce and must be regarded as joint designs.

Dates given are those of working drawings wherever available.

1812   ★Greenock Assembly rooms.

1813   North Leith Parish Church, Edinburgh; Gallanach, Argyll.

1816   Greenock Customs House; St John's Episcopal Church, Edinburgh; ★Merchant Maiden Hospital, Edinburgh.

1818   Saltoun, East Lothian [R]; Dundas Castle, West Lothian; Dunfermline (Abbey) Parish Church.

1819   Adderstone, Northumberland; Barrogil (Castle of Mey), Caithness [A].

1820   Blairquhan, Ayrshire.

1821   Melville Monument, Edinburgh; George Stiel's Hospital, Tranent; ★Port Glasgow Customs House; ★Elgin (Masonic) Assembly Rooms; Carstairs, Lanarkshire; Camperdown, Angus; 105–23 Lothian Road and 6–32 Morrison Street, Edinburgh.

1822   Murray Royal Asylum, Perth; Luffness House, East Lothian [A].

1823   Edinburgh Academy; ★Riccarton, Midlothian [R]; ★Niddrie Marischal, Midlothian [R]; Lochend, East Lothian; Union (now Royal) Bank, Murraygate, Dundee; Claremont Crescent, Edinburgh; Bridge of Earn Village, Perthshire.

1824   Ratho, Midlothian; ★Snaigow, Perthshire; Strathendrie, Fife; Brodie, Moray [A]; ★Dundee Asylum [A and R]; ★Dundee East Church [Rn]; replanning of central Dundee; ★Episcopal Church, St Andrews, Fife; Mount Stuart Lodge and Kingarth Church, Bute; Kinnoull Church, Perth; ★Edinburgh Oil Gas Works, Tanfield (later Tanfield Hall), Edinburgh.

1825   Lauriston, Edinburgh; Freeland, Perthshire [R]; ★Drumfinn (Aros), Argyll; Dalhousie, Midlothian [R]; Pinkie, Midlothian [A]; Pitfour, Perthshire [A]; Killiecrankie Cottage, Perthshire; John Watson's Hospital, Edinburgh [R]; 2–42 Henderson Row, Edinburgh; ★Kirkcaldy Town House and Prison, Fife; Moncrieff Lodge, Perthshire; Teasses, Fife; Balnamoon, Angus [A].

1826   ★Garscube, Dunbartonshire; Duntrune, Angus; ★Hoddam, Dumfriesshire [A]; Fettercairn, Kincardineshire [R]; St Monance Church, Fife [R and A].

1827   ★Cliveden, Buckinghamshire; Pitcairns, Perthshire; Balcaskie, Fife [A]; Sir William Forbes's Bank, Parliament Square, Edinburgh; Corstorphine Church, Edinburgh [Rn]; Abdie Church, Fife; Ardnamurchan Church, Argyll; gate, lodge and other buildings, Dalkeith, Midlothian; Whittinghame, East Lothian [A].

1828   ★Dupplin, Perthshire; ★Pilrig, Edinburgh

[A]; Gilmerton, East Lothian [A]; Belleisle, Ayr [R, attributed]; Bank of Scotland, Ingram Street, Glasgow; Cramond Church, Midlothian [A].

1829 St Giles Church, Edinburgh [R]; Faskally, Perthshire; *St Fort, Fife; Raehills, Dumfriesshire[A]; *Milton Lockhart, Lanarkshire; Tyninghame, East Lothian [R]; Thurso Church, Caithness; Tynron Church, Dumfriesshire; Stenton Church, East Lothian.

1830 Drumlanrig, Dumfriesshire [A and much estate work]; Kirkmichael, Dumfriesshire; Spott, East Lothian [R]; Aytoun, Perthshire [A]; Pitcaple, Aberdeenshire [A]; *Edmonstone, Midlothian [A]; *Hamilton Palace Stables, Lanarkshire; Cassillis, Ayrshire [A, attribution]; *Theatre Royal, Edinburgh [A]; Schaw's Hospital, Prestonpans; Minigaff Church, Kirkcudbright; Peebles Episcopal Church; Lothian Road Church, Edinburgh (design by Bryce); Blanerne, Berwickshire.

1831 Madras College and Schoolhouses, St Andrews, Fife; Urrard, Perthshire; Kilconquhar, Fife [R]; Auchmacoy, Aberdeenshire; Bowhill, Selkirkshire [A]; Ardgowan, Renfrewshire [A]; Lord Blantyre's Monument, Erskine, Renfrewshire; Hopeton Mausoleum, West Lothian.

1832 Auchterarder, Perthshire; Dalkeith, Midlothian [A]; *Spottiswoode, Berwickshire; *Gosford (Old House), East Lothian [R]; Posso (Dawyck), Peeblesshire; *Newburgh Church, Fife; Aberdalgie Manse, Perthshire; Charleton, Fife [A].

1833 County Buildings, Haddington, East Lothian; County Buildings, Inverness; The Gart, Perthshire; Netherby, Cumberland [R]; Bank of Scotland, Stirling; Bank of Scotland, Kirkcaldy, Fife; Teviotbank, Roxburgh; The Knowes (now Teviot Bank), Roxburghshire; Inverawe (Ardanaseig), Argyll.

1834 Dumfries Asylum; *New Club, Princes Street, Edinburgh; *Marchmont, Berwickshire [A]; *Thurso Castle, Caithness [A]; Monkrigg, East Lothian; *Handley Lodge (Hanley House), Midlothian; Meigle, Perthshire [A]; Murray Royal Asylum, Perth [A]; Signet Library (staircase), Edinburgh [IR].

1835 Dornoch Cathedral [R]; *Macbiehill, Pebblesshire [R]; Tyneholme, East Lothian; *Aboyne, Aberdeenshire [A]; Havra, Shetland (now deserted, query if executed); Parkhill, Stirlingshire [A]; Kirkcudbright Church; **Bourhouse, East Lothian; Caroline Park, Edinburgh (repairs); Courthouse, Cupar, Fife [IR].

1836 *Stenhouse, Stirlingshire [R]; *Arthurstone, Perthshire [A]; Anton's Hill, Berwickshire; *Duncrub, Perthshire [R]; Irvine, Dumfriesshire [A]; Knowsley, Lancashire (proposals); *Young Street Church, Edinburgh; Ettrick Bridge Church, Selkirkshire; *Royal Bank, Edinburgh [A]; Carmyle Cottage, Lanarkshire; Newbattle, Midlothian [A].

1837 Invergowrie, Angus [R]; Branxholme, Roxburgh [A]; Lude, Perthshire; Dalkeith West Church, Midlothian; Bank of Scotland, Greenock; Knowsley, boat-house, Croxteth and Hayton Lodges, Lancashire; Restalrig Church, Edinburgh [Rn]; Faskally, Perthshire [A]; Achnacarry, Inverness-shire [completion].

1838 Balcarres, Fife [R]; Jura, Argyll [*A and mausoleum at Killearnadale]; Ardarroch, Dunbartonshire; Harlaxton, Lincolnshire [A]; Peninghame Church, Wigtownshire; *Gladsmuir Church, East Lothian; Northesk Church, Musselburgh, Midlothian; Orchard and Ormskirk Lodges, Knowsley, Lancashire.

1839 Falkland (or Nuthill), Fife; Whitehill, Midlothian; Muckross, Kerry; Finnart, Perthshire [?]; *Nine Wells, Berwickshire; Castle Menzies, Perthshire [A]; West House, Morningside Asylum, Edinburgh; St Mary, St Andrews, Fife; Morton Church, Dumfriesshire; Bank of Scotland, High Street, Montrose, Angus; Granton Square, Edinburgh.

1840 Thirlestane, Berwickshire [A]; Cardona, Peeblesshire; Oxenford, Midlothian [A]; *Redcastle, Ross-shire [A]; Music Hall (addition to Assembly Rooms), Edinburgh; East Bank Church, Hawick; Portpatrick Church, Wigtownshire; Loughborough Lodge, Knowsley, Lancashire.

1841 Stoke Rochford and South Stoke Village, Lincolnshire; *Seacliff, East Lothian; *North British Insurance Office, 64, 65 Princes Street, Edinburgh.

1842 Galloway, Wigtownshire [A]; Rauceby, Lincolnshire; Bank of Scotland, Reform Street, Dundee; St Mary (East Church), Dundee; Liverpool Lodge, Knowsley, Lancashire.

1843 Carnell, Ayrshire [R]; Mertoun, Berwickshire [A]; Prestwold, Leicestershire [R]; Bamff, Perthshire [R]; **Dalkeith Episcopal Church, Midlothian; *Langholm Church, Dumfriesshire; **Edinburgh Life Assurance Building, 22, 24 George Street, Edinburgh.

1844 Revesby, Lincolnshire; Raby Castle, Durham [A]; **Carradale, Argyll; *Dartrey, Monaghan; Redrice, Hampshire [R]; Boughton Park, Northamptonshire.

1845 ***Inchdairnie, Fife [R]; **Leny, Perthshire [R]; **Clatto, Fife; ***Ladykirk, Berwickshire [A]; ***Western Bank, Miller Street, Glasgow [A]; **Middle Church, Dundee; **New Greyfriars, Edinburgh [Rn].

1846 *Eaton Hall, Cheshire [R]; Calwich, Staffordshire; *Creedy, Devon [A]; *1 Carlton House Terrace, London [R]; Knowsley, Lancashire [A and stables].

1847 Bangor (now Town Hall), Down; Gorhambury, Hertfordshire [A]; **Gilltown (Gillstown, Meath?); Lincoln Deanery; Tamnagh Chapel (Ireland ?).

1848 Clandeboye, Down [Helen's Tower (built 1862) and unexecuted proposals]; Eastwell, Kent [*R only part executed and lodge]; Idsworth, Hampshire; Knowsley, Lancashire

(Gate Lodge, Bridge, Gardener's House); ★★St Nicholas (East), Dalkeith.

1849 Moor Park, Hertfordshire [A]; ★Poltalloch (Calton Mohr), Argyll; Arundel, Sussex [A]; Beechwood, Hertfordshire [A]; ★★★Register House, Edinburgh [A].

1850 Pepper, Arden, Yorkshire [A]; Babworth, Nottinghamshire [A]; South Stoke almshouses, Lincolnshire.

1851 ★Dunira, Perthshire; Hirsel, Berwickshire [A]; Sandon, Staffordshire; ★Roehampton Grove, Surrey [A]; Stoneleigh, Warwickshire [A]; Rampton, Nottinghamshire.

1852 Kilruddery, Wicklow [A]; Branksome Tower, Dorset.

1853 ★Buchanan, Stirlingshire; ★Godmersham, Kent [A]; Holkham, Norfolk (Stables, Steward's Offices, North and South Gates, etc.); Orwell, Suffolk [A]; Knowsley, Lancashire (bakehouse and cottage); Kinmel Park, Denbighshire (stables and other buildings).

1854 Castlewellan, Down; Hamilton House, 22 Arlington Street, London [A].

1855 Abbotsford, Roxburghshire [A]; Patshull, Staffordshire [A]; Taplow, Buckinghamshire [R]; Amport, Hampshire; ★Surrenden Dering, Kent [A]; ★Post Office, George Square, Glasgow.

1856 ★Fonthill House, Wiltshire; Brodick, Arran [A]; Brawl, Caithness.

1857 Lynford, Norfolk; Sandbeck, Yorkshire [A]; cottages, Sheerwater, Surrey.

1858 ★Chevely Park, Cambridgeshire [A]; ★Tusmore, Oxfordshire [A]; ★Wishaw, Lanarkshire [A].

1859 ★Montagu House, London; ★Junior United Service Club, London [A?]; Balentore, Angus; ★Stanway, Gloucestershire [A]; Boltby Chapel, Yorkshire.

1860 Blythfield Staffordshire [A]; Dogmersfield, Hampshire; Narford, Norfolk [A, further work 1868].

1861 ★Tehidy Park, Cornwall [A]; Leys, Herefordshire [A]; Lamport, Northamptonshire [A]; Eildon Hall, Roxburgh [R to 1867].

1862 ★Packington, Warwickshire [A].

1863 ★Ganton, Yorkshire; ★Polmaise, Stirlingshire; Shirburn, Oxfordshire [A]; 18 Carlton House Terrace, London.

1864 Spye, Wiltshire; Swanbourne, Buckinghamshire; Kimbolton, Huntingdonshire [A]; ★17 Grosvenor Square, London [A]; Blickling, Norfolk [A]; Roehampton Grove Mausoleum, Surrey.

1865 ★Whittlebury, Northamptonshire; ★Powerscourt, Wicklow [A].

1866 Weston Park, Staffordshire [A]; Wickham Court, Kent [A]; 7 Grosvenor Place, London [IW]; High Woods, Mortimer, Berkshire.

1867 Oaklands (now Lockerley), Hampshire.

1868 Pendlesham, Suffolk; ★Ottershaw, Surrey [A]; ★Brocklesby, Lincolnshire [A]; ★Somerley, Hampshire [A].

1869 Crichel, Dorset [A].

1870 Barrington Park, Gloucestershire [A].

The principal unexecuted designs by Burn which went to working drawings and which have sometimes been listed as executed works, are as follows: George Watson's Hospital, Edinburgh, reconstruction, 1820; New Club, Princes Street, Edinburgh, 1821; Garscube, Neo-Greek scheme, 1826; Gordon's Hospital, Aberdeen, 1827; Fintray House, Aberdeenshire, 1827; Dunskey, 1830, Liff Church, 1837; Monymusk [A], 1838; Beaufort, 1839; Dartrey, classical scheme, 1843 (drawings destroyed at RIBA); Inverness Prison, 1843; Fonthill, first design, 1849; Watcombe (for I. K. Brunel), 1854; Caledonian Station, Glasgow; Tottenham Wiltshire, 1858; Blankney, Crown Point and Bearwood, all 1864. In addition Donaldson mentions alterations to Trinity Hospital, 1845; but this probably relates to a pre-demolition survey for compensation purposes.

The Caledonian Station design was the only known occasion on which he broke his rule never to enter competitions subsequent to his early disappointment at Edinburgh University. It was not built; the temporary timber structure survived until final closure and demolition.

Burn and Bryce: other work prior to 1850. As Bryce's office papers appear to have been dispersed it is not possible to be as definitive as might be wished. Prior to 1843 Bryce carried on a small private practice apart from Burn's, from his house at 53 Castle Street. Most if not all of the following were done in his own name:

1829 Newtonhall House, Fife.

1831 Currie Schoolhouse, Midlothian.

1835 St Mark's Unitarian Church, Edinburgh; 87 George Street, Edinburgh, interior.

1836 Coylton Church, Ayrshire.

1837 Monkton Parish Church and St Cuthbert's, Prestwick, both Ayrshire; Colinton Church Tower, Currie Manse, Midlothian.

1839 Keithick, Perthshire [A].

1840 Insurance Company of Scotland Building, 95 George Street, Edinburgh; Caledonian Insurance Building, George Street, Edinburgh (since altered as George Hotel); Edinburgh and Leith Bank (now Clydesdale Bank), George Street, Edinburgh.

1842 Luscar, Fife.

The following were commissioned from the partnership but are generally attributed to Bryce alone. Which, if any, of the 1850 works were actually commissioned before the break-up of the partnership is uncertain.

1844 Hamilton Mausoleum (taken over from D. Hamilton).

1845 ★Armadale, Inverness-shire [A]; Strathendry, Fife (stables); ★Western Bank (later Scottish Widows), St Andrews Square, Edinburgh.

1846 Exchange Bank of Scotland (No. 23) and British Linen Bank, both St Andrews Square, Edinburgh; Balfour, Orkney.

1847 Edinburgh and Leith Bank [A, then Edinburgh and Glasgow, now Clydesdale], George Street, Edinburgh; Invermark, Angus; Tollcross, Glasgow; Ardarroch, Dunbartonshire; 71 Hanover Street, Edinburgh.

1848 Falkland Church, Fife; Allanbank, Berwickshire.

1849 Guthrie, Angus [R]; Cameron Bridge House, Fife; Dargavel, Renfrewshire [R, since R again].

1850 Surgical Hospital (now Natural Philosophy Dept), Edinburgh; Berstane, Orkney; Clifton, Midlothian; Portmore, Peeblesshire; Stronvar, Perthshire; Sunderland, Selkirkshire.

As the illustrations of the present book are necessarily limited, I append a list of recent publications where more pictures of works by Burn may be found.

Mark Girouard, *The Victorian Country House*, London, 1971: Buchanan, Fonthill, Prestwold, Kinmel Stables.

Christopher Hussey, *English Country Houses: late Georgian*, London, 1958: Harlaxton.

James Macaulay, *The Gothic Revival 1745–1845*, Edinburgh, 1975: Dundas Castle, Carstairs, Ratho Park, Blairquhan, Fettercairn, Auchmacoy, Falkland.

Roy Strong, Marcus Binney, John Harris, *The Destruction of the Country House*, London, 1974: Surrenden Dering, Calwich, Fonthill Abbey, Whittlebury Lodge.

Catalogue of the Drawings Collection of the Royal Institute of British Architects, Volume B, 1972: Bearwood, Buchanan, Dalkeith, Fonthill, Montagu, Dawyck, Sandon.

Henry-Russell Hitchcock, *Early Victorian Architecture*, London, 1954.
 Buchanan, drawings of first scheme, pl. VIII 29.
 Fonthill, drawing of first scheme, pl. VIII 30.
 Fonthill, as built, pl. VIII 31.
 Baltentore, project drawing, pl. VIII 33.

Royal Commission on Ancient and Historical Monuments Stirlingshire.
 Stenhouse, pl. 102.

Royal Commission on Ancient and Historical Monuments Argyll 2 Lorn.
 Ardanaiseig, pls. 85–6.
 Gallanach, pls. 92–3.

Sheila Forman, *Scottish Country Houses and Castles*.
 Thirlestane, pp. 91–3.

II Philip and Philip Charles Hardwick
(a) Philip Hardwick

1822–25 Christ Church, Lisson Grove, London.

1825 Warehouses. St Katharine's Dock, London.

1829–35 Goldsmiths' Hall, London.

1830–31 Grammar School, Stockport.

1832 Rebuilt Babraham House, Cambridgeshire, for J. Adeane.

1832–33 New Clubhouse for City of London Club, Old Broad Street, London.

1833 Alterations to Bishop's Palace, Hereford.

1834 Gateway, St Bartholomew's Hospital, London.

1834–35 Medical theatre, anatomical museum, St Bartholomew's Hospital, London.

1836 Globe Insurance Office, Pall Mall, London.

1837 Globe Insurance Office, Cornhill, London.

1838 London and Birmingham Railway: Euston Grove terminus, London, and Curzon Street terminus, Birmingham.

1838–40 Victoria and Adelaide Hotels (later Euston Hotel), London.

1839–43 New Hall and Library, Lincoln's Inn, London (supervised and completed by Philip Charles in his father's name, 1843–45, plus additional buildings, gateway etc, designed by Philip Charles).

1840 Alterations and modernization of Westwood House, Worcestershire.

1842 New ward block, St Bartholomew's Hospital, London. Sefton House, Belgrave Square, London, for Earl Sefton.

1843 Alterations and repairs to chapel, Lincoln's Inn, London. Rebuilt Wycliffe Hall, Birmingham.

1843–45 Completed Stone Buildings, Lincoln's Inn, to original design.

1844 Design for Hall, near Barnstaple, Devon (completed by Philip Charles 1847–49).

1845 Additions to Stratfieldsaye.

1846–47 Designed extensions to Euston Station (completed by Philip Charles 1847–48).

1847–50 Redecorations at Spencer House, for Earl Spencer.

1850–54 Alterations to Apsley House, for Duke of Wellington.

1851 Recased Gibbs's buildings at St Bartholomew's Hospital, London.

1851–54 Restored St Anne, Limehouse, London, after fire. New Offices for Merchant Taylors' Company in Threadneedle Street, London.

(b) Philip Charles Hardwick

1843 Bank for Jones, Lloyd and Co., Lothbury.

1848–51 Aldermaston Court, Berkshire, for Higford Burr.

1849 Town Hall, Durham. Also refitted Great Dormitory of Abbey Buildings as Library and worked on Markets.

1850 School at Little Brington, for Earl Spencer.

1850–62 Completion of Adare Manor, Co. Limerick, for third Earl of Dunraven. Also restoration of medieval abbeys at Adare. Designed Roman Catholic Cathedral in Limerick.

1851 Royal Freemasons' School, Wandsworth. Billiard Room at Althorp, for Earl Spencer.

1851–52 Restoration of St Mary, Lambeth.

1851–53 Great Western Hotel, Paddington

Station.

1852 College of St Columba, Dublin. Gilston Park, Hertfordshire, for Mr Hodgson. Work at Althorp for Earl Spencer.

1853 Restoration of St Nicholas, Elstree, Hertfordshire.

1853–55 St Martin, Birmingham: restoration of tower.

1853–58 Ship Hotel, Greenwich.

1854 London and Australian Bank, Threadneedle Street, London. Robarts Bank, 15 Lombard Street, London. Clergy Orphan Schools, Canterbury. Lodge at Laverstoke Park, Hants.

1855 St John, Lewisham Way, Deptford. St Mark, Surbiton. St James, Upper Stowe. Altered Uxbridge House, Burlington Gardens, into branch of Bank of England. Branches in Whitefriargate, Hull, and South Parade, Leeds.

1855–56 All Saints, Haggerston Road.

1855–59 Work at Wynyard, County Durham; also on proposed mausoleum at Long Newton, and on Seaham Church, County Durham.

1856 Addington Park, Buckinghamshire, for J. G. Hubbard. The Abbots, Sompting, for Captain Crofts. St John, Little Brington, for Earl Spencer.

1856–57 Riding School, Knightsbridge, for Duke of Wellington.

1858 House at Adhurst St Mary, for Mr Bonham Carter. St Thomas, Portman Square, and school.

1859–60 All Saints, Aston Ubthorpe.

1861 Rebuilt West Smithfield frontage of St Bartholomew's Hospital, London.

1862 Chapel at Hartham Park, Wiltshire.

1862–63 St Leonard, and Almshouses, Newland, near Malvern, Worcestershire.

1863 All Saints, Aldershot. Design for Albert Memorial.

1863–85 Madresfield Court, Worcestershire, for Earl Beauchamp.

1864–67. Rendcomb House, Cirencester, Gloucestershire, for Sir Francis Goldsmith.

1864 Barclay and Bevan's Bank, 54 Lombard Street, London.

1865 Union Bank of London, Poultry.

1865–72 Charterhouse School, near Godalming, Surrey.

1866 Crown Bank, Norwich, for Harvey and Hudson. Sandgate, Church of England School.

1867 St Barnabas, Mayland.

1868 Hassobury House, Farnham, Essex.

c. 1870 House at Milton Heath, Dorking, Surrey, for Mr Powell.

III   Sydney Smirke

1829 Bridewell Hospital, Blackfriars, London. (Alterations)

1830 Custom House, Shoreham, Sussex.

c. 1830 Custom House, Gloucester. Oakley Park, Suffolk, for Sir Edward Kerrison. (Demolished). Wroxton Abbey, Oxfordshire, library.

c. 1832 Alterations at Clumber Park, for Duke of Newcastle.

1832–42 Brickwall, Northiam, Sussex, additions for Thomas Frewen Turner.

1833–34 Reconstruction of Oxford Street Pantheon. (Demolished)

1834 Gunnersbury Park, Ealing, Middlesex.

1834–37 Westminster Hall. (Restoration)

1835 Medway Bathing Establishment, Rochester.

1835–38 Oxford and Cambridge Club (mainly façade).

1836 Custom House, Bristol.

c. 1837 Thornham Hall, Suffolk, for Lord Henniker. (Demolished).

1837 St Mary, Northiam, Sussex. (Additions)

1838 The Rocks, Uckfield, Sussex. Holy Trinity, Leicester (remodelled 1855 and 1871).

1838–46 Bedlam Hospital, Southwark. (Extension)

c. 1840 Custom House, Newcastle upon Tyne. Wellington Pit, Whitehaven, Cumberland.

1840–43 Temple Church, London. (Completed restoration)

1840–45 York Minster. (Restoration)

1840–46 St Mary the Virgin, Andover, Hampshire.

1841 Prototype design for 'a public lodging-house'. Gloucester House, Park Lane, London, conservatory.

1842 Knowsley Hall, Lancashire, alterations for the Earl of Derby. House for R. Earle, near Knowsley, Lancashire.

1842–43 Holy Trinity, Bickerstaffe, Lancashire, altered 1860, 1895. Savoy Chapel, London (Restoration; also 1864–65).

1843 Luton Hoo, Bedfordshire. Reconstruction. Since altered.

1843–44 Exeter Change, Strand, London. Bielefield's Papier Mache works, and *Morning Post* office, Wellington Street, Strand. Parkhurst Juvenile Reformatory, Isle of Wight.

1843–45 Conservative Club, St James's Street, London (with Basevi).

1844 Holy Trinity, Penrhos, Montgomeryshire.

1844–45 Halsall, near Ormskirk, Lancashire rectory.

1844–46 Edmond Castle, Cumberland. (Additions)

1844–48 Portrait gallery, Drayton Manor, Staffordshire, for Sir Robert Peel. (Demolished)

1844–66 Mausoleum for Thomas Frewen Turner, St Mary's, Northiam, Sussex.

c. 1845 School, Eastnor, Herefordshire.

1845–56 Carlton Club, Pall Mall, London. (Demolished)

1846 St John the Baptist, Loughton, Essex, enlarged 1877. The Park, Ealing, Middlesex.

c. 1846 St Mary, Battle, Sussex. (Alterations)

1846–47 Assembly Rooms, hotel and Athenaeum, Bury, Lancashire.

1847 Hunting box, Barleythorpe, Rutland, for the Earl of Lonsdale.

1847–48   Extension of Paper Buildings, Inner Temple, London.

1848   Burscough, near Ormskirk, Lancashire parsonage.

1849   Royal Agricultural Society, design for cottages.

1850   St Mary, Theydon Bois, Essex. Christ Church, Folkestone, Kent (altered 1880–84).

c. 1850   Folkestone, Kent. Radnor Estate.

1850–51   St James, Westhead, near Lathom, Lancashire.

1850–55   School House, Oakham, Rutland.

1851   Grammar School, Tamworth.

1852–54   Kensington Palace Gardens, London, mansions for C. de Murrieta and Au de Arroyave.

1853–57   Began restoration of Lichfield Cathedral (finished by G. G. Scott).

1854–56   Brookwood Cemetery, near Woking, Surrey.

1854–57   Round Reading Room, British Museum, London.

1855   Christ Church, Treales, Lancashire.

1856   20 Irish Street, Whitehaven.

1857–58   Dr Johnson's Buildings, Inner Temple, London.

1858   Treales, Lancashire, parsonage.

1859–62   Galleries of Horticultural Society, Kensington. (Demolished)

1859–74   Burlington House: Academy Schools and Exhibition Galleries built 1867–68; second storey to Burlington House, 1872.

1862   Reconstruction of Lambton Castle, Co. Durham.

1863–64   Radcliffe Camera, Oxford. (Steps and lower library).

1867   King Edward's School, Witley, Surrey.

1867–70   Inner Temple Hall, London. (Demolished)

IV   J. L. Pearson

1846–47   North Ferriby, East Riding, Yorkshire.

1846–48   Weybridge, Surrey (spire added 1855; later alterations by Pearson).

1848–50   Church and house (Treberfedd), Llangasty-tal-y-llyn, Breconshire.

1848–50   Holy Trinity, Bessborough Gardens, London (destroyed by bombing).

1851–56   Restoration at Stow, Lincolnshire.

1855   Eastoft, Yorkshire–Lincolnshire border.

1857–58   Catherston Leweston, near Charmouth, Dorset.

1857–59   Scorborough, East Riding, Yorkshire.

1858–61   Dalton Holme (or South Dalton), East Riding, Yorkshire.

1859–61   Daylesford, Gloucestershire.

1859–61   Titsey, Surrey.

1860–65   St Peter, Vauxhall, London; plus adjoining vicarage and St Peter's House (both later).

1866–68   Sutton Veny, Wiltshire.

1863–66   Appleton-le-Moors, North Riding, Yorkshire.

1865–66   Restoration at Over Wallop, Hampshire.

1868   Roundwick House, near Kirdford, Sussex.

1868–73   Freeland, Oxfordshire, with vicarage and school.

1870–*c.* 77   St Augustine, Kilburn, London (spire later).

1874–78   St John, Red Lion Square, London (destroyed by bombing).

1874–75   Chute Forest, Wiltshire.

1875–87   St John, Norwood, London.

1876–85   St Michael, Croydon.

1877–83   St Margaret, Horsforth, near Leeds.

1879   Restoration at Lastingham, Yorkshire.

1879–81   St Alban, Birmingham.

1879 *et seq.*   Restorations at Westminster Abbey and Hall. Work on Peterborough Cathedral.

1880   Design for Truro Cathedral (work completed by son in 1910). Work on Lincoln Cathedral from 1870 onwards.

1881–98   St Stephen, Bournemouth.

1882–85   St Agnes, Sefton Park, Liverpool.

1882–84   Cullercoats, Northumberland.

1882–98   Work on Bristol Cathedral.

1883–90   St Michael, Headingley, Leeds.

1885–87   Thurstaston, Cheshire.

1886–87   Restoration at Abbey church of Shrewsbury; chancel vault at Hythe, Kent.

1887–89   Restoration at Lord Mayor's Chapel, Bristol.

1888 *et seq.*   Work on Rochester Cathedral.

1889 *et seq.*   Restorations at St Margaret, Westminster. Alterations to St John, Redhill, Surrey, including spire.

1889–1901   All Saints, Hove.

1889–1902   St John, Friern Barnet (also later work).

1890–95   Work on Norwich Cathedral.

1897–1901   Work on Chichester Cathedral (completed by son).

V   George Frederick Bodley

1854   St Michael and All Angels, Bussage, Gloucestershire; south aisle.

1854   School at St Paul's College, Cheltenham, Gloucestershire.

1854   School at Bisley, Gloucestershire.

1854–56   Christ Church, Long Grove, Herefordshire.

1854–57   St John the Baptist, France Lynch, Gloucestershire.

1855–56   Holy Trinity, Cuckfield, Sussex; restoration.

1857   St Andrew, Histon, Cambridgeshire; aisle windows, west window, clerestory, roof.

1858–61   Queens' College, Cambridge; redecoration and new library ceiling.

1858–61   St James, Bicknor, Kent; restoration.
1858–62   St Michael and All Angels, Brighton (now south aisle of new church).
1858–62   All Saints, Selsley, Gloucestershire.
1859   Christ Church, Pendlebury, Lancashire; tower.
1860–61   St James, Canon Frome, Herefordshire (except for 1680 tower).
1861–63   St Martin-on-the-Hill, Scarborough.
1862   St Mary Magdalene, Bread Street, Brighton (demolished).
1862–63   St Stephen, Guernsey.
1863   St Martin, Bridlington, Yorkshire.
1863   All Saints, Dedworth, Berkshire.
1863–65   St Wilfred, Haywards Heath, Sussex.
1863–70   All Saints, Jesus Lane, Cambridge.
1864–69   Jesus College Chapel, Cambridge; restoration and new ceiling.
1864   St James, Wigmore, Herefordshire; restoration.
1865   All Saints, Coddington, Nottinghamshire; restoration and chancel.
1865–70   St Salvador, Dundee.
1866–68   St Michael, Kingsland, Herefordshire; chancel, roof and restoration.
1867   St Saviour, Valley End, Windlesham, Surrey.
1868   All Saints, Scarborough.
1868   All Saints, Warwick; additions.
1868–71   St John the Baptist, Tue Brook, Liverpool.
1868–94   Hobart Cathedral, Tasmania (also 1903).
1869   Cefn Bryntalch, Welshpool.
1869   St Nicholas, South Kilworth, Leicestershire; restoration.
1869   Houses at Malvern Link.
1869   St James, Kinnersley, Herefordshire; nave and chancel decoration, and organ case.

1869   *Partnership with Garner began*

1870–74   St Augustine, Pendlebury, Lancashire.
1872–76   Holy Angels, Hoar Cross, Staffordshire.
1872   St Botolph, Cambridge; rebuilt chancel and vestry.
1872   St Michael, Lyonshall, Herefordshire; restoration.
1872   St Laurence, Rowington, Warwick; restoration.
1873   St Mark, Bilton, Warwick; restoration.
1873–74   St Mary, Plumtree, Nottinghamshire; restoration.
1873–83   St Michael and All Angels, Folkestone.
1874   St Paul, Brighton; narthex, rood screen.
1874   Oxford Cathedral; restoration.
1874   St Mary, Cheshunt, Hertfordshire; restoration.
1874–77   St Helen, Brant Broughton, Lincolnshire; restoration and chancel.
1875   Queens' College Hall, Cambridge.
1876   St George, King's Stanley, Gloucestershire; restoration and organ.

1876–77   St Peter, Cassington, Oxon; restoration.
1876–79   Christ Church, Oxford; Tom Quad, etc.
1876–81   St Michael, Camden Town, London.
1877   St James, West Hackney, London; reredos.
1879   River House, Chelsea Embankment.
1879   University College, Oxford; Master's Lodgings.
1880   St Mary of Eton, Hackney Wick, London.
1880–82   St Peter and St Paul, Tring, Hertfordshire; restoration.
1880–83   St Laurence, Frodsham, Cheshire; restoration.
1880–84   Magdalen College, Oxford; St Swithun's Buildings and President's Lodgings.
1881   All Saints, Clewer, Berkshire.
1881   St Oswald, New Bilton, Rugby.
1881   St Bartholomew, Reading; chancel.
1882   St Mary Magdalene, Lincoln (old exterior walls used).
1882   All Saints, Nettleham, Lincolnshire; chancel restoration and lengthening, decorated windows.
1882–83   St Andrew, Canwick Road, Lincoln; chancel decoration.
1882–1904   York Minster; restoration.
1883–84   St Laurence, Corringham, Lincolnshire; redecoration, organ case and screen.
1883–84   St German, Roath, Cardiff.
1883–86   Marlborough School Chapel.
1884   Jesus College, Oxford; additions to Principal's Lodgings.
1884   Exeter College Chapel stalls, Oxford.
1884   St Peter in Eastgate, Lincoln; chancel decoration.
1884   Westminster Abbey, London; monument to G. E. Street.
1885   Ely Cathedral; Bishop Woodford tomb.
1885   Stewart Memorial Gateway, Winchester.
1885   Holy Trinity, Market Street, Cambridge; chancel redecorated.
1885   St Mary, Saffron Walden; organ case.
1885   Magdalen College gateway.
1885   All Saints, Wroxton; restoration.
1885–87   St Mary, Nottingham; reredos and chancel screen.
1885–87   St Stephen, Sneinton, Nottingham.
1885–88   Lincoln Cathedral; tomb of Bishop Wordsworth.
1886   St Mary, Chigwell, Essex; chancel decoration and pulpit.
1886   St Laurence, Ecchinswell, Hampshire.
1886–87   St Mary, Pulham St Mary, Norfolk; organ case, chancel decoration.
1886–87   St Alban, Sneinton, Nottingham.
1886–89   St Mary, Clumber, Nottinghamshire.
1887   St Giles, Wimborne, Dorset; interior gothicized (complete restoration by Comper after fire 1908).
1887   St Manarck, Lanreath, Cornwall; restoration.

1887–88   St John the Baptist, Tibshelf, Derbyshire.

1887–88   St Saviour, Roath, Cardiff.

1888   St Augustine, Stepney, London; complete restoration.

1888   St Mary, Hemel Hempstead, Hertfordshire; chancel decoration.

1888   Holy Trinity, Stratford-on-Avon; restoration.

1888–90   All Saints, Bedworth, Warwickshire.

1889–92   St Chad, Hanmer, Flint; restoration.

1889–1909   St John the Baptist, Epping, Essex.

1890   St Saviour, Leeds; Pusey chapel.

1890   St Mary, Bromfield, Shropshire; south windows.

1890   St Julian, Wellow, Somerset; chancel.

1890   St Michael, Tatenhill, Staffordshire; restoration, reredos, pulpit.

c. 1890   Jesus College Chapel, Cambridge; organ case.

1890–91   Queens' College Chapel, Cambridge; Walnut Tree Court.

1891   St Peter, Bournemouth; painted roof.

1891–92   The Ascension, Woodlands, Dorset.

1891–95   St Mary, Primrose Hill, London; reredos and furnishings.

1891–98   Winchester Cathedral; reredos and restoration of figures.

1891–1904   St Michael and All Angels, Croydon, Surrey; font, pulpit, organ case, hanging rood.

1892   St Mary the Virgin, Great Bardfield, Essex; stone rood-screen restoration (figures above ogee arch).

1892   Holy Trinity, Mark Beech, Kent; chancel.

1892   St Paul, Wilton Place, London; chancel decoration and screen.

1892   All Saints, Dane Hill, Sussex.

1892   St Mary, Burghfield, Berkshire; chancel.

1892–93   St Mary, Horbury, Yorkshire.

1892–94   St John, Peasedown St John, Somerset.

1892–94   St Aldhelm, Branksome, Dorset. West end completed 1911 by Hare.

1893   St Luke, Warrington, Lancashire.

1893   St Barnabas, Pimlico, London; reredos.

1893   St Matthew, Great Peter Street, London; rood-loft and screen.

1893   King's College, Cambridge; Bodley's Buildings.

1894   All Saints, Laughton, Lincolnshire; chancel, south porch, roof, screen, reredos, organ case.

1894–95   St Catherine's College Chapel, Cambridge; alterations.

1894–95   Holy Innocents, South Norwood.

1894–95   St Aidan, Skelmanthorpe, Yorkshire.

1894–1902   St John the Evangelist, Cowley, Oxford; also Mission House and chapel.

1894–1902   St John the Baptist, Penshurst, Kent; chancel screen.

1895   St Mary the Virgin, Saffron Walden, Essex; organ case.

1895   All Saints, Rangemore, Staffordshire; chancel.

1895   St Martin, Womersley, Yorkshire; rood screen and loft, nave and chancel roofs.

1895–97   Christ's College Library, Cambridge.

1896   St Nicholas, Chislehurst; reredos.

1897   *Garner became R. C. and left Bodley*

1897   St Helen, Abingdon, Berkshire; reredos.

1897   Leicester Cathedral; south porch.

1897   Coggeshall Abbey, Essex; restoration of Gatehouse Chapel.

1897   St George, Kirk White Street West, Nottingham; chancel.

1897–98   St Matthew, Chapel Allerton, Leeds.

1898   Canterbury Cathedral; pulpit in nave.

1898   St Margaret, Oxford; tower porch, screen and pulpit.

1898   Christ Church, Mold Green, Huddersfield; chancel.

1898   Wilmslow Parish church, Cheshire; chancel and chapel.

1898   Bishop's Palace chapel, Lincoln.

1898   St Martin, Lincoln; vestries.

1898   St Michael, Camden Town, London; screen.

1898   St Alban, Sneinton, Nottingham; Lady Chapel.

c. 1898   St Bartholomew, Reading; chancel and chapel.

1898–1902   All Saints, Weston-super-Mare, Somerset.

1899   Christ's College Chapel, Cambridge; ceiling.

1899   St Mary, Eccleston, Cheshire.

1899   St Mary, Leicester; reredos.

1899   St Margaret, King's Lynn, Norfolk; reredos.

1899–1902   St Margaret, Oxford; steeple.

1900   Dunstable Priory, Bedfordshire; west front restoration.

1900   Sisters of Charity Chapel, Knowle, Somerset.

1900–01   St Andrew, Ham, Surrey; chancel.

1901   St Mary, Whitkirk, Yorkshire; chancel rebuilt.

1901   Little Bowden, Leicestershire; restoration.

1901   St Mary, Godmanchester; reredos and rood screen.

1901   House of Mercy Chapel, Clewer, Berkshire; monument to Canon T. T. Carter.

1902   Westminster Abbey, London; south transept rose window and two tiers of lancets below, for Burlison and Grylls.

1902   Holy Trinity; Prince Consort Road, London; chancel, nave and south aisle.

1902   Peterborough Cathedral; reredos.

1902   Beaumaris, Anglesey; restoration.

1902–03   Holy Rood, Shillingstone, Dorset; roof decorations.

1902–03   Oxford Cathedral; reredos, font cover.

1903   St Chad, Burton-on-Trent, Staffordshire.

1903   Bristol Cathedral; pulpit.

1903   All Saints, Gainsborough, Lincolnshire;

155

north and south vestries.

1903   Ripon Cathedral; reredos.

1903   St Agnes, Sefton Park, Liverpool; Lady Chapel screen and reredos.

1903–04   St Edward, Holbeck, Leeds.

1903–04   St Aidan, Nag's Head Hill, Bristol.

1903–06   St Andrew, Sonning, Berkshire; chancel decoration.

1903–07   St Bride, Kelvinside, Glasgow.

1904   St Mary Magdalene, Richmond, Surrey; chancel.

1904   St Boniface, Chandlers Ford, Hampshire.

1904–06   All Souls, Aylestone Road, Leicester.

1905   York Minster; presbytery nave reredos.

1905   St Bartholomew, Elvaston, Derby; chancel extended and decorated.

1905   Marlow Parish church, Buckinghamshire; panelling.

1905   St Giles, Stony Stratford, Buckinghamshire; rood-screen.

1905   St Nicholas, Boston, Lincolnshire; alterations and restoration.

1905   Boer War Cross, Duncombe Place, York.

1905–06   The Paraclete, Hom Green, Ross-on-Wye, Herefordshire.

1906   St Saviour, Oxton, Cheshire; reredos.

1906   St Paul, Bedford; screen.

1906   All Saints, Kedleston, Derby; north aisle.

1906   St James, Great Grimsby, Lincolnshire; Lady Chapel.

1906   Christ Church, Ealing, Middlesex; decoration.

1906   St Barnabas, Pimlico, London; rood-screen.

1906   Holy Trinity, Kensington Gore, London; north aisle.

1906   St Peter and St Paul Cathedral, Washington, D.C. (with Vaughan and Hare).

1906   Holy Angels, Parkstone, Dorset; rood, choir stalls and organ case.

1906   Christ Church, Lichfield; reredos.

1906–15   San Francisco Cathedral, California (completed by Hare★).

1907   St Faith, Brentford, Middlesex.

1907   Bedford School Chapel. Built *c.* 1908–09.

1907   St John the Baptist, Epping, Essex; tower, north aisle, porch and reredos.

★There is no record of a partnership between Bodley and Hare; but Hare appears to have used the name 'Bodley and Hare' after Bodley's death. He inherited Bodley's office, and since his death in 1932 very few Bodley drawings have ever come to light.

VI   Alfred Waterhouse

1854   Rothay Holme, Ambleside, Westmorland, for Elizabeth Head.

1856   Hinderton, Hooton, Cheshire, for Christopher Bushell.

1857   Bradford Banking Company, Bradford.

1858   Barcombe Cottage, Fallowfield, Manchester, for Alfred Waterhouse Jr.

1859   Manchester Assize Courts, Manchester.

1861   Royal Insurance Building, Manchester.

1862   Pilmore Hall, Darlington, for A. Backhouse.

1863   Salford County Gaol, Strangeways, Manchester.

1864   Hutton Hall, Guisborough, for J. W. Pease. Clydesdale and North Scotland Bank, London.

1865   New University Club, London.

1866   Foxhill. Whiteknights, Berkshire, for himself.

1867   Allerton Priory, Liverpool, for John Grant Morris. Balliol College, south front, Oxford. North-Western Hotel, Liverpool.

1868   Gonville and Caius College Tree Court, Cambridge. Manchester Town Hall, Manchester. Jesus College, detached range, Cambridge.

1869   Owens College, Manchester. Blackmoor House, Blackmoor, Hampshire, for Roundel Palmer, MP.

1870   Eaton Hall, Eaton, Cheshire, for Earl Grosvenor.

1871   Seamen's Orphan Institution, Liverpool.

1872   Girton College, Cambridge. Natural History Museum, London.

1873   Reading Grammar School Chapel, Reading.

1874   St Elisabeth's Parsonage, Reddish, Stockport, for W. H. Houldsworth. Balliol College, New Hall, Oxford. Pembroke College, New Hall and Library, Cambridge.

1875   New Court, Carey Street, London.

1876   House, Sheffield Terrace, London, for Edward C. Sterling. St Mary, Twyford, Hampshire.

1877   House, Iwerne Minster, Dorset, for Lord Wolverton. Prudential Assurance Buildings, Holborn Bars, London.

1878   Bedford Assize Courts and Shire Hall, Bedford. Yattendon Court, Yattendon, for himself.

1879   Hove Town Hall, Hove.

1880   St Elisabeth, Reddish, Stockport. 1 Old Bond Street, London.

1881   St Paul's School, Hammersmith Road, London. City and Guilds of London Central Technical Institution, London.

1882   Turner Memorial Home, Dingle Head, Liverpool.

1883   Lyndhurst Road Congregational Church, Hampstead.

1884   National Liberal Club, London.

1886   Liverpool Royal Infirmary, Liverpool.

1888   University College, London, Library Block and Jubilee Tower. Hotel Metropole, Brighton.

1889   King's Weigh House Chapel, London.

1890   St Peter, North Hagbourne, Berkshire.

1891   Foster's Bank (now Lloyds), Sydney Street, Cambridge.

1892   National Provincial Bank, Piccadilly, London.

1893   St Mary's Hospital, Manchester.

1894   St Margaret's Clergy Orphan School, Bushey, Hertfordshire.
1895   Prudential Assurance Company Offices, Edinburgh.
1896   University College Hospital, London.
1898   Royal Alexandra Hospital, Rhyl.
1901   Staple Inn Buildings, London.

VII   Edwin Lutyens

No list of Lutyens buildings is provided partly because this is readily accessible in Hussey and Butler (see Note 1) and partly because the essay does not attempt to cover the whole of Lutyens' career.

Sources of Illustrations

We are extremely grateful to Mr David B. Waterhouse for permission to reproduce the photograph of his great grandfather (ill. 92) and the details from his sketchbooks (ill. 94). We should also like to thank the following for supplying illustrations:

Architects' Journal (W. J. Toomey) 49; Christopher Ashdown 87; James Austin 77; G. L. Barnes 61–69, 76, 79, 80, 82, 84, 90; J. Brandon-Jones 111; British Museum 59; Cleaverhume Ltd 42; Commonwealth War Graves Commission 116, 119; Country Life 18, 46, 54, 110, 112; Dundee Public Library 2, 3; the vicar of St John the Baptist, France Lynch 78; Greater London Council 32; Hermione Hobhouse 33, 44, 45, 47, 48; Paul Joyce 117; A. F. Kersting 55, 71; the Mother Superior, Knowle 91; MacMonagle, Killarney 21; Manchester Central Library (H. Milligan) 99; University of Manchester, School of Architecture (D. Wheeler) 103; National Monuments Record 22, 36, 52, 72 (H. Felton), 81, 85, 86, 88, 89, 100 (G. B. Mason), 102; National Monuments Record of Scotland 6, 7, 15, 16, 24, 25; National Portrait Gallery, London 106; Perth Art Gallery 12; Royal Academy 37; Royal Institute of British Architects 29, 35, 38, 39, 43, 57; the vicar of St Augustine's, Pendlebury 83; Gavin Stamp 107; Stuart Allen Smith 104; W. J. Toomey 70; Valentine and Sons Ltd 19; Watts and Co. 87; J. B. White Ltd 11; Worshipful Company of Goldsmiths 30, 31, 34.

The drawings have been prepared by Peter Bridgewater 101; Dianne Clegg 96; Roderick Gradidge 114; David Walker 4, 5, 9, 13, 14, 17, 20.

Illustrations 40, 41, 51, 93, 95, 97, 105, 108, 115 are reproduced from the *Builder*; 53 from the *Gentleman's Magazine*; 118 from Robert Lutyens, *Sir Edwin Lutyens*; 109 from R. Phéne Spiers, *Architectural Drawing*.

Index

Numbers in italics refer to illustrations. The Check Lists of Chief Works (pp. 148–56) are not included in the Index.

Abbots, Sompting, The 44; *43*
Adam, Robert 14
Adare, Co. Limerick, 46; *46*
Adderstone, Northumberland, 13
Aldermaston Court 40, 42–43; *42*
Aldin, Cecil 133
Althorp 46
Andover, St Mary, 53, 54
Appleton-le-Moors, Christ Church, 70; *65, 66*
Arthurstone 23

Ashridge 14
Atkinson, William 14, 15, 20
Auchmacoy 21, 22
Auchterarder 22

Baker, Herbert 122, 147 (n. 6)
Balcarres 23
Balmoral 21
Bangor Castle 28
Barcombe Cottage 107–08; *96*
Barry, Charles, Jr 31
Basevi, George 59
Beaufort 25
Billings, R. W. 30
Birmingham, St Alban, 76
Blackmoor 118
Blairquhan 14, 15

Blore, Edward 19, 20, 25, 40
Blow, Detmar 131
Bodley, George Frederick 84–101; *75*
Bois des Moutiers, Varengeville, 123; *107*
Bonaly 23
Bonomi, Ignatius 66, 144 (n. 1)
Bournemouth, St Stephen, 77
Bradford Old Bank 106–07
Brighton, St Michael 87; *79*
Bristol, Cathedral, 145 (n. 29)
   Convent of the Sisters of Charity, 99; *91*
   Mayor's Chapel, 79
Britton, John 18
Brodie 20

Brookwood Cemetery 63
Bryce, David 29, 30, 31
Bryce, John 25, 29
Buchanan 31
Burn, William 8–31; *1*
Burton-on-Trent, St Chad, 99
Bury, Assembly Rooms, 57
Bussage church 84–85

Caldicott, Rudolph 133
Calton Mohr 28
Calwich 28
Cambridge, All Saints, 89
  King's College, 100
Camperdown, Dundee, 13,
  14; *4*
Canterbury, Clergy Orphans'
  School, 49
Carradale 30
Carstairs 15; *8*
Castle Drogo 123
Castle Menzies 22
Catherston Leweston church
  68
Charterhouse School 49; *49*
Chichester Cathedral 145
  (n. 28)
Chute Forest church 76
Clarke, T. H. 18
Clatto 30
Clumber, St Mary, 97–98; *88,
  89*
Cockburn, Lord 22, 23
Cockerell, C. R. 8, 61
Comper, Ninian 84, 92, 95, 96
Cowley, St John the Evan-
  gelist, 99
Crabbet Park 131
Crooksbury 124; *108*
Croydon, St Michael, 76; *70*
Cullercoats church 78

Dalhousie 20
Dalkeith Palace 23, 25
Dalton Holme, St Mary,
  68–69; *62*
Darlington, St Hilda, 80
Dartrey 28; *23*
Dawber, Guy 132
Dawyck 22
Daylesford, St Peter, 70; *67*
Deanery Garden, Sonning,
  129
Dobson, John 16, 18, 51, 53
Donaldson, T. L. 10, 15, 30,
  31, 112, 114
Drumfinn 16
Drumlanrig 23
Dublin, St Columba's Col-
  lege, 49
Duncrub 23
Dundas Castle 12; *4*
Dundee, St Salvador, 89
Dunraven, Earl of 46

Duntrune 20
Dupplin 16, 18, 19; *2, 3*

Earp, Thomas 86
Eastoft church 68
Eastwell 28
Eaton Hall 115–18; *100, 101,
  102*
Eccleston, St Mary, 98; *90*
Edinburgh, Merchant Maiden
  Hospital, 8
  St John, 8
  University, 8
Edmond Castle, Cumberland,
  18
Elliot, Archibald 14

Falkland 25, 26; *19*
Faskally 21
Fettercairn 17
Finnart 30
Folkestone, Christ Church, 53
Fonthill 31; *26*
Fowke, Francis 63–64, 110–11
France Lynch, St John the
  Baptist, 86–87; *77, 78*
Freeland 19; *12*
Freeland, St Mary, 73; *69*
Fulbrook 127

Gallanach, Argyll, 8
Garner, Thomas 91, 92–94, 96
Garscube 16; *4, 9*
Gart 23; *4*
Garton-on-the-Wolds church
  144 (n. 8)
George, Ernest 124
Gilston Park 44
Graham, James Gillespie 18
Greenock, Custom House, 8
  Exchange Assembly Rooms,
  8
Gregory, Gregory 23, 24
Guildford, Hillier's Alms-
  houses, 124; *109*
Gunnersbury Park 58

Hall 40
Hardwick, Philip 32–41, 66;
  27
Hardwick, Philip Charles
  36–49; *28*
Hardwick, Thomas 32
Harlaxton 23–25; *18*
Hascombe, Hoe Farm, 123
Haywards Heath, St Wilfrid,
  88
Headingley, St Michael, 78
Heathcote 130
Hewell Grange 96
Hinderton 106; *95*
Hoar Cross, Holy Angels,
  93–94; *85, 86*
Homewood 127–29; *112, 114*

Hove, All Saints, 78; *71*
Huis ter Heide, Utrecht, 147
  (n. 29); *113*
Hythe church 79

Idsworth 31
Inchdairnie 30
Ingram, Mrs Meynell 93, 96
Invergowrie House 22
Inverness County Buildings
  23

Jekyll, Gertrude 123, 124, 126
Joldwynds 127; *111*

Keble, Thomas 84, 86
Kempe, C. E. 90, 93, 97, 98
Kerr, Robert 8, 138 (n. 25)
Kilconquhar 22, 30
Kimmerghame 17; *10*
Kinfauns 18

Lambton Castle 53, 55
Lane, Richard 102
Lastingham church 77
Lauriston 15, 20
Leny 30
Lethaby, W. R. 125, 131, 132
Lilburn Tower 16, 18
Lincoln Cathedral 145 (n. 25)
Lindisfarne 123
Littlecote Hall 46, 140 (n. 61)
Little Brington 46
Liverpool, Royal Infirmary
  119–20
  St Agnes, 75, 78
  St John the Baptist, Tu
  Brook, 89–90; *81*
London, Barclay and Bevan
  Bank, 42; *41*
  Bethlehem Hospital, 57
  British Museum Reading
  Room 53, 65; *51*
  Burlington House, 61–62
  58
  Carlton Club, 59–60; *57*
  Cenotaph, 133, 134
  City Club, 35–36; *32*
  Conservative Club, 59–60
  56
  Euston Hotel, 41
  Euston Station, 40–41; *29
  37*
  Fishmongers' Hall, 96
  Goldsmiths' Hall, 34–35; *3
  31*
  Great Western Hotel, Pad
  dington, 37, 41–42; *38, 3*
  Holy Trinity, Bessboroug
  Gardens, 68
  Horticultural Society Ga
  dens, 63; *59*
  Inner Temple, 55
  Lincoln's Inn, 38–40; *36*

London School Board, 96
Lord Sefton's House, Belgrave Square, 36; *33*
Natural History Museum, 111–12; *98*
Oxford and Cambridge Club, 58; *55*
Pantheon Bazaar, 50, 55–56; *53*
Prudential Insurance, 119; *104*
River House, Chelsea, 96
St Augustine, Kilburn, 73–75; *61*
St Bartholomew's Hospital, 36
St John, Friern Barnet, 80
St John, Norwood, 76
St Katherine's Dock, 34
St Michael, Camden Town, 96–97
St Peter, Vauxhall, 71–73, 144 (n. 11); *68*
Savoy Chapel, 54
Union Bank, 42; *40*
University College Hospital, 120; *105*
Wandsworth Royal Freemasons' School, 48
Westminster Abbey, 80, 145 (n. 30)
Westminster Hall, 55, 81–82; *74*
Long Grove church 85
Loughton, St John the Baptist, 53
Lowther 14
Lude 22, 23; *17*
Lugar, Robert 18
Lutyens, Edwin 122–36; *106*
Lutyens, Robert 135
Lynford 28, 31

Macartney, Mervyn 131
Madox Brown, Ford 88
Madresfield Court 40, 48; *48*
Manchester, Assize Courts, 108; *93, 97*
Town Hall, 112–14; *99*
May, E. J. 131
Milton Lockhart 20; *4, 16*
Minto 14
Montagu House 31
Morris, William 88, 89, 126
Morrison, Sir Richard 15
Muckross, Co. Kerry, 25, 27; *21*
Munstead Wood 124, 129
Muthesius, Hermann 125

Narford 31
Netherby, Cumberland, 23
New Delhi 133
New Place, Welwyn, 127;

110
Newlands Almshouses 48; *47*
Newton, Ernest 131–32
Niddrie Marischal 18, 20
North Ferriby church 66
North Leith church 8
Northcairn, St Mary, 54
Norwich Cathedral 145 (n. 26)
Nottingham, St Bartholomew, 80

Oakley Park 58; *54*
Orchards 127
Overstrand, Overstrand Hall, 123
The Pleasaunce, 123, 129
Oxford, Campion Hall, 124
Magdalen College, 96

Panizzi, Anthony 65
Papworth, J. B. 15
Pearson, John Loughborough 39, 66–83, 140 (n. 30); *60*
Pendlebury, Christchurch, 87
St Augustine, 91–93; *76, 83, 84*
Pennethorne, James 62
Peterborough Cathedral 81; *73*
Pickering, W. G. 66, 144 (n. 2)
Pinkie 20
Pitcairns 20
Playfair, W. H. 8, 23, 137
Poltalloch 28, 29; *24, 25*
Porden, William 116
Prestwold 28
Prior, E. S. 123, 131
Pugin, A. W. N. 109–10

Quennell, C. H. B. 132

Raby Castle 28
Ratho 16; *4*
Rauceby 27, 28
Redcourt, Haslemere, 131–32; *115*
Reddish, St Elisabeth, 118; *103*
Redrice 28
Reid, Robert 18
Rendcomb 44–46; *44, 45*
Repton, Humphry 15
Revesby Abbey 27, 28
Riccarton 15, 20; *14*
Rickman, Thomas 18
Roberts, Henry 8, 53
Rochester Cathedral 145 (n. 27)
Rothay Holme, Ambleside, 104
Ruskin, John 84, 109

St Andrews, Madras College,

19, 25
St Fort 19; *4, 11*
Saltoun 8, 12; *5, 6, 7*
Salvin, Anthony 23–25
Sandon 31
Scarborough, St Martin-on-the-Hill, 88
Vicarage, 90; *82*
Schulz, Robert Weir 26
Scone 14, 15
Scorborough, St Leonard, 69–70; *63, 64*
Scott, George Gilbert 39, 84, 110, 112
Scott, Giles Gilbert 123, 126
Seacliff 30
Selsley, All Saints, 87–88; *80*
Shaw, Richard Norman 125
Small 15
Smirke, Robert 8, 14, 17, 18, 23, 51, 52, 54
Smirke, Sydney 50–65; *50*
Smith, John 21
Snaigow 19; *4, 13*
Spottiswoode *4*
Sprott 21
Standen 130
Stenhouse 22
Stockport School 37; *34*
Stoke Rochford 25, 27; *22*
Stokes, Leonard 123
Stow church 68
Street, G. E. 84, 110, 112, 114, 124, 134, 148 (n. 47)
Sutton, Frederick 93
Sutton Veny church 71

Tapper, Walter 96
Telford, Thomas 34
Theydon Bois, St Mary, 53
Thiepval Memorial Arch 133–36; *116, 119*
Thurstaston church 78–79
Tigbourne 127
Troup, F. W. 131
Truro Cathedral 80; *72*
Tyninghame 21; *15*

Upper Stowe, St James, 46
Uppingham, Memorial Hall, 132

Van t'Hoff, Robert 147 (n. 29)
Varengeville, *see* Bois des Moutiers
Vaughan, Henry 100

Warren, Edward 89, 92
Washington Cathedral 100
Waterhouse, Alfred 102–21; *92*
Watts and Co. 96; *87*
Webb, Philip 88, 90, 91, 106, 124, 125, 126, 127, 129, 130

159

Webster, George 18
Wentworth church 75–76
Westwood Park 37; *35*
Weybridge church 66, 144
  (n. 6)

Wheatley, St Mary, 134; *117*
Whitehill 25, 26; *4, 20*
Wilkins, William 14, 15
Willement, Thomas 54
Worthington, Thomas 114

Wyatt, Benjamin Dean 37
Wyatt, James 14

York Minster 54; *52*